The Great Texas Banking Crash

THE GREAT TEXAS BANKING CRASH

AN INSIDER'S ACCOUNT

Joseph M. Grant

UNIVERSITY OF TEXAS PRESS
Austin

Printed in the United States of America
First University of Texas Press edition, 1996

∞
The paper used in this publication meets the minimum requirements of American National Standard for Information Sciences–Permanence of Paper for Printed Library Materials, ANSI Z39.48-1984.

Library of Congress Cataloging-in-Publication Data

Grant, Joseph M.
The great Texas banking crash : an insider's account / by Joseph M. Grant.
p. cm.
Includes index.
ISBN 0-292-72791-7 (alk. paper)
1. Texas American Bancshares, Inc. 2. National Bancshares of Texas of San Antonio. 3. Bank failures–Texas. 4. Bank holding companies–Texas. 5. Federal Deposit Insurance Corporation.
I. Title
HG2613.F73G73 1996
332.1'6–dc20 96-10331

Dedication

To my loving wife, Sheila, for her unwavering support, devotion, and encouragement during the most difficult times, and to our children, Lisa and Clay, for their understanding and caring.

AND

To all the Texas bankers who had the courage and spirit to try to weather the financial hurricane that swept through Texas and, particularly, to the loyal men and women of Texas American Bancshares and of National Bancshares of Texas, who worked diligently trying to preserve their companies against insurmountable odds.

CONTENTS

William M. Isaac

FOREWORD

The Great Texas Banking Crash is not just another book about banking. In telling his story, Jody Grant gives a compelling and dynamic personal account of the demise of Texas American Bancshares (TAB) and other major banks in Texas. Hundreds of Texas banks, including nine of the ten largest, were forced out of business, most through failure, during the late 1980s. The near-total collapse of a state's banking system, particularly a state as powerful and populous as Texas, has no parallel in U.S. history.

When Jody Grant became chairman and CEO of TAB in 1986, he could not have imagined what the next four years of his life would be like. He could not have known that his bank and most of the other major banks in Texas were in a death spiral. He could not have anticipated the agony, frustration, and financial devastation that he, his family, and his colleagues were about to experience. Had he any idea of what was in store, one suspects he would have declined the "honor" of commanding the sixth largest bank in Texas.

I was privileged to work at Jody's side throughout this period as he struggled tirelessly to prevent the collapse of TAB. After serving as chairman of the Federal Deposit Insurance Corporation (FDIC) from 1981 through 1985, I formed The Secura Group, a consulting firm that in late 1986 was hired to help National Bancshares Corporation in San Antonio (NBC) cope with its deteriorating financial condition. In the course of a meeting with the FDIC to discuss NBC's plight, FDIC officials suggested that NBC consider merging with TAB, a merger the FDIC would support financially.

Following that meeting, NBC's two top officials, Richard Calvert and Mark Johnson, and I met with Jody Grant and his colleagues at TAB to discuss the plan suggested by the FDIC. Overcoming a fair amount of skepticism, the management and boards of the two banks decided to put their fates in the hands of the FDIC.

At the outset, I told each bank's management and board that the journey on which they were embarking would be arduous, with many emotional highs and lows along the way and no guarantee of success. My warning was prophetic, albeit greatly understated. The journey was far more difficult and the emotional swings far more extreme than anticipated; the ultimate outcome was bitterly disappointing.

The Great Texas Banking Crash is must reading for government policymakers and students of banking. It contains all the elements of a suspense novel, as indecisiveness, poor decisions, and Washington politics frustrate efforts to save the bank in time. Jody Grant brings the reader inside board rooms, executive offices, and government meeting rooms for a blow-by-blow account of a government assistance plan gone awry.

Other participants in the episode might have different views on what happened and why. No participant, however, was more central than Jody, nor has any labored more diligently to chronicle the events and put them in context.

The banking problems confronting the FDIC in the 1980s were perhaps the most severe in our nation's history. The FDIC handled far more and far greater bank failures during this period than during its entire prior history. Without the heroic efforts of the agency's staff in the face of overwhelming pressures, the depositing public might well have lost confidence in the banking system.

The agency's overall record during this period is remarkable, but mistakes were made. The FDIC's handling of TAB and NBC–indeed, of the entire Texas banking crisis–was not one of its prouder moments. This book provides insights that will be invaluable to those who seek to learn from the past.

Not much good came out of this sad episode, but for me one positive aspect was the opportunity to work side-by-side with some of the finest, most honorable, and most dedicated people I have ever known–Jody Grant and his colleagues at TAB and Richard Calvert, Mark Johnson, and their colleagues at NBC. Friendships forged in adversity endure a lifetime.

ACKNOWLEDGMENTS

I started writing this book in May 1988 from the diaries I was keeping at the time. Eight years later, it has finally come to fruition. In the interim, I received encouragement and help from so many people that it would be difficult to acknowledge them all.

In particular, I am deeply grateful to Libby Dotson, my loyal and hard-working administrative assistant at Texas American Bancshares (TAB), for her involvement in the early stages of the manuscript. I am also greatly indebted to Debbie Sheppis, my secretary at TAB, who spent so much of her spare time formatting this manuscript, and who over the years patiently taught me how to use several different word processors. I owe a special thanks to Robert D. Mettlen, professor of finance at The University of Texas at Austin, for his careful reading of the manuscript and for his many helpful suggestions, particularly related to the chapter dealing with the savings and loan crisis in Texas and in the nation.

I am especially grateful to my wife Sheila for her many suggestions and careful editing. She read all eight versions and improved each one through her insightful and constructive criticism. She also endured many hours alone to allow me to pursue my goal of recording for history the events contained in this book. I cannot thank her enough.

INTRODUCTION

From the mid-1980s through 1992 was an unprecedented period in the history of Texas: a period during which the financial landscape of the state was drastically and permanently changed. During this time, nine of the ten largest bank holding companies in Texas failed to survive. They were either acquired by out-of-state banks or dealt to the top bidder by the Federal Deposit Insurance Corporation (FDIC), in one of the highest-stakes poker games ever played.

The oil boom, which began with the Arab oil embargo of 1973, had pushed the Texas real estate and energy economy to giddy heights. Money poured into the state, resulting in prosperity and a spending binge that were unparalleled in Texas history, if not in the history of the United States. Inevitably, boom was followed by bust, creating a tidal wave that rolled over the state and left shattered companies and careers in its wake.

The resulting depression produced the worst real estate debacle in Texas history. In the major metropolitan areas, vacant skyscrapers and empty shopping centers stood as ghostly monuments to overzealous developers and investors. Real estate prices plummeted, destroying billions of dollars of value in the process. The havoc that resulted in the commercial banking industry is the principal focus of this book, although the story is told in the context of efforts to save the sixth-largest banking company, Texas American Bancshares (TAB), based in Fort Worth. I served as chairman and chief executive officer of TAB during the crisis days from April 24, 1986, to July 20, 1989.

The story of TAB's struggle for survival chronicles the proposed "shotgun" merger arranged by the FDIC between TAB and the state's seventh-largest bank, San Antonio–based National Bancshares of Texas (NBC).

It also chronicles the battle for control of TAB and NBC between financial titans Richard Rainwater of Fort Worth, former financial advisor to the multibillion-dollar Bass family of Fort Worth, and Carl Pohlad of Minneapolis, 40 percent owner of the Minnesota Twins baseball team and frequent partner of the glamorous, 1980s corporate takeover artist, Irwin Jacobs.

A principal protagonist in this saga was the FDIC, whose autocratic chairman, L. William Seidman, presided over an incredible series of blunders, false starts, and ever-changing agendas in dealing with TAB and NBC. Indeed, in most cases, the policies of the FDIC assured the ultimate failure rather than the resurrection of troubled banks, at a tremendous expense to the FDIC's insurance fund and, thus, to the American taxpayer.

With the second seizure in four years of the banks of First City Bancorporation of Houston on October 30, 1992, and their subsequent sale on January 27, 1993, the cycle of failures in Texas was complete. Only a decade earlier, at a time when Texas had more powerhouse banks than any other region of the United States, the state had been on its way to becoming the next great banking and money market center in the country.

Of the ten largest banking organizations, with approximately $116 billion in assets, only the $3 billion Cullen/Frost Bankers of San Antonio remains. Among the vanquished were RepublicBank Corporation, MCorp, and InterFirst Corporation of Dallas; Texas Commerce Bancshares, Allied Bancshares, and First City Bancorporation of Houston; and TAB. These banks were, respectively, the nation's eighteenth, twentieth, twenty-fifth, twenty-sixth, thirty-fourth, forty-seventh, and seventy-third largest banking organizations. Although not rated in the top one hundred bank holding companies, NBC, ranked eighth in Texas, and BancTexas Group, ranked tenth, also failed to survive.

The loss of Texas's major commercial banks is totally unprecedented in the history of the United States. Even during the Great Depression, no state suffered such financial devastation. Texas, the third-largest industrial state, has been left void of a major home-based financial institution. As a consequence, Texas has lost the engine of capital that spawned the third-largest industrial economy in the nation, built the gleaming modern skylines of its major cities, and bankrolled its entrepreneurs who created some of the nation's most preeminent businesses.

Most importantly, though, Texas has lost the institutional base that produced many of its most notable business and civic leaders. Indeed, the executive training and community outreach programs of these major banks served as incubators for leaders, and the executive offices and boardrooms of major banks were seats of power where many of the most critical decisions affecting their communities were made. With the demise of these institutions, and the concomitant displacement of their executives and boards of directors, a generation of leaders was disenfranchised. Such a vacuum cannot be easily filled. Additionally, many important matters, heretofore decided locally, will in the future be determined in the headquarter cities of new out-of-state owners. Consequently, philanthropy, community support, and financial decisionmaking will be severely impacted.

Unfortunately, it is too late for federal regulatory reforms and policy initiatives to save TAB or the other major Texas banks, or to avoid the billions of dollars in unnecessary costs to taxpayers that are associated with the Texas bank failures.

Yielding to political pressure, federal regulators adopted a much more lenient stance in dealing with problem banks in the East and on the West Coast. With the failure on January 6, 1991, of the $22 billion Bank of New England, based in Boston, it appeared that New England was in danger of losing its three largest banking organizations. Responding to a hue and cry from local business and political leaders, regulators spared the much troubled $32.5 billion Bank of Boston Corporation, based in Boston, and the $22.9 billion Shawmut National Corporation, located in Boston and in Hartford, Connecticut. Informed sources familiar with the assets of both banks claim that they were at least as troubled as their Texas counterparts, which had already failed. Similar leniency was shown in addressing the problems of the $56.2 billion Wells Fargo Bank, based in San Francisco, and of the $84.7 billion Security Pacific Corporation, which was allowed to merge on April 22, 1992, with the $110.8 billion Bank of America, both of Los Angeles. The troubles of all of these banks stemmed from problem real estate loans.

The lessons of history seem to be difficult to learn. Bankers have repeatedly made the same mistakes: inflating balance sheets and failing to adequately diversify during the boom phases of business cycles and then suffering the unhappy consequences of their actions during the busts. Even though the situation in Texas was unique in the annals of history, the temptations afforded by boom cycles will be repeated in another place at another time. The lessons of Texas during the 1980s, as depicted in this book, should serve as a further reminder to future generations of bankers to adhere to sound fundamentals of bank management and to avoid being seduced by Wall Street into attempting to meet their insatiable demand for unsustainably high performance.

In telling the story of TAB, NBC, and the other major Texas banks, I have attempted to be as meticulous to detail as possible. Much of the source material is from my files and library compiled over the last two decades and from my recollections as a principal protagonist in the story. Dialogue and other quotations with no citations were reconstructed from my memory, detailed diaries, and notes taken contemporaneously with events as they occurred. While I believe these sources are essentially correct and express the thoughts conveyed at the time, they are not all 100 percent accurate. To the extent there are errors or misstatements, they are inadvertent.

ONE

DEEP IN THE HEART OF TEXAS

As I turned onto Fourth Street in downtown Fort Worth to attend a bankers' meeting in March 1974, I looked ahead through the mist. I was awed by the gleaming silver tower that loomed before me. Shaped like an octagon and flared at the base, it looked like a giant spaceship ready to take flight. TAB's new, ultramodern, thirty-seven-story building, designed by prominent Atlanta architect John Portman, dominated the skyline. The building was a picture of strength, a fitting image for the banking organization it housed.

Texas American: Steeped in Tradition

Texas American Bancshares had its beginning in 1873, with the opening of Tidball and Wilson Bankers, the first bank to be formed in Fort Worth. By 1883, the city's banking needs exceeded those that could be provided by a private bank, and on March 4, 1884, the bank was issued a national charter and became The Fort Worth National Bank, a name it held until 1983, when its name was changed to Texas American Bank/Fort Worth.

From its inception, the progress of the bank and the city of Fort Worth were intertwined. The growth of the bank was spurred by the arrival of the railroad in 1876, the establishment of the city as a major shipping center for cattle and cotton, and the building of the Armour and the Swift meat packing plants in 1902.

While the bank benefited from the growth of Fort Worth, much of Fort Worth's growth was financed by the bank. Perhaps the greatest single event to spur the growth of the bank and that of Fort Worth was the discovery of oil in West Texas in 1911, when ranchers drilling for water struck oil on the W. T. Waggoner ranch near Wichita Falls. Fort Worth was the closest major city to the new oil field, and by 1912, two oil refineries had been built in the city. In 1917, wildcatters operating out of Fort Worth hit the mother lode with the discovery of a major new field in Ranger, Texas. A year later, major oil fields were found near the one-horse towns of Desdemona and Burkburnett in West Texas. As a consequence, Fort Worth became a hotbed of activity in the booming oil industry, and The Fort Worth National Bank played a major role in financing the development of the industry, gaining a national reputation for its proficiency in petroleum lending.

During the 1920s, Fort Worth enjoyed an unprecedented building boom, fueled primarily by the continuing oil activity. By 1922, nine oil refineries were operating in Fort Worth, and many new landmarks were added to the city's skyline during the decade. The Fort Worth National Bank's prominence was enhanced in 1927 when it merged with the Farmers and Mechanics National Bank and moved into a new twenty-four-story office tower, proclaimed to be the tallest in the Southwest.

The Great Depression, which began with the collapse of the stock market on October 29, 1929, and gripped the nation during much of the 1930s, was relatively less severe in Texas. This is due primarily to two factors: the strength and diversification of Texas's agriculture and the continued growth of the Texas oil industry. Oil production, for example, increased by 36 percent from 1929 to 1933, although its value declined due to lower prices.

During the depression, the building boom in Fort Worth ended, but The Fort Worth National Bank never suffered an operating loss or an interruption in business, except during the nationwide banking holiday proclaimed by President Franklin D. Roosevelt from March 6 to March 9, 1933. In fact, in one respect, the bank benefited; in 1934, it received the deposits of the liquidated Stockyards National Bank. By the end of 1938, deposits stood at more than $41 million after having dropped to $26 million in 1932.

As the nation recovered from the depression and entered World War II, both The Fort Worth National Bank and the city of Fort Worth prospered. By 1950, Fort Worth was a booming city of 300,000 people, and the bank was well established as its largest and leading financial institution.

On March 26, 1959, the bank elected Lewis H. Bond as its fourth president. Bond, who was a petroleum engineer by background, became president at the age of thirty-nine, upon the unexpected early death of his predecessor. At the time, Bond's title was vice president and petroleum engineer.

Bond's selection as president was a far cry from the way executives are selected today. It was done by straw poll. A hat and blank pieces of paper were passed among the senior officers of the bank, who were asked to write the name of their preference for president. When the ballots were tabulated, the same name appeared on every one: Lewis Bond. Bond later reflected, "I was pretty surprised and greatly awed. . . . Everyone was quite tolerant of my lack of knowledge in banking, and was quite understanding and helpful."[1]

Bond was an imposing person, with a full head of prematurely white hair, making him appear somewhat older than his age. He spoke articulately and commanded a presence of authority. He had a reputation as a sound and conservative banker and as a man of the highest character and integrity.

During Lewis Bond's tenure, the bank enjoyed unprecedented growth and was the first major bank in Texas to convert to a holding company structure when The Fort Worth National Corporation was organized in 1970. Under this structure, the parent company, The Fort Worth National Corporation, owned all of the common voting stock of six bank subsidiaries. This structure enabled the company to operate banks in more than one location, a substitute for branch banking, which was prohibited at this time by the Texas Constitution of 1876.

During the same year the holding company was formed, the company sought permission to acquire The Mutual Savings and Loan Association of Fort Worth. In a closely followed, nationwide, precedent-setting case, the Federal Reserve Board denied the application. This action henceforth affirmed the separate distinction between commercial banks and savings and loan associations (S&Ls), which were formed specifically to make long-term mortgage loans on homes.

The Fort Worth National Corporation's name was changed to Texas American Bancshares, Inc. (TAB) in 1974. At that time, it was the sixth-largest banking organization in Texas, with banking subsidiaries in Fort Worth, Dallas, Houston, Amarillo, Midland, and Levelland. At year-end 1974, TAB had total assets of $1.5 billion and shareholders equity of $97 million.

Lewis Bond's second-in-command in the formative years of the holding company was Bayard Friedman, president of The Fort Worth National Bank, lead bank of TAB. Bayard Friedman is one of those instantly likeable people. He is extremely warm and friendly, and he has an infectious laugh and magnetic personality. His dark unruly eyebrows and deep-set eyes, which have a mischievous glint, are part of his charm. In 1975, at age forty-nine, he was a devoted tennis player and still had the physique of an athlete.

Friedman, who possesses a politician's charisma, had served a two-year term as mayor of Fort Worth, the youngest in the city's history. Not surprisingly, he is a great salesman and was originally hired by the bank to head up business development and marketing. Prior to becoming mayor, he had practiced law and was associated with the second-largest firm in Fort Worth, which, incidentally, represented the bank.

In January 1975, Friedman invited me to join him for lunch in Austin, where I was then serving as president of the Capital National of Austin, the city's second largest bank. After four months of discussions, I agreed to join The Fort Worth National Bank. Since Friedman professed to have no interest in Lewis Bond's job, there was a clear shot to the top position upon Bond's retirement. This was an opportunity I felt I couldn't refuse.

In June 1975, I moved to Fort Worth with my wife, Sheila, and our two children. Six months later, in January 1976, at age thirty-seven, I was elected the sixth president of TAB's lead bank, The Fort Worth National Bank. The bank was the largest and most profitable in Fort Worth and the seventh-largest in Texas. Indeed, I had joined a venerable and proud organization, steeped in tradition.

Texas American under Siege

In the decade immediately following my election as president of The Fort Worth National Bank, TAB experienced extraordinary prosperity and tranquility. During this period, Lewis Bond's reign at the helm of the company went unchallenged, with one exception.

On July 22, 1983, Bond received an unsolicited offer from Ben Love, chairman and CEO of Texas Commerce Bancshares of Houston, for TAB to merge with Texas Commerce: the combination would produce the state's largest banking organization. Bond's face was ashen and his voice trembled with anger when he told our executive management about the offer. As he handed us copies of the letter, he said, "Love sent us a letter after I told him we didn't want an offer. Hell, when we met here last week, I couldn't have made it any clearer. He won't take no for an answer. I guess we're going to have to hit him with a sledgehammer."

With those words, war had been declared. I was in a unique position to assess the ensuing battle. After five years working for Citibank in New

York City and three years earning a Ph.D. in economics and finance at the University of Texas at Austin, I joined Texas Commerce in August 1970. Until I resigned at the end of 1973, I reported to Love, who had hired me and whom I found to be a remarkable individual.

Ben Love, who is larger than life, epitomizes Texas. He is six feet four inches tall and looks even taller because of his erect carriage. When I joined the bank in 1970, Love was strikingly good looking, with piercing blue eyes. He has a sharp wit and an intellect exceeding that of anyone I had worked with. In fact, his intellect–an ability for almost total recall of statistical and financial facts–and his quick retorts were intimidating to many of his colleagues.

As soon as I learned of Love's offer for TAB, I knew we were in for a fight. He would pursue TAB as he did everything, with a well-scripted plan and dogged determination. I also knew the plan. Ironically, while I worked at Texas Commerce, I had planned the expansion strategy that was now threatening TAB. It was also ironic that my friend Ben Love had become Lewis Bond's arch enemy.

Love's aggressive offer, unprecedented in Texas banking, rocked Bond's world to its epicenter. It was an unwanted intrusion into a situation Bond had dominated for the previous twenty-four years. Love's offer was a threat to Bond's very existence, and Bond would fight with all the resources he could muster to preserve the company's independence.

At the called TAB board meeting of July 26, Bond urged the directors to turn down the offer:

> Gentlemen, we have to make a decision. Here are the facts. First, Texas Commerce's offer is less favorable than InterFirst's offer for First United [First United Bancorporation, TAB's principal competitor in Fort Worth]; but it is more favorable than MCorp's offer for Southwest Bancshares in Houston. The InterFirst deal is probably more comparable given that it is for another Fort Worth company.
>
> Secondly, interstate banking is on the horizon. Several states in the East and Southeast have already approved some form of interstate banking. It is only a matter of time before the barriers come down in Texas, and when they do, we can expect acquisition multiples to increase considerably. So, based on that, now is too soon. If we wait for interstate banking, we can get a higher price.
>
> But, the most important reason is Ben Love. I just don't think his philosophy and ours are compatible. He's very aggressive, and his record of keeping senior people is questionable. Recently, TCB's president,

> John Cater, resigned in a dispute with Love. Before him, vice chairman Les Peacock left. And we understand that Bill Heiligbrodt, the current president, is in trouble. To merge with Texas Commerce would be a risky proposition for our people.
>
> It is your decision, gentlemen, but my strong recommendation is that we inform Love that we are not interested now or in the future and that we are not looking for a higher offer.

The board rejected the bid without debate or a dissenting vote. In a July 27, 1983, article reporting the action, the *Wall Street Journal* related that the suitor had not ruled out the possibility of another, higher bid. But it also quoted Lewis Bond as having said in an interview, "I think I made it pretty clear that we are strongly inclined to stay independent."[2]

On August 3, the *New York Times* printed a postmortem article, titled "Merger Spree of Texas Banks," about Texas Commerce's attempt to acquire TAB and about the other mergers between major Texas banks that had been announced. It referenced the attempt on TAB as "the most colorful and divisive merger move to date," which, it said, "is shaping up as a bitter struggle to stay independent." It cited a "stinging" letter released by Lewis Bond calling Texas Commerce's bid "unsolicited" and "unwanted," and reported that Bond "dislikes Texas Commerce's aggressive chairman, Ben F. Love." It further stated that "the proposed combination of the two banks is shaping up as a nasty personal battle between Mr. Love, Texas Commerce's chairman, and Mr. Bond, chief of Texas American."[3]

From my perspective, the *Times* article was off base in attempting to portray the struggle as a personal feud between Bond and Love. The issues were more a matter of turf and personality. Lewis Bond would have attempted to preserve TAB's independence from any intruder. In this instance, however, the two men were complete opposites. Bond was an introvert, with a quiet introspective style, whereas Love was extroverted, dynamic, and charismatic. Love would have totally overshadowed Bond, and that would have created a problem. They could not have coexisted.

From the outset, even though Texas Commerce was expected to put up a tough fight, there was little question as to the outcome of this contest: TAB would retain its independence. Lewis Bond had very carefully selected the members of the board of directors, and there was no doubt that they would support him.

Later I learned from the Texas Commerce camp that they were shocked that TAB's shareholders hadn't filed a suit forcing Bond to negotiate. As far as I know, there was never even a hint of such action.

As history would determine, TAB's decision to reject the Texas Commerce offer was extremely regrettable. Years later, after Bond's death, Ben Love told me that a very influential TAB director and a close confidant of Lewis Bond, William Fuller, confided to Love that the decision to reject Texas Commerce's offer was the worst business decision of his life.

A Time of Growth

From the time I joined TAB on May 12, 1975, until I was promoted to chairman and CEO on April 24, 1986, TAB grew from an organization with six subsidiary banks and $1.5 billion in assets to thirty-five subsidiary banks and $6.4 billion in assets. Earnings, likewise, increased significantly from $12 million in 1974 to $26.2 million in 1985, after having peaked at $47 million in 1982. Furthermore, the outlook for TAB in the future appeared even more favorable than it had in the past.

The nation's economy had recovered from the devastating recession of 1981–1982 and was continuing to improve. The growth in real Gross Domestic Product (GDP) of the nation had averaged 4.4 percent in 1983–1985, compared to the long-term trend of 3.0 percent, considered to be the maximum sustainable growth rate while maintaining stable prices. Unemployment, inflation, and the prime lending rate (the rate which commercial banks charge to their most credit-worthy customers) all had declined significantly. Moreover, most economists believed the outlook was for continued prosperity for the foreseeable future.

While the outlook for the nation was favorable, the expectations for Texas were exceptional. Projections called for Texas, California, and Florida to be the three fastest-growing states in the country over the next several decades, and Texas, with its central location, would receive more than its fair share of the growth. Texas had everything going for it, including its strategic location in the sunbelt; a favorable tax structure, with no corporate or individual income tax; an abundant low-cost energy supply; a well-developed transportation system and infrastructure; low-cost labor; and, most importantly, people with an indomitable will and an unbridled entrepreneurial spirit. Texas also had two of the most dynamic metropolitan areas in the country: Dallas/Fort Worth and Houston.

The outlook for Texas's financial institutions was at least as favorable as that for the economy, since one is the mirror image of the other. Having labored under antiquated laws prohibiting branch banking since the Texas

Constitution of 1876, the banks had been unshackled with the advent of multibank holding companies in Texas beginning in 1970. The passage of the Bank Holding Company Act in 1956 had permitted one-bank holding companies. Amendments to the act in 1970 allowed a single holding company to own more than one bank, thus providing a structure for the creation of banking "systems" under common ownership, which provided an alternative to branch banking in unit-banking states such as Texas. Subsequently, large holding-company systems of banks were formed in Texas through mergers and acquisitions.

On June 30, 1986, RepublicBank Corporation, Dallas, was the largest, with assets of $22.5 billion, followed closely by MCorp, Dallas, with assets of $21.7 billion; InterFirst Corporation, Dallas, with assets of $19.2 billion; Texas Commerce Bancshares, Houston, with assets of $18.8 billion; and First City Bancorporation of Texas, Houston, with assets of $14.4 billion. These organizations ranked eighteenth, twentieth, twenty-fifth, twenty-sixth, and thirty-fourth in the United States, respectively. Allied Bancshares, Houston, with assets of $9.8 billion, and TAB, with assets of $6.1 billion, ranked forty-seventh and seventy-third in the nation, and sixth and seventh in the state. In comparison, NCNB Corporation in Charlotte, North Carolina, and Banc One Corporation in Columbus, Ohio, which would play major roles in Texas banking in the future, were ranked seventeenth and thirty-ninth in the nation, with assets of $23.9 billion and $11.2 billion, respectively.

TAB enjoyed excellent prospects for growth, with its headquarters in downtown Fort Worth and strategically positioned in the heart of the Dallas/Fort Worth metropolitan area. The lead bank, which was larger than its two largest competitors combined, was the dominant bank in Fort Worth. TAB/Fort Worth financed much of the city's growth. It gave millions of dollars in charitable contributions supporting civic, cultural, and economic causes, and its executives were the leaders of the community. Fort Worth was predicted by all the experts to enjoy exceptional growth and prosperity due to its location thirty miles from Dallas and twenty-two miles from the Dallas/Fort Worth International Airport.

The Dallas franchise, albeit relatively much smaller than Fort Worth, was strategically located in the growth path of the northern half of Dallas. TAB also had an attractive franchise in Austin, with the largest bank located outside the central business district in the rapidly growing northwest quadrant of the city. The company's presence in Houston was very small, but well positioned for expansion, with its lead bank located in the prestigious and dynamic Galleria shopping mall as the anchor.

Financially, TAB was also poised for expansion. The downturn in earnings in 1983 and 1984, after the peak in 1982, was due to problems in TAB's oil loan portfolio. By the beginning of 1986, exposure to the oil industry had been reduced significantly, with oil loans having declined from 22 percent of total loans in 1981 to 6 percent in 1985. Additionally, we had recognized our oil loan problems, based on a reasonable view of the oil industry and the economy for 1986 and beyond, by taking large charges to earnings in 1983–1985 to augment TAB's loan loss reserves.

TAB had also avoided significant problems with loans to lesser-developed countries (LDCs). Money-center banks and regional banks across the country had aggressively expanded international loans in the 1970s. Loans to LDCs–particularly to Argentina, Brazil, and Mexico–became a serious problem in the 1980s as a result of huge budget deficits and a negative balance of international payments in these countries. TAB had largely avoided LDC loans, with a total of about $7 million outstanding, less than one-half of one percent of total loans. While LDC loans were a major problem for some of the nation's largest banks, they were not a significant problem in Texas.

During the early to mid-1980s, it was difficult to envision anything derailing an exceedingly prosperous and successful future for Texas and its major banks, and particularly for TAB. At that time, no one could have foreseen the crash in oil prices in the first quarter of 1986 or the passage of the Tax Reform Act of 1986, which led to the subsequent crash in the real estate markets.

Changes at the Top

On September 7, 1982, Bayard Friedman announced his intention to retire on January 1, 1983, when he would become chairman of TAB/Fort Worth's Executive Committee, while remaining on the boards of the holding company and the bank. It was also announced that I would assume the titles of chairman and CEO, in addition to retaining the title of president. At the same time, I was elected vice chairman of TAB, a clear signal that I was in line to succeed Lewis Bond as chairman and CEO of TAB upon his scheduled mandatory retirement in July 1986.

A Promising but Uncertain Future

In late January 1986, I convened TAB's management committee to reassess our plans for my coming administration. Although we had completed our formal budgeting and profit-planning process the previous fall, I didn't feel comfortable about the glowing projections that had been developed for 1986.

Regardless, I opened the meeting on an optimistic note, reiterating my enthusiasm for working with the group. Then, as I customarily did in such meetings, I asked each person at the table to give their assessment of our chances for achieving our planned profit objectives for the year. As each person voiced their opinion, a litany of pessimism pervaded the meeting, and there was unanimity as to the scenario.

Everyone had spoken except for Gene Gray, TAB's senior credit officer. Gene had expressed his concerns to me privately. Now I wanted the entire group to hear his opinion.

> Jody, we've been through hell. I don't know what it was like during the Depression, but it couldn't have been much worse, and it damn sure isn't over yet. We survived the crash in oil and in agriculture in pretty good shape, but this thing we're in right now–no one knows where it's going. Only thirty days ago, oil was at $30 a barrel, now it's at $20. Hell, it could go to $10 in another thirty days. If that happens–and, I think it could very easily–what's that likely to do to the rest of our energy portfolio? And, then, what's going to be the effect on the rest of the economy? Real estate could go much deeper into the tank than it already is. I think we'd better get ready for the biggest Texas tornado we've ever seen, because its going to tear this state apart.

As Gray spoke, I observed the reaction of the others turn from incredulity to grave concern. While I felt he was perhaps being overly pessimistic, I knew there was a reasonable possibility that his gloomy assessment was right. Certainly, the stage had been set. From the dizzying heights of the late 1970s and early 1980s, the break in oil prices engineered by Saudi Arabia beginning in late 1981 had sent the Texas oil economy into a tailspin. As a consequence, the oil-based cities of Houston, Midland, and Odessa were devastated, as were their banks. First City Bancorporation of Houston was reeling from the punches it had taken, and the four independent banks in Midland and three of the four independent banks in Odessa had failed. Additionally, banks throughout Texas and the nation that had lent money in the "oil patch" had taken severe losses.

Now, with oil prices in a free-fall, we could only expect the crisis to deepen and spread to the rest of the economy. Real estate, we believed, was particularly vulnerable. By now, the excesses of the S&Ls, following their deregulation in the early 1980s, were well known. Many of the S&Ls were insolvent–even though they remained open due to regulatory forbearance–and real estate values, which had been driven to unsustainable heights by the S&Ls' freewheeling lending and investing, were poised for a fall. With TAB's large concentration in real estate, we were especially vulnerable. All we could do would be to erect all our defenses and hope we could weather the storm. The thought of the consequences was sobering and depressing, not the kind of upbeat outlook one would hope to have in anticipation of taking on the CEO job of a major company.

We were comforted, however, by the fundamental strength of the company. In spite of some lackluster earnings years, TAB was heavily capitalized. We had been examined by the Office of the Comptroller of the Currency (OCC) in the spring of 1985 and had received a good report.[4] And, in response to growing concerns about the viability of the real estate markets, we had curtailed lending to all but the home mortgage sector of that market.

We knew the challenges were considerable, but we were confident that the 113-year-old TAB organization could withstand nearly any test. But at that time there was no way to anticipate the depth of turmoil the Texas economy would experience, or the impact the economy would have on TAB. Nor could anyone have anticipated the Achilles' heel our real estate portfolio would prove to be. Even Gene Gray's dire concerns vastly understated what reality brought.

TWO

BOOM AND BUST, TEXAS STYLE

While most of the nation and much of Texas basked in the glow of recovery from the 1981–1982 national recession, the effects were certainly not felt uniformly. Drastically declining oil prices beginning in 1981, and the accompanying reduction in exploration, drilling, servicing, and supplying activities, devastated areas heavily influenced by the oil industry. Those regions particularly hard hit were the oil-production states of the Southwest and the Rocky Mountains. In Texas, communities in the oil patch, such as Midland and Odessa, were especially affected, as was Houston, the petroleum capital of the nation.

The Seeds of Crisis

The birth of the oil industry in Texas occurred with the eruption of the legendary Spindletop gusher near Beaumont in Southeast Texas on January 10, 1901. Reports of the well, which spewed thousands of gallons of oil before it could be capped, created a sensation throughout the world. In its first year of production, Spindletop produced over seventeen million barrels of oil, which was 94 percent of the state's total production.

Consequently, a "black gold" rush occurred in Texas, reminiscent of the California gold rush of 1849. Subsequent discoveries in West Texas during 1911–1919, and in East Texas in 1930, transformed Texas into the predominate energy state in the nation. As a result, the state's agrarian economy was changed into an oil-driven industrial juggernaut.

As the year 1973 dawned in Texas, there was no hint of the oil crisis that was to follow. Before the year was concluded, however, Saudi Arabia had cut off the flow of oil to the consuming nations.

Prior to the embargo, the average price of oil was $3.50 per barrel, and the total value of the oil produced in Texas was $4.5 billion per year. By contrast, less than a decade later in 1981, the price of oil averaged $35 per barrel and the total value of the oil and gas produced was $45 billion. Texas led the nation in oil and gas production, accounting for about one-third of the total, and produced twice as much as second-place Alaska. For 1970–1986, the total value added to the Texas economy through oil and gas production was an astounding $367 billion.[1]

The increase in oil and gas prices stimulated a boom of epic proportions. The frenetic pace of activity created a tidal wave that rolled over nearly every segment of the Texas economy. In the 1970s and early 1980s, Texas was the second fastest-growing state in the nation behind Florida, having surpassed California. Texas was also the third most-populous state behind California and New York, and was projected to pass New York in the early 1990s.

Growth produced more growth, as increases in population created demands for goods and services, which in turn produced additional jobs and further stimulated the economy. Not surprisingly, the frenzied economic activity, with the excessive demand for goods, services, and housing, escalated the prices of everything at a dizzying pace.

The Real Estate Boom

With a value system deeply rooted in the land and a proclivity for risk, Texans were eager participants in the real estate boom that was kicked off by the fever pitch of the energy economy. Those who were not involved in the oil business, but who wanted to jump on the bandwagon, looked upon real estate as the vehicle with the most upside potential and the least downside risk. It was unthinkable that real estate values, which were relatively low compared to other markets nationwide, wouldn't continue their upward march.

As a consequence, a flood of money from both domestic and foreign sources poured into the state, from large commercial banks, insurance companies, pension funds, investment banking houses, other institutional investors, and wealthy individuals. Additionally, the vaults of federal savings and loan associations had been thrown open by the passage of the Garn-St. Germain Depository Institutions Act of 1982, which significantly expanded the loan and investment authority of federally chartered S&Ls. State laws governing S&Ls were already liberal. However, with the passage of the Garn-St. Germain act, state lawmakers and regulators made them even more permissive in an effort to be competitive. Billions of dollars were made available for loans and direct equity investments in commercial real estate and in raw land.

The largest factors in the market were the Texas developers and investors. Because Texas had experienced uninterrupted growth since World War II, there was a cadre of well-financed and experienced developers in the state. In fact, Trammell Crow Company, Vantage Company, and Lincoln Property Company, all of Dallas, and Gerald Hines of Houston were ranked among the top ten developers in the country in the 1980s. Behind them were a host of other well-capitalized developers and legions of less-substantial developers and of aspiring entrants. So great was the attraction to participate in the building of Texas, many successful businessmen, lawyers, doctors, and other professionals abandoned lucrative businesses and practices to enter the real estate business.

Texas commercial banks, which had experienced a large and unreplenished runoff of loans from the energy and agriculture sectors of the economy, rushed headlong to supply acquisition and construction loans to their real estate customers. Like most of the major Texas banking companies, TAB numbered among its customers virtually all the giant developers.

The Oil Boom Turns Sour

The decline in the price of oil beginning in late 1981 caught by surprise not only the oil and gas industry, but also the entire world. For years, Saudi Arabia, the richest of the Organization of Petroleum Exporting Countries (OPEC) in oil reserves, had curtailed oil production to prop up world oil prices, diminishing its own revenues and subsidizing the other members of OPEC in the process. At the beginning of 1986, Saudi Arabia reached the limit of its tolerance and greatly increased production, flooding the world oil market.

The Saudi's action had a catastrophic effect on the price of oil. As indicated by Graph 1, the average price per barrel of oil declined from $27.00 in 1985 to $14.72 in 1986. But the decline was even worse than indicated by the averages, as the price fell from a high of $30.00 in December 1985 to a low of $9.75 in April 1986. This was an unprecedented drop in the price of oil, and its consequences for Texas's oil, real estate, and banking industries were disastrous.

Petroleum economists and engineers alike had predicted that the price of oil would reach in the $70-per-barrel range by the end of the 1980s.

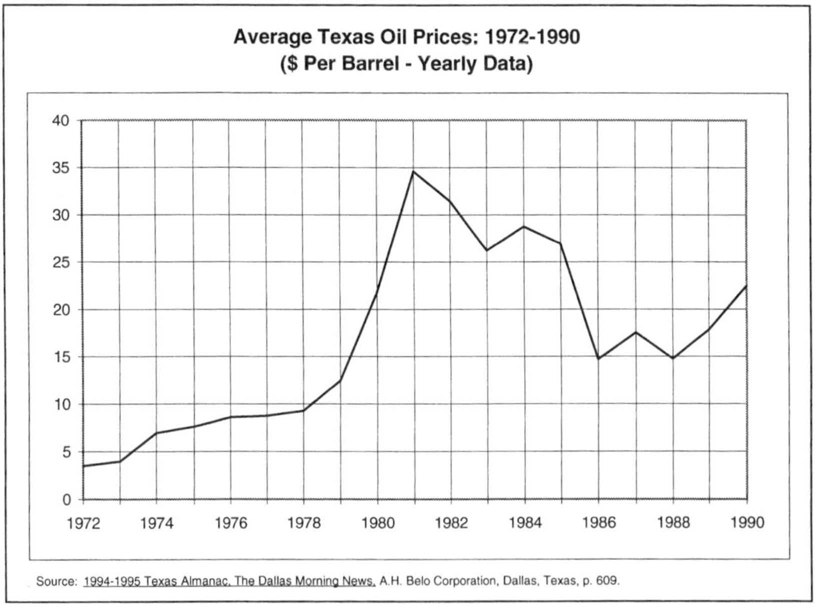

Graph 1

The industry and its suppliers had built their operations accordingly: they continued to gear up for ever-increasing demand, ordering more drilling rigs and inventorying drilling pipe, other supplies, and equipment in huge quantities. To finance these purchases, large amounts of funds were borrowed from banks and other lenders.

Consequently, as prices started to drop, the industry suffered from excess capacity and inventories, and it was overleveraged. Banks and other lenders had made loans predicated on continued expansion and rising prices. When the opposite occurred, the lenders found their collateral vastly undervalued and borrowers unable to meet debt service requirements.

As was the case when oil and gas prices were increasing, the impact of their decline was profound. For instance, the number of active rotary drilling rigs working in the U.S. declined from 4,520 in December 1981 to 686 in July 1986.

The fate of The Western Company of North America typifies the battering taken by the industry's service and supply companies. From the company's 1981 peak, its revenues declined from $726 million to $176 million in 1987; cumulative losses for 1982–1987 aggregated $627 million; stockholders equity declined from a high of $382 million in 1982 to a negative $273 million in 1987; and the price of the company's stock fell from a high of $32 per share in 1981 to a low of $.25 in 1986. The chairman, Eddie Chiles, retired as the company's chief executive officer in 1987, after witnessing the company he had spent his life building reduced to shambles. TAB had participated in a line of credit to The Western Company, with TAB's share being $7.5 million, on which in excess of $4 million was lost.

Perhaps no communities were more heavily affected by the reversal in world oil markets than Midland and Odessa, the principal cities of the Permian Basin and the economic centers of the oil and gas business of West Texas. From its peak in 1983, employment declined one-fourth by 1987. New construction nearly evaporated, and literally thousands of homes were for sale. The price of homes in the resale market dropped by one-half, if they could be sold at all. Foreclosures and bankruptcies were at an all-time high, as high-flying oilmen, as well as conservative and well-respected businessmen, were brought to their knees.[2]

The Real Estate Bust

During the 1960s and 1970s, Texans had been conditioned to regard their state as recession proof. While the rest of the country struggled during the recessions of 1969–1970 and 1974–1975, the Texas economy scarcely missed a beat. Petroleum and agriculture formed the foundation upon which the economy rested, and the demand for each was considered to be stable, irrespective of the nation's business cycles. This myth was shattered forever with the oil, real estate, and financial disaster of the 1980s.

By the end of 1985, the office and retail markets were gorged with millions of square feet of vacant space, and real estate prices had inflated to unsustainable levels. The markets were poised for a collapse and only needed a catalyst to start the avalanche. The plunge in oil prices in the first quarter of 1986 provided that catalyst, driving nails into the coffin of the construction industry.

While the initial break in oil prices in 1981 had called into question the invincibility of the Texas economy, the crash of 1986 confirmed its vulnerability. With their confidence in the economy shaken, investors and lenders fled to the sidelines, in effect redlining the state.

Domestic investors also were discouraged from investing in real estate by the passage of the Tax Reform Act of 1986. Until then, a significant amount of the funds flowing into real estate had been tax motivated. Individuals with substantial incomes were allowed to significantly reduce their tax liability by investing in tax shelters, usually in the form of a limited partnership, that offered losses or tax credits generated by a particular business or activity, irrespective of the individual's level of participation in the day-to-day operations of the shelter. Real estate was a particularly attractive investment because of the availability of large tax credits from interest expense on borrowed funds and from depreciation on the improvements to the property and on furniture and fixtures.

With the passage of the Tax Reform Act, individuals, estates, trusts, closely held corporations, and personal service corporations were prohibited from deducting losses generated by passive activities (defined as any trade or business in which the investor did not materially participate). The Tax Reform Act not only applied to future real estate investments, but was also retroactive to include losses on previous investments. This unusual feature of the act destroyed the economics for investors on many prior transactions and was a major factor in the subsequent decline in real estate values.

Another deterrent to lenders was the opinion of federal officials and regulators that the real estate markets were overblown and needed a dose of restraint. This was evident in the attitude of the Office of the Comptroller of the Currency (OCC) toward TAB during the third quarter of 1985. Although the saber-rattling was somewhat subdued at the time, the message was very clear that the OCC believed real estate markets were headed for a fall and banks should curtail their lending to the industry. In fact, TAB had already taken such action in August 1985 on its own initiative.

It wasn't until February 1987 that the regulators overtly took action. In a letter dated February 6, the OCC informed TAB and the other large banks in the Southwest that it would immediately begin target examinations to assess the extent of problem real estate assets.[3]

It was clear that these requests and initiatives were intended to send TAB and the rest of the Texas banks a message that real estate lending should be curtailed. In retrospect, the regulators were right in their judgments about the real estate market; however, it is also clear that they were no smarter than the bankers in anticipating the market collapse.

Moreover, many prominent bankers, real estate developers, and investors believe that the regulators were a major factor in accelerating and deepening the problem with their heavy-handed approach in supervising the real estate lenders, which cut off the flow of funds to the liquidity-starved markets. I share that opinion and believe that the OCC's attitude about TAB was largely unwarranted. Our concentration in real estate loans, at about 40 percent, was in line with banks in the growth states of California and Florida, and a substantial percentage of our portfolio was in stable home mortgages. Additionally, our underwriting standards had been relatively conservative, and we had already stopped making new real estate loans.

By the summer of 1986, a multitude of events and circumstances were conspiring to produce a real estate catastrophe. As a consequence, the real estate markets crashed into a deep and protracted depression, with profound repercussions for the state.

What was previously thought of as temporary impairment in the real estate markets was now regarded as a longer-term problem. In the case of an office building that had been built for $100 million in expectation of obtaining rents of $25 per square foot, the investor or developer now faced the realization that it could only obtain rents of $10 to $12 per square foot. With the income from the project cut in half, the value of the building, based on the amount of cash flow available for debt service, was also only half as much.

Because construction activity had been so robust prior to 1985 and the subsequent fall so sharp, by mid-1987 the amount of vacant office space in the major markets was overwhelming. In the five major metropolitan areas in Texas–Austin, Dallas, Fort Worth, Houston, and San Antonio–there was a total of 311.5 million square feet of office space, of which 91.2 million, or over 29 percent, was vacant. Houston alone had nearly half the total and a vacancy rate of 31 percent.[4]

Cavernous high-rise office buildings, often constructed to satisfy someone's "edifice" complex, stood completely empty. Euphemistically referred to as "see throughs," many were padlocked to await better days. Plans for new buildings were shelved as the amount of vacant office space accumulated. Some buildings in very early stages of construction were abandoned, leaving eerie skeletons of framed steel or gaping holes in the ground as testimonials to the times.

The landscape was also replete with ghostly looking, half-completed shopping centers, anxiously awaiting tenants so bays could be finished. Shopping centers that had been built expecting $20-per-square-foot rentals were now bringing $8. Some high-quality centers that had been constructed at more than $100 per square foot were now worth less than half that much.

Since most of the commercial projects were financed without mortgage loan commitments from permanent lenders, the financial institution that financed the construction was stuck with the loan. With either no cash flow or insufficient cash flow, the borrower had to "come out of pocket" with debt service. Even the most strongly capitalized found this extremely painful and debilitating. The lesser-capitalized developers surrendered one by one.

To the lender, it was a simple process to determine when the developer would run out of funds and incur a liquidity crisis. From the borrower's cash flow projection, which matched all expected future sources of funds against all known cash requirements, the year and month the developer would run out of cash could be anticipated. In most instances, once the borrower was out of funds, the lender foreclosed on the property, taking, in addition, a promissory note or other assets from the borrower for the deficiency in settlement of the debt. Rather than agree to such a settlement, many developers and investors declared bankruptcy. Others, in an attempt to preserve their reputation and credit standing, eagerly settled.

A Disastrous Scenario

The accumulation of billions of dollars of real estate by commercial banks and S&Ls created a disastrous scenario for the Texas economy–the specter of massive "fire sale" dumping of foreclosed real estate, which would drive values down even further. Due to the inability of the already financially crippled banks and S&Ls to take losses and further deplete capital, most reluctantly withheld the most-distressed properties from the market, or they refused to price properties at salable values. The Federal Home Loan Bank Board, under its chairman, M. Danny Wall, recognized this problem and structured incentives for S&Ls to hold real estate in its S&L rescue plan, known as the Southwest Plan.

The terrible plight of both borrowers and lenders created havoc on both sides. Financial institutions failed in unprecedented numbers, and bankruptcies–both formal and informal, "out-of-court" restructurings–were at an all-time high in Texas. For many of the executives of failed banks and S&Ls, it meant the end of careers and financial ruin. For the borrowers, fortunes were wiped out and businesses that had taken years to establish were liquidated. Lives were irrevocably changed; I don't believe anyone outside of Texas realized how deep the problems ran, or how critical the situation was.

But the financial failures masked the real casualties in these situations. Individuals' spirits were broken, their confidence was shattered, and they sank into despair and depression. Confrontations between borrowers and lenders led to inordinate pressure and stress on both sides. It was not uncommon for the borrower, facing financial ruin, to break down in tears in the lender's office. In the most-severe situations, alcoholism, drug addiction, nervous breakdowns, and even suicide were the end result.

The Banking Depression

Before the ravages of Texas's economic collapse could filter down to the banks, the nation and the state were sensitized to the links between the health of the nation's oil economies and the banks that served those economies.

On July 5, 1982, the failure of the Penn Square Bank in Oklahoma City shocked the United States into awareness of the troubles of the oil and gas industry and its lenders. Penn Square Bank had been promoted into one of the most aggressive and largest oil and gas lenders in the nation. So voracious was its appetite, it not only generated loans for its own portfolio, but it also supplied approximately $2 billion in loans to other banks, namely Seattle-First National Bank (SeaFirst) and Continental Illinois National Bank and Trust in Chicago (Continental).[5]

Even though Penn Square's problems had been chronicled in local and banking industry newspapers for months, the depth of the graft and mismanagement that contributed to its failure was shocking. As the story unfolded, it became more and more bizarre: accounts of lavish entertaining by Bill Patterson, the bank's chief lending officer, which included such antics as drinking beer out of his cowboy boot, were particularly outlandish. Unfortunately, the "self-dealing" on the part of the involved bankers reflected poorly on the entire industry. The improprieties were so audacious and the ramifications so widespread that they were reported in the media for years following the bank's demise and were the subject of several books.

Shortly after the demise of Penn Square came the failure of another bank highly involved in lending to the oil and gas industry. On August 6, 1982, Abilene National Bank, Abilene, Texas, with assets of $450 million, was forced to merge with Mercantile Texas Corporation, the predecessor of MCorp of Dallas, the second-largest banking organization in Texas.[6]

Abilene National was the second-largest bank behind Penn Square to fail in 1982, and the circumstances of its failure were very similar to Penn Square. Both banks had grown very rapidly by lending to the oil and gas industry, and many of the loans proved uncollectible as a result of the unexpected downturn in oil prices and drilling activity. Abilene National also suffered from a run when it lost about 12 percent of its deposits in a three-day period in mid-July following a negative article in the *Dallas Morning News*, which alleged that many of the bank's loans were bad.

It wasn't long after the failure of Penn Square that the repercussions were felt at Continental. In July 1982, Continental disclosed that it had purchased approximately $1 billion in energy loans from Penn Square. In the ensuing two years, Continental was buffeted by rumors, which led to repeated runs by domestic and foreign depositors. Finally, on July 26, 1984, the government engineered a bailout of the liquidity-insolvent bank.

In a highly controversial move, William M. Isaac, chairman of the FDIC, in effect nationalized the bank. This was the first of the modern-day "open bank" transactions utilized by the FDIC to shore up a bank to prevent its failure. In the case of Continental, the FDIC injected $1.5 billion in capital into the bank, giving the FDIC controlling interest and significantly diluting existing shareholders. The rescue of Continental was the largest in U.S. history up until that time, and, in retrospect, it would ultimately be regarded as one of the most successful bailouts in the experience of the FDIC.

In 1983, only three banks failed in Texas, and all three were located in Midland and Odessa, a clear indication of the depth of the problems in those economies.

The failure on October 14, 1983, of The First National Bank of Midland was by far the most notable of the three, stunning bankers in Texas and the nation alike. The collapse of First National, with $1.4 billion in assets, was the second-largest failure in U.S. history, behind the 1974 failure of Franklin National Bank in New York, with $3.6 billion in assets.[7]

The First National Bank of Midland was an impressive institution, with one of the highest capital ratios (capital as a percent of total capital plus liabilities) of any bank in Texas. C. J. Kelly, the bank's president, was almost legendary for his abilities as an energy lender and a collector of western art. And, indeed, under Kelly's watchful eye, the bank had accumulated what was reputed to be one of the finest private art collections in the country.

But Kelly had retired during the 1970s, and his successors had steered the bank away from traditional, conservative energy-production loans, secured by oil and gas reserves, and toward loans to finance oil field equipment, most notably drilling rigs. When the drilling business collapsed in 1982, rigs no longer in use or in demand could not bring $.10 on the dollar at auction.

The growth of First National during the post-Kelly years was meteoric. Once considerably smaller than TAB/Fort Worth, by the end of 1981 it was nipping at our heels to supplant us as the seventh-largest bank in Texas. But rumors were rampant that the rapid growth had been achieved through aggressive lending and that the bank was heading for a downfall. In fact, months before it failed, it was known to be in deep trouble. Nonetheless, the banking community was stunned when its doors actually closed. How could such a venerable institution, so steeped in conservative traditions, have deteriorated so rapidly? It was an unsettling question.

The experience of the banks in Midland and Odessa patently demonstrates the impact a deteriorating dominant industry can have on a community and on its financial institutions. At the outset of 1982, Midland had seven banks, four independents and three holding-company subsidiaries. Odessa, also, had seven banks, three independents and four holding-company banks. At the close of 1987, all four independents in Midland and three of the four independents in Odessa had failed. In all likelihood, the holding company subsidiaries would have succumbed to a similar fate had it not been for the willingness of their parent companies to provide needed capital injections to keep them afloat. This was certainly the case with TAB's bank, Texas American Bank/Midland, whose loan losses over the 1982–1985 period had depleted its capital and reserves.

During 1982–1985, there were 289 bank failures in the United States, of which only 28, or approximately 10 percent, were in Texas. Most of the others were either in energy-dependent or agricultural-dependent states.[8]

With the precipitous decline in oil prices in the first quarter of 1986, there was an immediate impact on banks in oil-based communities. Two major Oklahoma banking companies were among the first fatalities.

The First National Bank & Trust Company of Oklahoma City, the third-largest bank in Oklahoma, failed on July 14, 1986, and was sold to First Interstate Bancorp, Los Angeles. Once the largest bank in Oklahoma, First National had been struggling since the beginning of the oil price slide in 1982 and was regarded as the most critically ill of the Southwest banks. With $1.6 billion in assets, First National was the second-largest failure in the U.S. behind Franklin National Bank in New York, replacing The First National Bank of Midland for that dubious distinction. (The rescue of Continental was not officially recorded as a failure since the bank never was officially declared insolvent and received "open bank" assistance.)[9]

One week later, on July 22, the *Wall Street Journal* reported that the second-largest banking organization in Oklahoma, BancOklahoma Corporation of Tulsa, with assets of $2.7 billion, was seeking assistance from the FDIC. The request was precipitated by the troubles of its Oklahoma

Commercial Bank Failures: 1983-1992
Texas and The United States

	Texas Failures		U.S. Failures		Texas % of U.S.	
Year	Number	Deposits ($ Billions)	Number	Deposits ($ Billions)	Number	Deposits
1983	3	0.7	48	5.4	6.3	12.5
1984	6	0.2	79	2.9	7.6	8.1
1985	12	0.3	120	8.1	10.0	3.5
1986	26	0.0	138	6.5	18.8	0.0
1987	50	1.9	184	6.3	27.2	30.2
1988	113	22.8	200	24.9	56.5	91.6
1989	133	18.5	206	24.1	64.6	76.8
1990	103	5.4	168	14.5	61.3	37.2
1991	31	1.1	124	53.8	25.0	2.0
1992	29	8.2	120	41.1	24.2	20.0

Source: The Banking Department of Texas and Annual Reports of the federal Deposit Insurance Corporation.

Table 1

City unit, Bank of Oklahoma, formerly known as Fidelity Bank, prior to its acquisition by BancOklahoma in 1984.[10] According to reports, approximately 20 percent of that unit's loans were nonperforming (loans on which neither interest nor principal was being collected).

On August 18, the FDIC announced the second "open bank" assistance transaction for an energy-beleaguered bank when it agreed to provide assistance of $130 million to Bank of Oklahoma, Oklahoma City. In return, the FDIC received convertible preferred stock for substantially all of the stock in Bank of Oklahoma, N.A., a new bank resulting from the merger of the Oklahoma City Bank with Bank of Oklahoma, Tulsa. In addition, the FDIC received warrants convertible into 55 percent of the common stock of the parent company, BancOklahoma Corporation.[11]

While The First National Bank & Trust Company of Oklahoma City and BancOklahoma were the first major Southwest banks to succumb to the aftermath of the 1986 oil price dive, they were only a precursor of many others to follow.

As evidenced by Table 1, 1986 was the worst year since the Great Depression for the nation's banking system. There were a total of 138 bank failures, mostly centered in the oil and agricultural states of the Southwest, Rocky Mountains, and Midwest. The banking industry of Texas was particularly hard hit with twenty-six bank failures, or 18.8 percent of the total, due to the heavy orientation of the Texas economy in both oil and agriculture.

However, the collapse of the real estate industry in 1987 and 1988 had an even more pronounced effect on the state's banks. Of the 184 bank failures in the nation in 1987, Texas accounted for 62, comprising 30.5 percent of the total. As the real estate depression deepened in 1988, so did the problems of the Texas banking industry, even though conditions in the rest of the nation were improving. As a result, total bank failures again set a record with 200 for the year. Of these, 118, or 53.4 percent of the total, were in Texas.

These statistics actually understate the severity of the situation. As a result of the oil and real estate crash, nine of the ten largest banking organizations, all of which survived the depression of the 1930s and which accounted for approximately 57 percent of the total banking assets of the state, either merged, failed, or were recapitalized with FDIC assistance during 1986–1989. In addition, virtually all of the major Texas S&Ls were insolvent and were restructured prior to 1989, or were taken over by the FDIC under their new powers introduced by President George Bush on February 6, 1989, and passed into law on August 4, 1989, with the enactment of the Financial Institutions Reform, Recovery, and Enforcement Act (FIRREA).

Indeed, the financial structure of Texas was altered profoundly and permanently.

THREE

THE S&L SCANDAL IN TEXAS

Although the problems in the oil industry rocked banks located in oil-predominant states and communities, a confluence of events in the early 1980s set the stage for excesses in the real estate markets that were beyond comprehension or imagination. The deregulation of the S&L industry, concomitant with lax supervision, permitted imprudent lending practices, self-dealing, and fraud, which amplified an explosion in real estate speculation and construction far exceeding existing demand, or any reasonable expectation of future demand. This problem was particularly acute in Texas, where S&L activities had a profound effect on real estate markets. Unfortunately, by the time regulators and the general public–including the management of the major Texas commercial banks–became aware of the extent of the damage, it was too late. The consequences for TAB would prove to be disastrous.

Awareness

In retrospect, it seems incredible that virtually no one saw the thrift crisis coming. Perhaps in Texas we were too close to the situation to realize what was happening. But, regardless of the reason, in the short period of two to three years following deregulation, the S&L industry engaged in reckless, irresponsible, and, in many cases, fraudulent activities that created a financial disaster of epic proportions.

My first awareness of possible irregularities in the Texas S&Ls began with a request for a credit report on Vernon Savings and Loan Association of Dallas. All we at TAB knew about the company was that it had been very active in lending on commercial real estate, but, with a few inquiries, we learned some disturbing facts.

Vernon was controlled and run by Don Ray Dixon, a real estate developer known for his "Dondi Homes" condominium developments and his flamboyant lifestyle. Apparently, Dixon and his associates were living off of Vernon Savings and Loan, extracting large salaries, unlimited expense accounts, and extravagant fringe benefits. Among the perks provided to Dixon by the thrift were a Ferrari "company car" and a fleet of six airplanes.

We advised our customer that having a developer running an S&L was like having a fox in the hen house, and that Vernon was providing perks far beyond anything reasonable. We couldn't point to anything illegal, but something just wasn't right. Vernon Savings failed on March 20, 1987.

Shortly after our inquiries concerning Vernon Savings, the media began a serial exposé about the abuses of Empire Savings & Loan of Mesquite, Texas. Empire, which had grown from $17 million in 1982 to $309 million when it was closed on March 14, 1984, failed because of loans used to finance the construction of thousands of condominiums in eastern Dallas County along Interstate 30 near Lake Ray Hubbard. In its indictments of the Empire owner Danny Faulkner, members of management, developers, and land appraisers, the government alleged that loans to finance the condos were based on inflated appraisals and that some of the proceeds went into the pockets of the accused parties.

In spite of the extensive media coverage of the I-30 excesses, the Empire case seemed to be a special isolated situation and not a precursor of problems endemic in the industry. Occasionally we would become aware of an S&L transaction that TAB had already rejected as unsound. An example was Vernon's financing of Stonegate in Fort Worth.

Stonegate was the name given to the Davis "family farm" by its purchaser, a Dallas-based developer. Consisting of 189 acres of undeveloped land in the affluent west side of Fort Worth, the $6 million, 19,000-square-foot mansion in the center of the farm was the scene of the well-publicized murders of Stan Farr and Andrea Wilborn. Farr was the lover of Priscilla Davis, the estranged wife of oil heir T. Cullen Davis, and Wilborn was Priscilla Davis's daughter. Cullen Davis was indicted for the murders but was found innocent in one of the longest and most widely publicized trials in Texas history. The colorful history of the property, and of the intent to use the mansion as the focal point of the proposed mixed-use development, gave the project added intrinsic value. Even so, we felt the proposed purchase price of $33 million, or $4.00 per square foot, was outrageous, and that it was worth about half that much.

TAB was approached to make the loan, which we declined. The developer finally received a commitment from Vernon for $64 million for the acquisition and development of the property. In return, Vernon received a 50 percent equity or profits participation, in addition to interest. Subsequent to Vernon's failure, Stonegate was foreclosed and later sold by federal regulators to the Bass family interests of Fort Worth.

Most of the properties financed by S&Ls were overpriced. However, information regarding S&Ls and their financing activities was highly fragmented, and it was impossible to see the whole picture. Bankers had no idea of the aggregate magnitude of the financings, nor of the impact they were having on the market. And, by the time the total impact was known, the damage was done.

A Bottomless Pit?

The depth of the S&L crisis was described by the *New York Times* on June 12, 1988, as "the biggest financial disaster of the post-war era . . . that could produce the largest Government bailout in history."[1] So deep was the problem that its ultimate cost defied accurate estimation. Forecasts ranged from $150 billion to $300 billion, including interest, the latter figure representing over $1,000 for every man, woman, and child in the U.S. However, the final cost will not be known until the federal government disposes of between $300 billion to $500 billion in real estate it inherited from failing S&Ls.

In Texas, where in 1989 approximately 80 percent of all thrifts were believed to be insolvent, the crisis was much more acute than in the rest of the nation.[2] In 1988, Texas thrifts lost $10.1 billion, or 83 percent of the nation's total of $12.1 billion.[3] According to the Federal Home Loan Bank Board chief economist, James Barth, "The state [Texas] was so hard-hit by bad loans that the size of the problem is overwhelming." Barth pointed out that of the twenty worst thrifts in the nation, one-half were in Texas.[4]

Deregulation

Because of anti-inflationary monetary policies–and concomitant, historically high interest rates–the nation's S&Ls suffered massive disintermediation of funds and severe losses in the late 1970s, which threatened to bankrupt the entire industry. In response, Congress passed legislation that effectively deregulated the S&L industry. First, in 1980, they enacted the Depository Institutions Deregulation and Monetary Control Act, phased out Regulation Q by lifting the 5.5 percent ceiling, and raised insurance coverage under the Federal Savings and Loan Insurance Corporation (FSLIC) and the FDIC from $40,000 to $100,000.[5] Many experts agree that lifting the ceilings on interest rates and raising deposit insurance coverage was a deadly combination, which contributed significantly to the S&L crisis.

Then, in 1982, Congress added insult to injury by passing the Garn-St. Germain Depository Institutions Act, which allowed the industry to diversify its loan portfolio away from home mortgages. The act permitted S&Ls to enter facets of the high-flying real estate business, which were prohibited to much more sophisticated commercial banks that had the necessary expertise and experience. Under their new powers, federal S&Ls could invest up to 10 percent of their assets in commercial loans, 30 percent in consumer loans, and 40 percent in commercial real estate. They could, thus, put their assets at risk in uncharted waters, a significant departure from the relatively safe harbor of loans on homes.[6] Additionally, they could take high front-end fees on loans, and a 50-percent equity interest in loans on real estate, as compensation in addition to interest.

The passage of the Garn-St. Germain act caused already liberal Texas laws governing state-chartered S&Ls to be liberalized even further. The Texas Savings and Loan Act stipulated that state-chartered associations could "make any loan or investment, perform any function, or engage in any activity permitted a federal association" domiciled in Texas.[7] Thus, the Garn-St. Germain act set the minimum standard.

An unusual quirk of the Garn-St. Germain act allowed real estate loans of up to 100 percent of appraised value. As a consequence, by obtaining liberal and fraudulent appraisals, borrowers were able to obtain loans far in excess of the amount actually paid for a real estate property and put the difference in their pockets. Although legal, it was a fraudulent concept.

However, the main factor in the creation of the S&L crisis was not deregulation: it was a complete breakdown in the regulatory system that allowed undesirable and unqualified individuals to enter the business as owners and managers and permitted them to abuse the system by making imprudent and illegal loans and investments. Additionally, neither the Federal Home Loan Bank (FHLB) nor the FSLIC had the resources or the experience to control a deregulated S&L industry.

Deregulation Attracts Undesirables

With deregulation, the lure of the S&Ls became irresistible to opportunists who recognized the advantages of the new powers under the Garn-St. Germain act. To the real estate entrepreneur, the only thing better than borrowing from an S&L was owning one. To the less than honest, owning an S&L was a license to steal.

Of all the slick, fast-buck artists who gained control of and then looted Texas S&Ls, none was more audacious than Edwin McBirney III, also known as "Fast Eddie."[8] McBirney, the son of a Philadelphia food-retailing executive, graduated from Southern Methodist University, where he started his own business leasing refrigerators while still in school. He married the daughter of a Texas S&L executive and became a millionaire helping real estate investment trusts work out troubled investments.

In 1982, McBirney, at age twenty-nine, combined six small Texas S&Ls–from such rural communities as Stephenville and Bonham–to form Sunbelt Savings Association of Texas. In the next two years, he dazzled the S&L world by increasing Sunbelt's assets from $190 million to $3.2 billion using nationwide telemarketing techniques to acquire out-of-territory and brokered federally insured deposits. Sunbelt's earnings peaked in 1985 at $34.5 million, before cascading into a sea of red ink during the next three years.

Ed McBirney ran his S&L like he lived: in the fast lane. Because of its "shoot-from-the-hip" lending style and reputation for outgunning the competition, Sunbelt acquired the moniker, "Gunbelt Savings." McBirney was a wheeler-dealer, who many referred to as "brilliant." He thought big and had the experience and financial sophistication to structure complicated commercial and real estate acquisition and development deals.

McBirney would frequently hold forth at Jason's, a North Dallas restaurant, entertaining friends and associates, including Don Dixon and Jarrett E. "Jerry" Woods, Jr., chairman, founder, and controlling shareholder of Western Savings Association. McBirney would diagram deals on the butcher-paper tablecloth, enthralling his guests with his financial wizardry. From these meetings, loans exceeding the legal lending limits of any one of the S&Ls would evolve into loan participations shared among the thrifts. In the final analysis, over $1 billion in loans were shared by Sunbelt, Vernon, and Western.

So loose were Sunbelt's lending practices that they once lent $125 million to Sam Ware, an inexperienced Dallas developer in his twenties;

$80 million of the loan later went into default. Ware had entered the real estate business in Dallas in 1980 at age twenty-two, after graduating from Abilene Christian College. In 1983 he started his own company and began borrowing money from Sunbelt. By his own estimate, he borrowed some $300 million in aggregate in the four-year life of his company. Ware, who couldn't qualify for a loan at a more conservative commercial bank, was welcome at Sunbelt, where he would have to pay a higher interest rate and two to three points in fees.[9]

One of Sunbelt's more unusual loans was to the Dallas luxury-car dealer Bob Roethlisberger, who, in a highly publicized transaction, bought eighty-four Rolls Royce automobiles from the Bhagwan Shree Rajineesh collection in Rancho Rajineesh, Oregon. Not only would such a large number of Rolls Royces be difficult for the Dallas market to assimilate, but thirty-six of them had been custom painted by the Bhagwan's staff with peacocks and geese in flight. The $3 million purchase was financed by a Sunbelt subsidiary, a ludicrous loan and a ludicrous investment.

McBirney's flamboyance in lending was exceeded only by his extravagance in entertaining. His parties were legendary in Dallas. For example, he dressed as a king to greet the guests for his 1984 Halloween party at his palatial North Dallas home. In the backyard, smoke machines created a surreal atmosphere, while the guests feasted on lion, antelope, and pheasant. A magician entertained with feats of levitation, and two huge disco performers called "Two Tons of Fun" provided the music. McBirney's 1984 Christmas party, held at a film studio in Las Colinas, featured Ben Vereen on a winter wonderland stage. The Halloween party the following year had a "jungle" theme, featuring a live elephant and entertainment by the rock-and-roll group, the Spinners. With each extravaganza, McBirney seemed to be trying to outdo himself.

In addition to entertaining in Dallas, McBirney frequently transported his friends–most of whom were either associates or Sunbelt customers–to resort destinations, such as Hawaii or Mexico. His last fling in March 1986, three months before regulators forced him out of Sunbelt, was perhaps the most excessive. With fifty of Sunbelt's closest friends and customers, McBirney boarded a Boeing 727 for Las Vegas. That evening, after arriving at the Dunes Hotel, the guests gathered at McBirney's luxurious and spacious suite for a cocktail party. Shortly thereafter, the entertainment arrived in the form of four exotic dancers, who immediately began a striptease act. "Once disrobed, they proceeded to perform sexual acts on some of the businessmen."[10]

McBirney's extravagance was also evidenced in the perks he and other

Sunbelt executives enjoyed. These were epitomized by Sunbelt's fleet of four aircraft consisting of two jets, a Gulfstream II, which is one of the top-of-the-line corporate airplanes, and a Falcon 10. McBirney would often use the jets to fly to Las Vegas, where Sunbelt had acquired a mortgage company, but also where McBirney was a regular at Caesar's Palace, the Stardust, and the Dunes.

The March 1986 trip to Las Vegas was McBirney's last hurrah. In June, he was out, and Thomas Wageman, who was handpicked by the FHLB, was in.

Among the many individuals attracted to the S&L industry, few were more controversial than George Aubin of Houston. I first met Aubin in mid-1974, shortly after I had been elected president of Capital National Bank in Austin. Aubin and his partner Bill Haley operating under the name "Aubin and Haley," were the general partners of an investor group that owned a "chain" of nine country and suburban Texas banks. The ownership group included some of Houston's most prominent and prosperous citizens, and one of its most prestigious law firms, Bracewell and Patterson, the former law firm of Comptroller of the Currency, Robert Clarke.

George Aubin can best be described as ordinary. He uses this quality to his advantage, because no one would suspect that behind this very ordinary facade is an extremely cunning and devious individual. Aubin is about five feet six inches tall, and pudgy, with a cherubic face. He dresses conservatively, without gold chains or bracelets, pinkie rings, or other flashy jewelry. In short, he is a perfectly respectable and credible-looking businessman, with a low-key, quiet, unassuming, and sincere personality–all carefully calculated to win friends and gain confidences.

Aubin was not a banker in the context professional bankers would judge him: he was an entrepreneur and an investor. With the board of directors of each bank under his control, Aubin would have himself elected chairman of each bank, with full loan authority. This was a mistake, which ultimately allowed Aubin to abuse his power. He was not an experienced lender. He had no formal training in making loans; he never went through a training program in bank lending or attended a banking school specializing in credit training.

One of the banks Aubin acquired was the $27 million Bank of Texas, Dallas, which had been purchased with interim financing of $2.5 million from Fannin Bank in Houston (now NationsBank-Fannin). Capital National Bank in Austin (now Texas Commerce Bank of Austin) assumed the loan from Fannin Bank in 1974.

Shortly thereafter, in early 1975, Capital National's monitoring of the bank revealed extensive unsecured "insider" loans made by the bank to Aubin, Aubin-controlled entities, and Aubin's friends. These loans, which were highly irregular, had been made under Aubin's authority as chairman or by the bank's president, J. B. Haralson, an Aubin appointee and confidant. Because of a voting trust, which Aubin controlled, Capital National was unable to remove him from a position of authority, and the Texas commissioner of banking refused to take action.

In the meantime, Aubin was able to keep his loans at the bank current with funds borrowed from other Aubin banks or from banks owned or controlled by the Waco attorney Michael J. Vaughn. Aubin reciprocated in a "you scratch my back and I'll scratch yours" relationship. According to E. Ridley Briggs, former president of the Aubin-controlled Paris Bank of Texas, the bank in Paris charged-off a loan to Vaughn in the amount of $125,000 in 1976. Briggs described Vaughn as a "fat" version of George Aubin, but with a law degree.[11]

In 1976, Bank of Texas, Dallas, essentially failed, leaving Capital National with a large loss. Only one of the Aubin banks officially failed, the South Texas Bank, Houston, with assets of approximately $8.9 million, which was closed on February 26, 1976.

In December 1976, a subcommittee of the U.S. House of Representatives Government Operations Committee identified Aubin, Vaughn, and Herman K. Beebe, Sr., of Bossier City, Louisiana, as the central figures of three separate but closely connected groups of banks, in what has become known as the Texas "Rent-A-Bank" scheme. The banks were bought on borrowed money, and subsequently abused for the benefit of the owners, primarily through "insider" loans. Although not convicted of a crime, Aubin was barred by federal regulators from any future participation in banking due to his part in the scheme.[12]

I didn't hear of Aubin again until I read about him in the October 13, 1986, edition of *Fortune* magazine in an article entitled, "How Hutton Took a Texas-Sized Bath."[13] According to *Fortune*, the investment firm, E. F. Hutton, filed a suit in July 1986 against Aubin alleging he had been the "mastermind" in an elaborate stock and commodity trading scam, which resulted in Aubin writing $46 million in bad checks to Hutton. To cover the checks, J. B. Haralson, former president of Bank of Texas in Dallas, offered his stock in Mercury Savings Association of Wichita Falls and in Ben Milam Savings and Loan Association of Cameron.

In March 1986, the FSLIC declared Mercury Savings and Ben Milam Savings insolvent. According to *Fortune*, the Texas savings and loan commissioner said Mercury Savings was engaged in "extremely dangerous and questionable practices at the thrifts. Among them were major loans to insiders, including George Aubin, and speculation on securities in a secret E. F. Hutton margin account."[14] Hutton maintained that, even though Haralson was the nominal owner of Mercury Savings and Ben Milam Savings, Aubin actually controlled both and ran them through Haralson and others.

Shortly after Hutton filed suit, Aubin countersued, alleging, among other things, that Hutton colluded with federal regulators to devalue the S&Ls they took as collateral. The judge hearing the case threw both suits out of court.

Subsequently, George Aubin, J. B. Haralson, Michael J. Vaughn, Herman K. Beebe, Sr., and Jerry Woods, who was a childhood friend and business associate of Aubin's, emerged as figures in the S&L crisis in the Southwest.[15]

Déjà Vu

As incredible as it might seem, what happened in Texas a decade earlier in the Texas "Rent-A-Bank" scheme served as the blueprint for the Texas S&L scandal. According to the *Dallas Morning News* series on the crisis, a "network of rogue financiers, entrepreneurs and confidence artists" presided over the loss of over $10 billion at fifty thrifts and banks in the South and Southwest.[16] The center of the network was in Texas and included as prominent participants George Aubin and Herman K. Beebe, Sr., two of the three principals identified as the protagonists in the "Rent-A-Bank" scheme.

In August 1987, amid public outrage and mounting pressure from Congress, the U.S. Justice Department announced that it was dispatching a special task force of prosecutors, FBI agents, and Internal Revenue Service agents to investigate fraud in the failure of financial institutions in Texas.

Ed McBirney, George Aubin, Herman Beebe, and Jerry Woods were named as targets, along with 286 other individuals identified by the special task force. Previously, the Justice Department had launched a massive effort to investigate the dealings of D. L. "Danny" Faulkner, the owner of Empire Savings. In 1985, Beebe had been convicted of fraud and received five years probation. He subsequently pleaded guilty on April 29, 1988, to two counts of bank fraud for which he received a one-year prison sentence.

On December 21, 1990, an agreement was reached. In a plea bargain, Ed McBirney agreed to plead guilty to federal criminal charges and to cooperate in future cases. In return, he received a reduced sentence of fifteen years, from a maximum of eighty-five years had he been convicted on all seventeen counts of the indictment.[17] Fifteen months later, on March 31, 1992, a federal jury convicted Jerry Woods on thirty-five counts of fraud, including charges that he used the thrifts' funds to pay off gambling debts he owed to Ed McBirney.[18] McBirney was one of the government's star witnesses against his former friend. Woods received a prison term of twenty-five years and was ordered to pay $37.9 million in restitution to the federal government "for losses he caused his failed thrift, Western Savings Association."[19]

Danny Faulkner was convicted on January 15, 1992, on forty-two counts of stealing millions from five S&Ls through bogus condominium and land deals.[20] Faulkner received a prison term of twenty years, and he and two other defendants were ordered to surrender $100 million they had earned illegally through their dealings.[21]

George Aubin was convicted of conspiracy and bank fraud on October 9, 1994, and was sentenced to ten years imprisonment. He was also ordered to pay restitution of $43.7 million to the Resolution Trust Corporation, the receiver for Western Savings, which Jerry Woods had owned and run. Aubin was charged with scheming to steal $31 million from Western Savings to purchase a horse farm in Kentucky and of hiding more than $14 million from the Internal Revenue Service by routing it to the Cayman Islands. Aubin said he would appeal his conviction to the Fifth U.S. Circuit Court of Appeals in New Orleans.[22]

On May 18, 1989, the FDIC reported that, after examining nearly 220 S&Ls throughout the nation, it had found evidence of criminal fraud and abuse in almost half of them.[23] Clearly, fraud was a major contributor to the S&L problem, and just as clearly the resources devoted to investigating and prosecuting the perpetrators were inadequate. Unfortunately, failure to promptly pursue the guilty parties only encouraged further abuses.

S&L Postmortem

The lesson has been an expensive one: the estimated cost to taxpayers is close to $300 billion, including interest, over a thirty-year period. Hopefully, it is a lesson well learned.

On August 4, 1989, President George Bush signed into law FIRREA, the sweeping S&L bailout and reform bill. The law raised capital requirements for thrifts; pushed thrifts back into the home mortgage business and out of risky investments in speculative commercial real estate ventures and junk bonds; placed the regulatory division of the Federal Home Loan Bank Board under the Office of Thrift Supervision; and moved the supervision for the FSLIC to the FDIC.[24]

Unfortunately, President Bush's actions came too late to save the majority of Texas's S&Ls. Of the 279 S&Ls in Texas as of December 31, 1987, only 50, or 17.9 percent survived; 225 either failed or were forced by state or federal regulators to merge due to insolvency. Two voluntarily merged into other institutions, and two were voluntarily liquidated by their boards of directors.

Only six of the top one hundred Texas S&Ls survived. They included Guardian Savings & Loan Association of Houston (ranked seventh, with assets of $3,338 million as of December 31, 1987), USAA Federal Savings Bank of San Antonio (ranked nineteenth, with assets of $1,050 million), and Colonial Savings & Loan Association of Fort Worth (ranked forty-third, with assets of $496 million).

Special circumstances accounted for most of the survivals. Guardian eschewed opportunities in the overheated commercial real-estate loan markets, and instead followed a strategy of originating and buying packages of single-family mortgages to take advantage of relatively high interest rates in the early to mid-1980s. USAA has no branches and makes no commercial loans; it issues credit cards, primarily to individuals in the U.S. armed forces throughout the world, and its loans consist mostly of credit outstanding on the cards. Colonial makes few commercial loans and engages mostly in single-family mortgage loans. The remaining three S&Ls that survived are Lufkin Federal Savings & Loan Association (ranked eighty-first), South Texas Savings Association of Victoria (ranked eighty-sixth), and Fort Bend Federal Savings & Loan Association of Rosenberg (ranked eighty-ninth). All are smaller S&Ls located in secondary cities where opportunities in commercial lending are limited.

As indicated in Table 2, S&L failures in Texas fall within two time periods: 1988, when 90 of the 225 failures occurred, and 1990–1991, when there were 127 failures. Eighty-eight of the ninety-one failures in 1988 were consolidated into seventeen groups under the Southwest Plan.[25]

The Southwest Plan was conceived and executed by the FHLB chairman M. Danny Wall in lieu of addressing the problem through the Federal Savings and Loan Insurance Corporation, which at the time had insufficient resources to handle the large number of insolvent thrifts. Under the plan, a group of insolvent S&Ls were combined by merger and then sold to outside investors, who would inject new capital. The FSLIC would guarantee the purchaser against losses accruing from the nonperforming

Savings and Loan Failures: 1983-1992
Texas and The United States

Year	Texas Failures		U.S. Failures		Texas % of U.S.	
	Number	Deposits ($ Billions)	Number	Deposits ($ Billions)	Number	Deposits
1983	1	0.1	36	4.6	2.8	2.1
1984	2	0.3	22	5.1	9.1	6.8
1985	1	0.2	31	6.4	3.2	2.7
1986	2	1.1	46	12.5	4.3	8.6
1987	4	1.5	47	10.7	8.5	14.1
1988	90	43.0	205	100.7	43.9	42.7
1989	8	3.9	47	10.3	17.0	38.3
1990	72	20.5	315	105.0	22.9	19.6
1991	55	20.1	232	87.4	23.7	23.0
1992	7	1.5	69	32.9	10.1	4.5

Source: Information Services Division of the Office of Thrift Supervision and the American Council of State Savings Supervisors, January 12, 1993.

Table 2

Texas Savings and Loan Associations: 1961-1992
($ Millions)

Year	No.	Total Assets	Net Worth	Year	No.	Total Assets	Net Worth
1992	64	$47,566	$2,918	1978	318	$27,934	$1,445
1991	80	53,500	2,257	1977	328	24,186	1,235
1990	131	72,041	(4,567)	1976	316	19,922	1,045
Conservatorship	51	14,952	(6,638)	1975	303	16,540	915
Privately Owned	80	57,089	2,071	1974	295	13,945	835
1989	196	90,606	(9,356)	1973	288	12,630	764
Conservatorship	81	22,160	(10,866)	1972	278	10,915	678
Privately Owned	115	68,446	1,510	1971	272	9,113	589
1988	204	110,499	(4,088)	1970	271	7,707	532
1987	279	99,614	(6,677)	1969	270	7,056	487
1986	281	96,920	110	1968	267	6,602	429
1985	273	91,799	3,904	1967	268	6,156	391
1984	273	77,544	2,938	1966	268	5,694	362
1983	273	56,685	2,387	1965	267	5,351	334
1982	288	42,506	1,631	1964	262	4,797	296
1981	311	38,344	1,494	1963	256	4,192	259
1980	318	34,954	1,711	1962	248	3,533	231
1979	310	31,280	1,640	1961	240	2,991	194

Source: 1994-1995 Texas Almanac, The Dallas Morning News, A.H. Belo Corporation, Dallas, Texas, p. 469.

Table 3

assets on the S&L's books, provide a guaranteed spread above the "Texas" cost of funds on their deposit liabilities, and allow the purchaser to utilize the tax benefits resulting from post-transaction operating losses and from the carryforward of pretransaction tax losses. As a consequence, the purchaser would receive a guaranteed profit on his original investment, which, in some cases, would be fully recovered through the tax benefits.

Critics of the Southwest Plan charged that it benefited a few wealthy individuals at the expense of the taxpayer. An outcry of protest occurred after a flurry of last-minute deals were consummated immediately prior to December 31, 1988, in order to take advantage of tax breaks expiring at year-end. The controversy was sparked by tax breaks, estimated to be $800 million to $900 million, given to the New York financier and takeover artist Ronald O. Perelman for investing $315 million in First Gibraltar Savings of Dallas.

The Southwest Plan was suspended immediately after President Bush announced his thrift rescue package on February 6, 1989. Danny Wall resigned under fire on December 4, 1989.[26]

Of the 120 Texas S&Ls that failed in 1990–1991, most had actually been placed under conservatorship by the FHLB during 1986–1988. Control of these was transferred to the FDIC on February 7, 1989, when bank and thrift regulators began merging insurance fund operations in accordance with President Bush's thrift rescue plan.

On December 7, 1989, new, more stringent capital requirements, mandated by President Bush's thrift bill (FIRREA) or promulgated by federal regulators under the authority of FIRREA, went into effect. Under the three-tiered requirements, it was estimated that 1,217 thrifts across the nation, with total assets of $795 billion, would fall short of the targets. Of these, 424 thrifts, with assets of $294 billion, failed to meet the minimum standards.[27]

A particularly controversial feature of the new capital requirements involved the treatment of "supervisory goodwill," an intangible asset, which represented the negative gap between the market value of assets and the book value of those assets at the time an S&L was purchased. Originally, regulators granted the purchasers forty years in which to write off this so-called goodwill. Under the new thrift regulations, acquirers were given only five years to write off goodwill, which accelerated losses and reduced capital.

In the early 1980s, when the S&Ls experienced huge losses on the sale of fixed-rate mortgages, regulators allowed them to operate with lower capital requirements by granting regulatory forbearance. For example, they were permitted to amortize the losses over the life of sold mortgage loans, rather than upon their sale, as would have been required under generally accepted accounting principles. This was a double-edged sword in that the S&Ls were burdened with these losses for twenty to thirty years, but, conversely, they were able to report higher capital ratios than otherwise would have been possible. Regulatory forbearance was granted routinely prior to February 1989 in order to allow the weak S&Ls to stay open and to preserve the assets of the FSLIC.

The new standards, that is, the more rapid write-off of supervisory goodwill and the elimination of forbearance, were widely criticized within the thrift industry, with many predicting that the industry was headed toward chaos and paralysis. While the new capital requirements may have hastened the demise of some marginally capitalized S&Ls, it is generally agreed that the practice of keeping insolvent S&Ls open deepened their losses and, thus, the cost of the bailout.

As indicated by Table 3, on December 31, 1987, there were 279 Texas S&Ls with total assets of $99.6 billion, whereas, on December 31, 1992, there were only 64 S&Ls in Texas with total assets of $47.6 billion. In the interim six years, $52 billion in assets had evaporated, mostly through loan write-offs.

For the Texas economy, real estate industry, and commercial banks, the results of the deregulation of the S&L industry and the excesses that followed were devastating. The flood of money that flowed into the state, together with the speculative fever that infected the entire spectrum of the industry, left a house of cards that was destined to collapse. The prices of real estate–especially that of raw land, retail developments, and office space–were driven to unsustainable levels, and the markets were bloated with an oversupply of inventory of all types.

The bacchanalian orgy of the mismanaged S&Ls produced a hangover of unprecedented proportions, leaving no participant untouched. The impact on Texas's major banks, all of which were active participants, was particularly severe.

This account of the impact of the S&Ls in Texas would be incomplete without pointing out that, during the 1980s, most of Texas's S&Ls were run by honest, reputable bankers who managed their organizations in a very prudent manner. In the September 10, 1990, edition of *Fortune* magazine, the consultant Bert Ely of Alexandria, Virginia, estimated that only 3 percent of the $147 billion, excluding interest, that he calculated as the present value of the cost of the bailout for the nation was due to fraud. More recently, a congressional commission found that about 15 percent of the number of thrift failures were caused by "out-and-out fraud."[28] In Texas, the percentage of both the cost and number of failures was probably slightly higher, since there was fraud involved in the failure of some of the largest institutions, including Empire, Sunbelt, Vernon, and Western.

Throughout their existence in Texas, S&Ls have made a significant contribution to the development of the state. Much, if not most, of the financing for single-family housing in Texas has been provided by the S&L industry, particularly since World War II.[29]

FOUR

BANKING THE OLD-FASHIONED WAY

When commercial banks were established in Texas in the late 1800s and early 1900s, the foundation of the system was trust. Communities were relatively small, the society wasn't very mobile, and everyone knew each other. Loans were typically based on a borrower's character: his word was the best collateral, and a handshake sealed a deal. The customer, in turn, placed his faith in the bank and in the people who owned and ran it.

This mutual trust was put to the test in Fort Worth on February 18, 1930, during the Great Depression. Minutes before closing time at the First National Bank–one of the city's two largest institutions–a thousand people, fed by rumors, arrived shouting for their money. In the back office, bank officials huddled with the civic leaders Amon Carter, Sr., and W. T. "Pappy" Waggoner, planning strategy.

A bank officer soon emerged from the meeting, displaying ebullient confidence, and proclaimed that the bank would remain open all night if needed to serve customers.

Carter then stepped into the lobby and declared, "I was sick in bed, and I couldn't believe this thing when I first heard it, and then I got up and here I am. This is the safest bank in the world and you'll soon find it out. It is paying off every dollar as fast as you are passing in your checks and for every dollar it is paying you it is taking in six more. Why, right now, $2,500,000 is coming from the Federal Reserve Bank in Dallas."

At that instant, as if on cue, the bank doors flew open and a convoy of armed guards carried in large United States currency pouches and smaller coin bags.

"See there," Carter shouted. "What did I tell you! You can't take your money out as fast as they can bring it in. Let's boost our city. Let's not go mad like this. Let's go home and in the morning your money will be right here for you."

Waggoner then joined in:

> I have been a cowman . . . and I have swung on many a cow's tail in a stampede, but this is the first stampede like this I ever saw. . . . I am here to tell you this stampede is worse than cattle stampeding, and I want you to stop it and go on home. This bank has been in business for fifty years and will be in business long after we are gone.
>
> I hereby pledge to you every cent I own and possess in this world that you shall not lose a single dollar in this bank. I will sell every cow and every oil well if necessary to pay for any money you lose here. Go home, I tell you, go on home.[1]

With Carter's pleading and Waggoner's pledge, the run abated. The influence of these two men and the trust the public had in them had turned the tide. During the Great Depression, displays of trust, similar to the one that saved the First National Bank in Fort Worth, were replicated throughout Texas. As a consequence, runs on Texas banks were not as prevalent as they were in other parts of the country.

At TAB/Fort Worth in 1975, mutual trust was still the foundation of banking, and loans continued to be made the old-fashioned way. Fort Worth had a small business community where a person's word and reputation were sacrosanct. Under these circumstances, sophisticated financial analysis wasn't considered necessary.

TAB/Fort Worth had prospered by betting on people and by taking a calculated risk in the process. The financing of the oil and gas industry, in its fledgling years in particular, required nerves of steel, as money was lent to wildcatters to drill discovery wells. The bank had "bankrolled" many of the early pioneer wildcatters. Perhaps the most prominent was Sid Richardson, patriarch of the Bass family of Fort Worth. During the Great Depression, Richardson owed The Fort Worth National Bank $350,000. At the time of the loan, Richardson had a monthly income of about $25,000; a year later, his income had declined to the point that he could no longer pay interest, much less the principal, on the loan. Ellison Harding, the president of the bank, said, "Sid, keep what little income you're getting to live on and pay on your loan when you can."[2] As an indication of Richardson's ongoing gratitude, he instructed his heirs to always "take care of" the bank. This relationship was based on mutual trust, where the bank's reliance on the borrower's character was the guiding principle.

TAB/Fort Worth was used to lending to the larger-than-life entrepreneurs who had helped build the city. Borrowers, likewise, were used to having financing available to fund their business projects. This partnership between lender and borrower had been a winning combination.

In 1975, loans were made by a committee of the bank's elders sitting around a large mahogany table. Cigar smoke clouded the room, and conversation was punctuated with four-letter expletives that added a western "cowtown" atmosphere to the meetings. The elders of the committee, several of whom were retired but who continued to attend and participate by special invitation, regaled other members with anecdotes about past borrowers.

In some cases, a loan was turned down simply based on family connections: "Hell, I wouldn't lend the son-of-a-bitch a nickel. His father reneged on the sale of a piece of land to my brother-in-law, and the son's no better." Or, rejection might be based on sheer dislike. In the case of one potential borrower, I can recall one of the elder committee members saying, "I wouldn't do business with that S.O.B. if he were the last borrower in town. To know him is to hate him." In other cases, potential customers might be rejected because of past loyalties to TAB's competition: "He's always been a customer of First National. I remember when he ran a full page ad congratulating First National when it temporarily passed us in size. I'd tell him to go to hell!"

In spite of some of the riskier practices of the Sid Richardson era and the "folksy" way of doing business, in 1975 TAB was a conservatively run organization that avoided inordinate risks. Loans were made almost exclusively to businesses and individuals who were either located in the markets we served or who did business in those markets. Each loan was approved by a loan committee consisting of the senior lenders in the company. If any committee member or executive officer had a strong objection to a particular credit, it would be denied.

TAB/Fort Worth was the biggest bank in the TAB system, accounting for about 50 percent of total assets, and it was the dominant bank in the Fort Worth market. As a result, its performance set the tone for TAB, and, in turn, its performance was influenced greatly by the Fort Worth economy.

By 1982, the basic business of Fort Worth was still rooted in oil and gas, agriculture, rail transportation, and defense spending. It lacked the depth, breadth, and diversification of Dallas, and TAB/Fort Worth's opportunities were limited accordingly. Under Lewis Bond, a petroleum engineer, oil and gas lending had been emphasized, and, as a result, loans to this industry, which had increased at 30 percent per year during 1978–1982, provided most of TAB's growth.

TAB's growth, fueled by an insatiable demand for loans, was explosive during 1975–1982, when its assets nearly tripled. The tidal wave of prosperity from the oil boom that had swept over Texas engulfed TAB, as well. A bank is a mirror image of the economy it serves, and the economies in all of TAB's markets were booming.

The Bloom Was Off the Rose

During the 1970s and early 1980s, all the major Texas banks had become extremely growth oriented. Their stocks had been widely touted by Wall Street, and institutions had bought large amounts of stock in Texas banks. As a consequence, performance had become the name of the game, and quarterly increases in earnings at a rate of close to 15 percent per annum were not only expected, but demanded by investors. TAB had not disappointed Wall Street, as its earnings had increased from $22.6 million in 1978 to $47 million in 1982. Likewise, the price of the company's common stock had increased from $21 per share to $35 per share over the same period.

As 1982 came to a close, the bloom was off the rose in relation to the oil and gas business. Prices were in a protracted decline and so was loan demand. In fact, most of our oil and gas customers had advised us they were discontinuing exploration, and loans would be running off as they were paid from existing production revenues. Consequently, we had to find new opportunities if we were to continue to grow.

In early 1982, a dramatic change was announced that would come back to haunt TAB years later. The company would henceforth concentrate its efforts on real estate lending, the area of greatest opportunity at that time.

It was clear that if TAB was to continue its record of increasing future earnings and satisfying the insatiable demands of Wall Street, it would have to replace the loan runoff from oil and gas. This was more than accomplished during the 1982–1985 period, when oil and gas loans declined from 18 percent of the total portfolio to 10 percent, and real estate loans increased from 23 percent to 44 percent. In 1982 alone, real estate construction loans grew 50 percent, setting the tone for the future. While much of the 1982–1985 increase resulted from the acquisition of fourteen banks, including several "real estate banks," the largest portion came from loans generated within the TAB system.

Real estate values, although rising rapidly, were not out of line with comparable properties in other parts of the country. Class A office space (the highest-quality office space), for example, at $25 per square foot, which was the top end of the range of assumptions on which new projects were being based, was a bargain compared to most other major markets.

By the early- to mid-1980s, most of the old-timers had retired, and TAB's managers and lenders were young and inexperienced. None of them had seen really tough times, and most had gained experience only during the highly inflationary days of the 1970s. In those days, it was hard to make a mistake, or at least mistakes were hard to recognize, as inflation bailed out one ill-advised deal after another. In relation to real estate, either land values or rental rates would rise enough to make a bad development or investment viable. In this environment, both borrowers and lenders began to regard themselves as bulletproof.

These circumstances, combined with the goal of growing the banks' assets sufficiently to assure the continued upward march of our earnings, proved to be a fatal combination.

The attitude of our borrowers was "go-go" (a slang expression used at the time to mean "aggressive"), and some of our lenders became infected with their optimism. At times, loan officers would become giddy with enthusiasm over a borrower and his projects. Objectivity would be thrown to the wind, with the end result that loans would be vastly oversold to the loan committee, both in terms of attractiveness and economic viability.

One such case involved a proposal to finance a "condo conversion" of an apartment building known as "2016 Main" in downtown Houston. The borrower was one with whom we had done numerous deals, and he was experienced in this type of transaction: buying an existing apartment house and converting it to condominiums by offering to sell the apartment units to the existing rental tenants. If the building and location were well established and attractive, the concept would work. The loan officer's enthusiasm in presenting the loan for 2016 Main was infectious: "This is a slam dunk. We have an experienced developer, a trophy property, and a solid financial partner. I'll stake my future on it."

The property at 2016 Main had been troubled since its construction in the 1960s. It was one of the first high-rise apartment buildings built in Houston, and one of the few apartment buildings to be built downtown. It had never enjoyed a high rate of occupancy as an apartment building, and it had failed as a hotel under Mexican ownership.

The loan officer presenting the loan had spent months studying the project; condo conversions were in vogue and had been highly successful elsewhere. We had participated in several that had been real winners, and there was no reason to think the same approach wouldn't work here.

Unfortunately, though, it didn't work. In order to renovate the property, we had to ask the tenants to move out–thereby dislocating our captive market–and few returned as purchasers of condo units after the renovation was completed. After the condo project failed, the building was converted back to apartments to let. By then, though, so much was invested in the building that the apartment concept couldn't support the cost structure. Additionally, TAB's financial partner, which was supposed to take our company out of the project by making the individual mortgages on the condo units, was Gill Savings and Loan of San Antonio, which regrettably would be one of the early casualties in the S&L fiasco.

While a valuable lesson was learned from this experience, if TAB wanted to be a contender in Southwest banking, we could not afford to turn down opportunities that any of our competitors would take. For every prospective loan, there were dozens of lenders. Either TAB competed or sat on the sidelines. Neither TAB's board, its shareholders, nor Wall Street would have stood for it.

Besides, there was a strong belief that, in the event of default and foreclosure, the repossessed property could be resold in the strong Texas real estate market with little if any loss. No one believed that values could drop enough to produce large losses, or that values could drop precipitously. How wrong we all were!

Real Estate Lending at TAB

With the inflation of the late 1970s and early 1980s and with the more permissible lending resulting from the enactment of the Garn-St. Germain act in 1982, the traditions that had governed real estate lending gave way to a new set of standards. This led to a greater concentration in real estate loans. Loans remained on the books longer, and it became commonplace for lenders to extend loans covering 100 percent of the cost of projects, including interest carry.

Moreover, because of the double-digit interest rates that prevailed at the time, real estate developers could no longer afford to lock into permanent fixed-rate mortgages, known as "take outs." As a result, take-out loans became a thing of the past. In their place, lenders extended "mini-perms," normally made on a floating rate basis for a period of up to five years. This gave the developer additional time to arrange for a permanent fixed-rate loan.

Unfortunately, even after interest rates declined to single-digit levels after 1982, lenders didn't revert to the prior practice of requiring take-outs. Without that discipline, other requirements were relaxed: pre-leasing standards became more lenient, and the borrower's balance sheet strength replaced the equity previously required. This meant increased risks for the lender.

At the same time, the distinction between acquiring raw land for development purposes and for speculation became blurred. Developers presented borrowers with glitzy feasibility studies and marketing plans on projects, which proved to be overly optimistic. As a result, the developments didn't sell out according to plan, and they remained on the lender's books longer than anticipated. In many cases, the projects were so outlandish, they were sheer speculation. In other cases, the lender threw caution to the wind and knowingly made loans to speculators who had no development intentions.

Egged on by Wall Street, lenders competed eagerly against each other to finance these projects. With profit margins having been squeezed during the tight credit period of the late 1970s and early 1980s, and with the increased competition for normal sources of loans, the fees available on real estate loans proved irresistible to most banks.

Additionally, the deregulation of the S&Ls in 1982 had changed the competitive landscape in Texas; the exclusive domain of the commercial banks had been challenged. Previously there had been a division of financing roles: the commercial banks financed most of the single-family real estate development and construction and virtually all of the commercial construction, whereas S&Ls supplied permanent home mortgage financing. For the first time, S&Ls were bidding aggressively for loans for the development and construction of residential properties and of commercial projects.

The debates at TAB during this time about whether or not to change its lending policies were extensive and ultimately convincing. The principal advocates for change were the real estate lenders.

Gene Gray, the senior credit officer of TAB and of TAB/Fort Worth, who had spent much of his career in the real estate lending department and was its manager during the last several years of his tenure there, was sympathetic to change. His opinion was respected; he knew the real estate business and had a great feel for the market. His intuition was usually right, and his endorsement of change carried considerable weight.

Gray argued,

> Hell, we're not competitive. The S&Ls and the big real estate banks are setting the standards and are dominating the market. They're eating our lunch. If we don't start making mini-perms, if we don't lend the full cost including interest, and if we don't agree to more lenient pre-leasing, we might as well get out of the business. In fact, we won't have to get out, we're out now, and we'll stay out by default.
>
> Our oil and gas loans are running off the books. We will lose over $200 million in the next year. The agricultural business is in the tank, and commercial loan demand is weak. We can't make any consumer loans because people won't fight the traffic and spend the time to come downtown when they can borrow at one of the neighborhood banks. If we don't get competitive, we won't put any new loans on the books to replace those we're losing, much less to continue to grow. We don't have any choice.

At this time, in early 1983, TAB had just experienced the best year in its history, and there was considerable pressure from TAB's CEO, Lewis Bond, to maintain the momentum. TAB was on the acquisition trail, and it was important to have a highly valued common stock to use as currency in purchasing other banks. As pointed out by Gene Gray, oil loans were being paid down rapidly and commercial loan demand was weak, as we were just coming out of the recession of 1981–1982. Being more aggressive in real estate lending seemed like the only alternative and a perfectly rational strategy.

Additionally, out-of-state financial institutions, primarily from the Midwest and the East Coast where the economies were lackluster, looked upon the fast-growing state of Texas as an attractive source for real estate loans.

The competition was fierce, and it was apparent that, if we were to compete, we had to conform to the new lending practices. Accordingly, we relented to the pressures of the market and adopted the more relaxed standards that had become commonplace in the industry.

TAB wasn't unique: virtually every major real estate lender in the country conformed. Bankers across the U.S. let competition, the quest for earnings, the need to show successive quarterly increases and 15 percent annual increases, and pressures from the investment community dictate actions.

A Harbinger of the Future

The first sign of weakness showed up in TAB's petroleum-lending portfolio. In particular, the sharp decline in drilling activity, beginning in 1982, had a harmful effect on the smaller, more thinly capitalized oil and gas companies, many of whom TAB had financed because they weren't large enough to be meaningful customers of larger Dallas and Houston banks. The domino effect from the slump in the oil and gas business was particularly severe in those communities that were heavily dependent on the industry. With banking offices in Houston, Fort Worth, Midland, and Longview, TAB was impacted severely. Consequently, loan losses increased from $12.8 million in 1982 to $31.1 million in 1983, and to $32 million in 1984. TAB's earnings also suffered, declining from $46.9 million in 1982 to $36.3 million in 1983, but rebounding to $43 million in 1984.

Of greater concern than the loan losses and the decline in earnings, however, was the large increase in nonperforming assets, which included nonaccrual loans and foreclosed assets. Nonaccrual loans were loans on which TAB was either no longer collecting interest and principal payments, or the ultimate collection was considered questionable. In these instances, the loan would be put on nonaccrual, which means that the bank would no longer record the collection of interest for accounting purposes: any interest actually received would be applied to the principal of the loan. Most of the foreclosed assets consisted of real estate and oil and gas properties.

The level of nonperforming assets was considered a harbinger of the future, because of the cost of carrying sterile nonearning assets and of the high probability of future losses on these assets.

Whereas nonperforming assets were only $18.2 million in 1981, with the break in oil prices in the latter part of that year, they had climbed to $43.4 million by the end of 1982. This, however, was only the beginning of an unending upward spiral. During 1983 and 1984, nonperforming assets increased to $83.4 million and $103.2 million, respectively.

During these years, real estate was not considered to be a significant problem as measured by nonperforming assets. For instance, foreclosed real estate and nonaccrual real estate loans accounted for 16.6 percent of nonperforming assets in 1983 and 22.8 percent in 1984.

In these two years, signs of overbuilding in some areas of the state and in some sectors of the real estate market were beginning to appear. As a result of increasing concerns about the trends, TAB made a conscientious decision as early as 1984 to avoid lending in some geographic areas where the markets were already satiated, and to avoid loans for the construction of office space regardless of location.

The year 1985 was a watershed for TAB. By then, the Texas banks were receiving national publicity due to their deteriorating condition. But TAB was outperforming the group. TAB had the smallest percentage of nonperforming loans of any major banking organization in the Southwest. It had fewer loans to the energy sector than any of the other banks, never made loans on drilling rigs, and made only a small amount to the service and supply companies. Also at that time, there were only a few signs of actual problems in the real estate markets, and these were confined to cities that had been hit heavily by the decline in oil prices.

But, as the year progressed, concerns grew about the oversupply of real estate. In July 1985, TAB decided to curtail all real estate lending. By then, however, real estate already constituted about 44 percent of TAB's total loan portfolio. TAB recognized that this concentration was too high, and the decision was made to reduce the amount to 35 percent by June 30, 1986. Unfortunately, this decision came too late, as confidence in the real estate markets deteriorated rapidly in the last half of 1985.

By year-end, no progress had been made toward the goal of reducing real estate loans. Additionally, from 1984 to 1985, loan losses had increased from $32 million to $53.3 million, and earnings had declined from $43 million to $26.2 million. Even more alarming, however, there was a whopping increase in nonperforming assets over the same period, from $103.2 million to $169.8 million, with real estate rising from 22.8 percent to 37.3 percent of the total. By this time, we were worried.

FIVE 5

THE GROWING CRISIS

Thursday, April 24, 1986, was the day of TAB's annual shareholders' meeting and the day I would be elected TAB's chairman and chief executive officer. A few weeks earlier, I had moved from my sixth-floor office to Lewis Bond's office on the sixteenth floor, with its rich, wood-paneled walls and private bathroom. Instead of the roof of Monnig's department store, I could now see the two gleaming towers built by the Bass family and the confluence of the "West Fork" and the "Clear Fork" of the Trinity River, where Fort Worth was founded. Bond had selected an appropriate view for the office of the chairman of the city's most important business enterprise.

That morning I took a little extra time getting dressed. I wanted to both look and be my best at the shareholders' meeting, primarily because my wife Sheila would be there. My election as chairman and CEO was just as important to her as it was to me, since she had worked just as hard to support my rise to the top.

The first order of business that morning was to address our officers' meeting, as I did every Thursday. But this meeting would be different–the mantle of power would change within hours, and a full contingent would show up to hear what the new chairman and CEO had to say. My comments reflected both my hopes and my concerns:

> The last nine months have been rough, but I believe that the worst is behind us now. We've had to take some strong action in order to stand up to the heavy blows that the present economy has dealt us. But I'm confident that we have done the best that we could under the cir-

cumstances, and we will emerge a leaner, meaner, stronger organization that is ready to face the challenges of the future.

Out of adversity comes opportunity. We have seen adversity, and we will see opportunity. But we must position TAB to take advantage of opportunities, such as interstate banking and possible acquisitions. We can't stick our heads in the sand. TAB is an attractive acquisition target. But our mission is the same whether we are the acquirer or the acquired: we must work to maximize the returns to the shareholders, the community, and the employees. The best way to accomplish this is to improve our earnings, and to see that improvement reflected in the price of our stock.[1]

Even though I expressed guarded optimism in my remarks, I was, by this time, extremely concerned and apprehensive about TAB's condition. Gene Gray's gravest fears of only three months ago had come to pass: the price of oil had continued its free fall, crashing through $10.00 per barrel, reaching a low of $9.75 on April 4, 1986. We didn't know the extent of the potential damage, but we did know that TAB wouldn't escape unscathed. Since the break in oil prices in late 1981, we had been observing with growing concern the decline of the oil industry and its impact on the banking business.

This was a particularly tough time, as the mighty ship, which we loved and which had withstood the toughest times, including the Great Depression, was taking on water and beginning to list.

Now, as prices plunged in the first quarter of 1986, we were repricing almost daily the value of the collateral behind our oil and gas loans. With each dollar's decline, our spirits wilted as we watched our collateral depreciate and the potential losses on our loans mount.

When the price of oil dipped below $10 per barrel, we knew we had no choice: we were forced into action that would produce the first loss the company had ever recorded. With future loan losses almost certain, we reduced our earnings by the amount of the expected losses, which we placed in a reserve pending their realization.

The timing of the loss couldn't have been worse: it would be announced at our annual shareholders' meeting. Under normal circumstances, Lewis Bond's retirement and my election to CEO, also announced at the meeting, would have been a time for great recognition and celebration. As it was, much of the luster was removed from the occasion. It was sad to listen to Lewis Bond announce the $21 million loss, and it was too bad his long and successful career had to end on such a sour note.

Redlined

TAB's problems actually began to surface publicly more than a month before the disclosure of the first-quarter loss at the shareholders' meeting.

Standard & Poor's Corporation had announced on March 18 that it was lowering its credit rating on TAB's $50 million in public debt, and we had started experiencing some resistance in negotiating renewals on our certificates of deposit (CDs).[2] With the announcement of the first-quarter loss, our fate was sealed: the door to out-of-state funds was slammed shut. TAB had been redlined by the rest of the country.

Given the severity of the situation, we moved quickly to develop contingency plans, including the affirmation of commitments for the continued purchase of overnight federal funds from our New York correspondent banks, with whom we had enjoyed long-standing relationships.

TAB, like most major banks, relied heavily on funds borrowed from other banks through the federal funds market. At the beginning of each business day, and continuously throughout the day, banks calculate whether they will have surplus funds or be in need of funds at the end of the day in order to balance their assets and liabilities. Typically, banks in high-growth areas with strong loan demand are in need of funds, whereas banks in slow-growth areas have surplus funds. Through an informal but highly developed market, known as the federal funds market, banks with a surplus sell funds to banks with a deficit. Settlement is made through book entry, in most cases at the twelve regional Federal Reserve Banks, where both the seller and the buyer maintain accounts. Once a contract is agreed upon, the seller's account is debited and the buyer's account is credited on the books of the Federal Reserve Bank. In some cases, where the seller maintains an account with the buyer (called a correspondent bank), or vice versa, the sales are handled directly on the books of the seller and the buyer and do not pass through the Federal Reserve System. Most transactions are for one day, and the transaction is reversed the following morning. The federal funds market provides an efficient structure for the transfer of excess funds from low-growth areas of the country to high-growth areas where they are needed for loans.

To plead our case, we decided to go to New York on May 5 and 6. I asked Lewis Bond to accompany Gary Cage and me on the trip, as he was well acquainted with the senior executives of some of the banks. Besides, Bond had been asked by the board to remain as chairman of the executive committees of TAB and TAB/Fort Worth, and he was drawing a $100,000-per-year consulting retainer for the two years until his mandatory retirement at age sixty-seven.

Gary Cage had been chief financial officer of TAB since the early 1970s, having joined the company from Price Waterhouse. He was regarded highly by his peers and was well connected with the bank analysts. Gary and I would work very closely together over the next several years.

Our first appointment in New York set the tone for the rest of the meetings. As we entered Chemical Bank's glass-sheathed tower on Park Avenue, with its greenhouse-looking lower facade, we were apprehensive but hopeful that our New York banking friends would remember our long-standing relationship and allegiance. We were greeted warmly by Dick Bryan, executive vice president, with whom we had lunch prior to a subsequent meeting with Walt Shipley, chairman, and Bob Callander, president.

During lunch our hopes began to fade as we listened to Bryan explain that they had all the Texas exposure they wanted. "We've had it up to here with Texas," he said, gesturing with his hands to indicate they were over their heads. "Through our offices in Dallas and Houston, we plunged headlong into oil and real estate, and we just can't take any more."

The meeting with Shipley and Callander was, thus, anticlimactic, since we had already gotten the message. Before leaving, we gave them a package containing TAB financial information. While they assured us they would review the material carefully, we knew this was only a courtesy.

Upon leaving, we were terribly discouraged. We said little, each of us buried in our own thoughts. The specter of being closed out of the national CD markets and the possibility of losing a critical bid to retain $90 million in deposits from the Dallas/Fort Worth International Airport, which would mature later in May, was haunting. How could we possibly meet our liquidity requirements if we were also shut out by the New York banks? The limo ride to Wall Street from midtown Manhattan for our next appointment at Chase Manhattan Bank seemed interminable. Lewis Bond's silence engulfed the car.

Unfortunately, the reception at Chase, Bankers Trust Company, and J. P. Morgan & Company mirrored that at Chemical. With the conclusion of each meeting, our spirits sagged further. This had to be particularly disheartening to Lewis, as he was extremely proud of the relationships he had built with these organizations.

In total, the trip was a sobering experience. Before this, whenever we went to New York, we were wined and dined, and we couldn't give them enough business. But, apparently, memories were short and so were loyalties. None of us had ever been on the other end of a loan rejection, and we didn't like the feeling.

On our return to LaGuardia Airport, we traveled through the Queens Midtown Tunnel, emerged onto the Long Island Expressway, and then passed what had to be the world's largest cemetery on both sides of the freeway. As I looked at the sea of gray grave markers, the symbolism was as inescapable as it was frightening. Would there be light at the end of the tunnel for TAB, or would we be buried under the weight of our liquidity problems?

As I shuddered over these possibilities, Lewis interrupted my train of thought. With his jaw set tightly, his teeth clenched, and his steel-blue eyes dark with anger, he said bitterly, "I thought we'd get a better reception. After all the years we've kept deposits with them, I would have thought we would deserve some loyalty." Gary Cage, forever a cynic but starkly realistic, said the last word on the subject as we continued our journey: "Lewis, I'm not surprised. These New York banks will help you only as long as you can help them. They know no loyalties and have no friends."

I was sure as I listened to Gary that he was thinking the same thing I was. Given the circumstances, the response of the New York banks was understandable. They were in a tough spot–forced to weigh past relationships against assuming more risk in a faraway state such as Texas. Neither of us would have said that to Lewis, though. His pride had been severely wounded, and there was no reason to add insult to injury.

On the flight back to Texas, thinking about our lack of success, I worried about what our next option was. TAB's predicament was worsening, and we had no place to turn in the event of a crisis. The reality was frightening.

Liquidity Crisis

Tuesday, May 28, 1986, began like most days since I had become chairman and CEO a little over a month before: the rush to get an early start on the day, a morning filled with numerous phone calls and committee meetings. But this day would be like none other in my twenty-five years in banking.

When Gary Cage came through the door of my office, the routine of the morning and my equilibrium were shattered. He was grim-faced and frowning. Even before he spoke, I knew something was wrong.

"Jody, I know you're in a hurry, but this can't wait. We've got to go into the Fed. We have a deficit of $105 million in our account there, which we can't cover. This morning we scoured the entire country for funds, and we just can't find any," he said, tightening his lips to mask his own emotion.

I felt a suffocating sense of panic as Cage spoke. Could this be the beginning of the end? Every banker's nightmare was a liquidity crisis. Having to borrow from the Fed could lead to a loss of public confidence and a run that could bring the entire organization down. Only a few years earlier, the FDIC had taken over Continental Illinois Bank & Trust in Chicago due to a liquidity crisis. Could this happen to us? The thought sent cold chills down my back.

Trying to regain my composure, I exclaimed, "Gary, I can't believe this."

"I know how you feel," he said. He drew a deep breath, his face pained, and continued. "We've been redlined–along with all the other banks in Texas. We can't find a bank in the country that'll sell us funds." He paused for a long moment, then added, "We're finding out who our fair-weather friends are: they were selling us funds hand over fist when times were good."

With Gary still in my office, my mouth dry, and my stomach tied in knots, I placed a telephone call to Robert Boykin, president of the Federal Reserve Bank of Dallas. I had previously advised Boykin of our possible liquidity problems, and, under the Fed's supervision, we had put all the procedures in place to facilitate possible borrowings, including sufficient collateral, in the event of such an emergency.

Previously, we had made routine borrowings at the Federal Reserve Bank, solely to take advantage of the more favorable borrowing rate afforded by the discount rate, which at times would be from a half point to a full point lower than rates available in the federal funds markets. These borrowings would be justified on the basis of liquidity, but there was never an instance when we couldn't have fulfilled our needs through federal funds purchases from our money-center correspondent banks.

Borrowing under emergency conditions was different, however. The amount we would require was substantially larger, as were the collateral requirements. Rather than transporting eligible collateral to the Federal Reserve, eligible customer loans had been segregated and secured on our premises. Additionally, borrowings during routine times wouldn't have been regarded by our customers, analysts, and the press as being a sign of weakness. Even so, we were always careful to have no Federal Reserve borrowings outstanding over quarter-end statement dates. Especially in this environment, the public would be scrutinizing our statements for any anomalies.

I greeted Boykin by getting right to the point. "Bob, I was hoping I wouldn't have to make this call, but we just ran out of liquidity. You are aware that we lost our bid to keep the $90 million Dallas/Fort Worth airport deposits. We've also been having trouble renewing deposits acquired in the national CD markets. We were confident we could cover the shortfall with Fed Funds [excess funds lent from one bank to another] from our correspondent banks. The Texas banks came through for us–as they always have–but our out-of-state banks cut us off." I paused, taking a deep breath. "We need to borrow $105 million. I'm sick about the situation, but that is unfortunately where we are."

Boykin is one of the nicest and most gentle men I know, and the tone of his response was totally in character. "Jody, that's what we're here for. We want to be helpful, and we'll see you through this crisis. How long do you think you'll need to borrow?"

"Bob, I don't have any idea. We have been absolutely cut off from all external sources of funds, but I promise you we will be working as hard as we can to get out before quarter-end."

"I know you will. Just keep us informed," Boykin said warmly as he hung up.

As I put down the phone, a sudden sense of urgency swept over me. If we were to avoid the same fate as Continental, I knew we would have to work our way out prior to the June 30 quarter-end, when Fed borrowings would be reported on our financial statements and published in the local newspaper as required by banking regulators. The very existence of the company depended on restoring and maintaining our liquidity. For a brief moment, I thought about the predicament I was suddenly in: I had been CEO for only thirty-four days, and we were in a life-or-death crisis.

The script to this story wasn't playing out the way I had planned. I had thought I would be taking over a financial Goliath poised to experience extraordinary growth and prosperity. Instead, I felt like the captain on the bridge of the Titanic, fighting to keep the ship afloat.

As Cage rushed out of my office to put the wheels in motion for the Fed borrowing, my thoughts turned to how to deal with the current crisis.

We didn't have a game plan for this emergency: we had just lost $90 million of Dallas/Fort Worth International Airport deposits, we had been cut off from all out-of-state sources of funds, and our loyal customers were rapidly drawing down their deposits to the maximum limit of $100,000 per account in coverage by the Federal Deposit Insurance Corporation. We were desperate and we were scrambling, using every gimmick we could think of to bring in deposits–and to keep the deposits we had.

Ironically, the answer to TAB's liquidity problem, and that of the other major Texas banking organizations, was rooted in Texas's archaic prohibition on branch banking imposed by the Constitution of 1876. We had been forced to use the holding company structure to expand into multiple locations: each location was a separate bank, with each having separate FDIC coverage. This structure, however, provided the solution: a "spread CD program" through which customers could maintain their deposits in excess of the $100,000 FDIC insurance limit. Under the program, a customer could deposit up to $3.5 million at any one of TAB's thirty-five separate subsidiary banks, to be spread to the other thirty-four banks in increments of $100,000, utilizing the FDIC limit in each bank.

As a result of a great sense of urgency and a herculean effort on the part of our staff, we were out of the Fed within three weeks. The amount of CDs spread through the system went from zero to over $600 million by the end of the summer.

Crisis Management

With Texas having been redlined, the oil business in a shambles, and an economy reverberating from the effects, we knew we had to take extraordinary measures to build our defenses. To develop a survival plan, we convened a crisis management session on the weekend of June 6 and 7, 1986, which included all members of our management team.

By this time, we were beginning to see visible signs of deterioration in our real estate loan portfolio. The crisis was deepening, as was our despair.

Loan quality was our most pressing problem. We had quit making real estate loans in August 1985 and recently had curtailed all other lending. However, the damage was already done as it related to loans already on the books. We were in a damage-control mode; our challenge was to collect existing loans and minimize further deterioration to the extent possible.

Under Lewis Bond, each unit in the TAB system was operated autonomously, which was an outgrowth of Texas's unit banking and holding company structure. Under this structure, each bank had to be operated as a separate entity, making it difficult for the parent company to effectively exercise control. It was obvious that tighter controls were needed in the existing environment.

In order to bring the company under tighter control, we decided to transform TAB into a highly centralized organization, basically removing much of the individual authority the banks and CEOs had enjoyed and vesting that authority in the head office or regionally. Under this restructuring, new committees and functions were created to centralize the loan approval process, problem loan collection and administration, and loan policy. Also, we set in motion a process to review and evaluate the effectiveness and efficiency of virtually every activity and function in the organization.

Not everyone immediately bought into this program. In a meeting held to implement the changes, one of our TAB/Dallas executives, who didn't fully appreciate the gravity of our problem, said, "You guys have a siege mentality."

As I heard him speak, I thought to myself, how naive these people are. We're at war, fighting for our lives, and they haven't got a clue. They couldn't see the forest for the trees. These were the same young bank officers who had experienced only the good times of the 1970s and early '80s–they had never seen real adversity.

"You're 100 percent right!" I exclaimed, pointing my finger at him. "We do have a siege mentality, and let there be no misunderstanding, we *are* under siege."

Thereafter, we had a very frank exchange about the seriousness of TAB's situation, and he finally understood our concerns, although within a year he left TAB for a position with a bank in Florida. This executive, however, wasn't the only member of TAB's senior-level management who felt we were overreacting; a number of our executives believed prosperity would continue. Considering that the Dallas/Fort Worth economies were still reasonably strong, this wasn't surprising.

Expense Control

Given the deteriorating Texas economy and our growing concern about the outlook for the oil and real estate industries–and, thus, TAB–I decided in the summer of 1985 that it was time to take draconian measures.

Using industry benchmarks, we concluded that expenses needed to be reduced by 15 percent to bring the company in line with its peers. Accordingly, on June 6, 1985, we announced sweeping expense cuts across the entire company. The programs were simple, but they were extraordinarily effective.

We used cash bonuses to reward people at all levels for their efforts. Our focus was both vertical from the top down, and horizontal across the entire company. We slashed advertising, eliminated company cars, and decreased the company's contribution to the health and life insurance plans. We adopted new policies related to physicals, overtime pay, vacations, holiday pay, travel, club memberships, and many other similar activities. We initiated an early retirement program under a special provision of our retirement plan, the major expense of which was borne by the plan. A large number of eligible employees volunteered.

Regretfully, all of this wasn't enough to save a sinking ship. We had no other alternative but to impose company-wide layoffs.

For a company that had known no adversity, the layoffs were particularly tough on everyone involved. Lewis Bond announced the first of our two layoffs in the spring of 1986 at an officer's meeting at TAB/Fort Worth. The script had been well planned and rehearsed, but, as soon as he started to speak, his voice broke. To Bond, who prided himself on his stoicism, this had to be a very difficult experience.

Over the next three years, total employment was reduced by 923 positions, nearly one-fourth of the total. Overall, from mid-1985 through 1988, expenses were reduced by 17.5 percent.

This was accomplished without seriously impacting employee morale. We fully explained why we had to do what we were doing; we used attrition to absorb displaced employees; we provided out-placement services; and we were as generous as possible in severance pay. As a result of doing everything we could to ease the burden, most who were displaced left without rancor. This also had an ameliorating effect on those who stayed: it gave them the confidence to continue and helped keep morale as high as possible. To those who helped us achieve the results, we promised they would share in the savings.

Report of Examination

For TAB's directors, the first half of 1986 had been sad and sobering, and, looking ahead, the storm clouds were growing ever darker. The extent of the damage caused by the precipitous decline in oil prices could only be imagined, and real estate values were becoming increasingly suspect.

Failures of commercial banks in Oklahoma were receiving wide publicity in the press. We couldn't help but wonder if and when this plague would migrate across the Red River and infect Texas's major banks.

Certainly, we were extremely apprehensive as the level of problem loans increased and loan losses mounted. TAB's board of directors was also becoming increasingly nervous.

On March 31, 1986, the OCC had commenced its regularly scheduled examination of TAB's banks. The results were devastating: "The company's overall condition is unsatisfactory. . . . Quality . . . is considered unsatisfactory. Liquidity is not adequate. . . . Earnings are poor. Capital is considered marginal."[3]

In the early months of my chairmanship, we were reacting to events, which were changing rapidly. We were behind the power curve and were playing catch-up. However, at our crisis management meeting of June 6 and 7, we had outlined an aggressive plan to proactively manage the company and address its problems. The implementation of this plan had begun immediately, and much of it was in place long before this report to the TAB board of directors. We got little credit for the positive actions that had been taken, with the exception of acknowledgment that "a stronger movement toward centralization" was occurring and "initial steps" had been taken to correct some of the deficiencies identified.[4]

It is interesting, however, that the previous report for the examination begun on January 28, 1985, using financial information for the period ended December 31, 1984, was laudatory of management and the directors–the same cadre of people who were so severely criticized a little over a year later.[5] At that time, the condition of TAB was rated "satisfactory," and supervision and administration of the company by management and the board was considered "good." The asset and liability management function was judged to be "sound," and liquidity was "adequate." What a difference one year and a deteriorating economy had made.

During this time, we had continued to observe with mounting alarm the deterioration of the Texas economy and our own financial condition along with it. As a precautionary measure, we had augmented our reserve for loan losses significantly in the first half of 1986. The reserve for loan losses is an asset account set up on the bank's balance sheet as an offset to loans. It represents management's estimate of future losses on loans and is deducted from total loans, the difference being "net loans" or collectible loans. In most banks, a separate departmental function, designated "loan review," is charged with continuously evaluating the quality of loans, their likelihood of being collected, and the adequacy of reserves against those loans. Additions to the loan loss reserve are deducted from earnings, and thus from equity capital, thereby providing a more accurate representation of both earnings and equity capital. Losses on loans are charged against the reserve for loan losses as they are realized. For the purposes of determining solvency, federal regulators include the reserve for loan losses, in addition to equity, surplus, and retained earnings, in their calculation of total capital.

In the third quarter of 1986, we still didn't feel comfortably reserved. Given the environment, it appeared that loan losses would continue at abnormally high rates. Additionally, we wanted to over-provide–to add enough to get ahead of events. We were using a technique widely used in turn-around situations, taking huge losses in an already poor year in order to set up the future for better results.

Accordingly, on September 26, 1986, we announced that the company would add $105 million to its loan loss reserve and would sustain a loss of close to $84 million for the third quarter.[6] We felt confident this action would set up 1987 for a turnaround.

The final financial tally for 1986 was dismal; TAB had lost $115.2 million, reducing its equity capital by one-third. In response, its stock had declined from $30 per share on January 1 to $14 5/8 at the end of the year. Surely, 1987 couldn't be any worse.

Commitment

It was my steadfast belief that management could not represent the interest of the shareholders unless they had a significant stake in the company. Likewise, I believed stock incentives were strong motivators to induce management to optimize earnings and to run the company as effectively as possible.

I had been accumulating shares in TAB since I joined the company, and, by April 1986, I owned a significant stake, with little debt. Upon taking the reins of the company, however, I wanted to make a statement: a demonstration of leadership, of an example for others to follow, and of a commitment to the company in these troubled times. I wanted to send a clear signal to employees, investment analysts, and potential investors that I had confidence in TAB and its management team. Accordingly, in the summer and early fall of 1986, I increased my holdings by nearly 200 percent, mostly from money borrowed through TAB's executive loan program and from a local bank. I now had all of my liquid assets and almost all of my net worth tied up in TAB stock, and I was the largest shareholder among the directors. In short, I had placed a huge bet on TAB.

SIX

THE QUEST FOR CAPITAL

At last, 1986 ended–it had been a miserable year–and we were looking forward to 1987, which was touted to both employees and shareholders as a transition year from the very poor economy and results of 1986 to much better times.

There was considerable evidence to support this point of view. The national economy had continued its uninterrupted expansion from the 1981–1982 recession. As indicated by Graph 2, the Texas economy was also showing signs of improvement, after the devastating impact of the crash in oil prices in the first quarter of 1986.

The Texas unemployment rate had peaked in mid-1986 at 10.3 percent and had stabilized at 9.1 to 9.5 percent by year-end. Retail sales, which had been declining from month-to-month during most of 1986, began to recover in September. Most importantly, oil prices had rebounded from the dismal lows of below $10 per barrel in April and had stabilized in the $15 to $18 per-barrel range. As an overall measure of economic activity, the Texas Index of Leading Economic Indicators had started increasing after the low reached in mid-1986.

Even though prospects for the economy were looking better, many of us were still deeply concerned. There are considerable lags between a turn in the economy and its impact on banking, and there was at least a fifty-fifty chance that the real estate sector would continue to slide rather than turn around. With TAB's large exposure to real estate loans, the company would be vulnerable, particularly considering its weakened capital position. Once hailed for its strength in capital, TAB was now only marginally capitalized due to the losses of 1986.

The progressive increase in TAB's nonperforming assets was also alarming: the ratio had doubled in the last year to 6.87 percent of total loans and foreclosed assets. Once this ratio exceeded 10 percent, it would be difficult to realize an operating profit, which meant TAB would have no chance to earn its way out of its problems. Unfortunately, it was likely that nonperforming assets would continue to increase with the continued deterioration of the real estate markets.

As an insurance policy against continuing losses, TAB needed more capital. By now, the obvious had become unmistakably clear–capital represents the Maginot line against insolvency–and TAB was capital deficient.

Management's mission was just as clear: to find additional capital in order to shore up our defenses and assure our continued survival. Given the rapid decline in the fortunes of the Texas economy and in the quality of TAB's assets, this task was enormous.

Interstate Banking

In September 1986, the Texas banks got some relief from an unexpected source. Texas passed legislation allowing out-of-state banks to enter the state through acquisition, throwing open Texas and its distressed, capital-starved banking market to new sources of capital.

On April 5 and 6, 1986, three weeks before I was elected chairman and CEO of TAB, I attended in Phoenix the annual meeting of the Association of Reserve City Bankers (now known as Bankers' Roundtable). Since representatives from all the major banking organizations in Texas were in attendance, it was a good opportunity for us to meet and discuss the challenges we faced. Although the mood at this meeting was one of general good cheer, there was a somber undertone. The performance of all the Texas banks had been lackluster for the past few years, and oil prices had been in a free-fall since the first of the year. Thus, there was the specter of much more difficult times ahead.

Against this backdrop, we discussed various strategies to bolster our companies and give us forward momentum. The conclusion reached was that we would launch an all-out effort to approve interstate banking in order to permit out-of-state banks to acquire banks located in Texas, thereby attracting the much-needed new capital. The barriers to interstate banking had been crumbling in states in the Northeast and Southeast, and we all believed this trend would eventually engulf Texas. My expectation was that this would occur within five years, and I needed that much time to maximize the value of TAB's franchise.

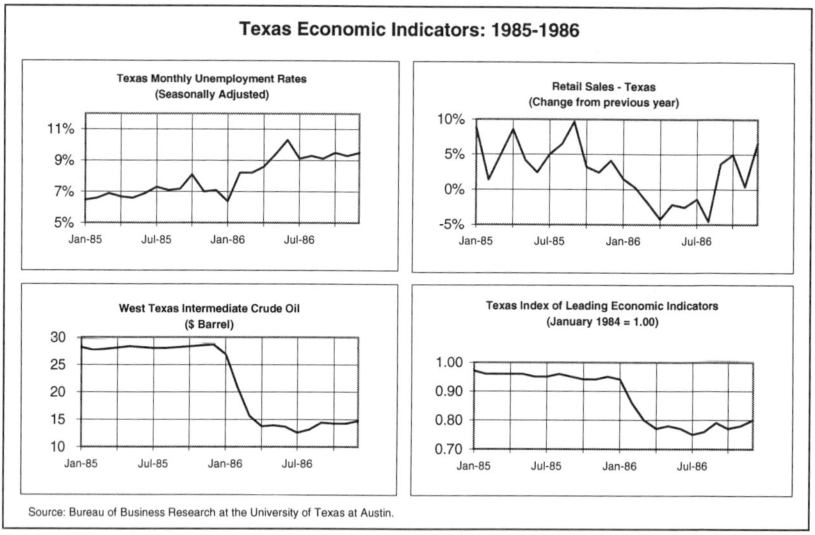

Graph 2

It was inevitable that TAB, or its successor, would be competing in an interstate banking environment. In the interim, however, I wanted to put TAB on a growth path that would help close the gap between us and our larger competitors. Unfortunately, we had done little to penetrate the consumer markets, a gaping hole in our strategy: this was a deficiency we had to correct. Even in the Fort Worth market, which we dominated, we only had six locations to serve a population of nearly one million. Additionally, TAB could be operated much more efficiently and, thus, more profitably than in the past. By centralizing our operations and by running our smaller banks as if they were branches, instead of as individual unit banks, the potential economies were enormous.

Once we had improved the profitability of the company, the option of joining with Allied Bancshares of Houston, National Bancshares of Texas in San Antonio (NBC), or one of the other major companies in a "merger of equals" would be feasible. By so doing, TAB could become part of a Texas-based organization that could be competitive in an interstate banking environment yet retain the marketing advantage of its Texas identity in its home state.

Although we would have preferred that interstate banking be delayed, we were sympathetic to those who needed capital urgently and wanted to have the opportunity to sell now. Consequently, TAB supported the effort.

Ben Love, chairman and CEO of Texas Commerce, was the principal proponent, and he received strong support from Robert H. Stewart III, chairman and CEO of InterFirst Corporation of Dallas.

Bobby Stewart looked particularly grim throughout this meeting, and he had every reason to be subdued. InterFirst had gone through extremely tough times since the First National Bank of Midland had failed in October 1983. In the wake of the ripples from the Midland failure and the burden of its own aggressive energy lending, InterFirst had suffered huge loan and operating losses. At times, it had seemed as though Stewart had been fighting what appeared to be a no-win battle. He was, understandably, tired. At one point in the meeting, he said, "I don't care what we do, as long as we do something; I just want out."

Through the efforts of the major holding companies, including all-out support from TAB, interstate banking was passed by the state legislature on August 26, 1986, and signed into law in September, to become effective January 1, 1987. The new law allowed out-of-state banks to purchase existing Texas banks; however, they were not allowed to establish branches in Texas or enter the state by chartering and establishing new banks, referred to as *de novo* entries.

On the same day the state legislature approved interstate banking, it also approved limited branch banking. This action was ratified by the voters in a special election on November 4, 1986. Under the new amendment to the Texas Constitution of 1876, banks were authorized to branch within the city and county of the domicile of its principal office. Banks that were acquired by out-of-state banks had the same branching privileges as in-state banks, but out-of-state banks were still precluded by federal law from branching across state lines. In early 1988, a federal judge ruled that national banks could branch statewide–instead of being restricted to their home city or county–because S&Ls were allowed statewide branching. In fall 1988, the state Finance Commission of Texas issued rules allowing state-chartered banks the same branching privileges as national banks. These rulings struck down the last barriers to branching in Texas.

Texas Commerce/Chemical

In spite of the new law allowing interstate banking, virtually the entire state was shocked by an announcement made on Monday, December 15, 1986: Texas Commerce Bancshares, the largest banking company in Houston and the third largest in Texas–with $19 billion in assets and seventy banking offices–would be acquired by Chemical New York Corporation, the nation's sixth-largest banking organization and parent of Chemical Bank. Their combination would produce the fifth-largest banking organization in the nation.

I was among those who were surprised by the announcement. Considering Love's fierce sense of independence and his strong allegiance to Houston and Texas, I thought he would have been one of the last to sell to an out-of-state interest.

Love was "Mr. Houston," if not "Mr. Texas": his efforts to promote both were legendary. Texas Commerce annually published and distributed *Houston Facts and Figures* and *Texas Facts and Figures*, extolling the salient economic features and advantages of Houston and of Texas. The name "Texas Commerce" was itself indicative of the bank's roots. The bank's emblem was the state flag, which every bank officer wore as a lapel pin and which appeared–embossed in red, white, and blue–on every bank publication and piece of stationary. Indeed, Texas Commerce seemed so intertwined with Texas that it was almost inconceivable that it could be sold to an out-of-state interest. I assumed that Love had worked so hard in order to obtain the authority to help banks that were already in dire straits, such as InterFirst and First City, and also to provide a backstop in the event his own bank's fortunes worsened.

Years later, Love confided to me that, in considering the future of Texas Commerce, he was haunted by his family's experience during the Great Depression. Love's father, a cotton broker, had watched the price of cotton drop in 1929 from around $.25 a pound to $.06 a pound. As the cotton price plummeted, Love's father, thinking it had reached the bottom, bought additional contracts to purchase cotton in the future at today's prices. Bet after bet was made, according to Love, and the price continued to decline. As the contracts matured, Love's father was forced to purchase at the contract price, a price considerably higher than the market price at the time, thus sustaining great losses in the process. Watching the losses accumulate and the family's finances erode had a profound and lasting impression on young Ben Love.

When Love looked at the Texas economy of the mid-1980s and saw many of the same forces at play as during the depression era, he vowed not to let what happened to his family fifty years earlier happen to Texas Commerce's shareholders. Whatever drove his decision, there is no question that affiliating with the prestigious New York Chemical Bank was good for the shareholders, and it provided a suitable capstone to Love's illustrious career.

In a news conference on Monday afternoon announcing the deal, Love said that the merger would provide consumer and corporate customers with new products, make it easier for Texas Commerce to raise funds, and help the Houston and Texas economies recover from the energy recession.[1] "Banks in this state could do a better job with consumers," explained Love. "We have been so preoccupied with commercial banking that we have not done a good job."[2] Love further elaborated that Chemical is a leader in consumer and electronic banking and in development of investment and merchant banking services. According to media reports, it was expected that Chemical, which operated 270 branches in the New York City area, would push Texas Commerce toward branching under the newly approved branch banking law in Texas.

It was expected that the combination would give Texas Commerce an immediate benefit from saving as much as fifteen basis points (.15 percent) on Texas Commerce's cost of funds. Due to the uncertainties about the Texas economy and the future prospects of its banks, Texas banks had been forced to pay a premium on their federal funds purchases and on their certificates of deposit.[3] In commenting on Texas Commerce's funding problems, Love said, "Texas banks have been, in essence, redlined over the past two years. It has been painful to us, and inhibited us."[4] He added that, as part of Chemical, the funding problem would evaporate. The savings would result because of Chemical's higher credit rating and their greater access to funding sources.

However, Moody's Investor Service, Inc., said that if the agreement were completed, it could lead to a possible downgrading of ratings on Chemical's $1.3 billion debt.[5] On Tuesday, December 16, Standard & Poor's did indeed place the debt of Chemical New York Corporation on credit watch with "negative implications," but simultaneously it put Texas Commerce Bancshares on credit watch with "positive implications."[6] As far as the credit rating agencies were concerned, the proposed acquisition was the proverbial double-edged sword insofar as the public debt holders of each company were concerned. Those holding Chemical debt were taking on more risk with the acquisition due to the weakness of the Texas economy and the uncertain prospects of Texas Commerce. To the contrary, the debt holders of Texas Commerce would benefit because of the added strength of Chemical.

In explaining the reasons for the merger, Love denied that the deal was a "bailout." "I don't think this could be characterized as a rescue from any perspective," Love said.[7]

However, Texas Commerce was suffering from the same malaise that afflicted the rest of the state's major banks. Located in Houston, and with banks in the other major oil centers of the state, Texas Commerce had taken the full brunt of the slide in oil prices since 1981 and of the free-fall in the first quarter of 1986. Their nonperforming assets had increased from $485 million in the first quarter of 1985 to $840 million in the third quarter of 1986, or from 3.6 percent of loans and foreclosed real estate to 6.5 percent.[8]

While the amount and the percentage of nonperforming assets by themselves were not alarming, the rapid growth and the trend were. With a total real estate portfolio of $4.1 billion, constituting approximately 31 percent of total loans, and the rapid deterioration in real estate values, these trends could only be expected to continue.

"If nothing else, I think Ben's a realist," said James Sexton, former Banking Commissioner of Texas, in commenting on the deal.[9] The reality that Love saw was earnings through September 30, 1986, cut in half from the same period a year earlier, and a future that was clouded by a worsening economy. "It's pretty hard not to get into trouble in Texas these days," observed Bill Isaac, former chairman of the FDIC.[10] But, to Love's credit, Texas Commerce's troubles surfaced later and seemed to be less severe than those of most of its peer banks in Texas.

Chemical, in recognition of the inherent risks in the transaction, chose a structure that partially shielded their shareholders and left much of the risk with the Texas Commerce shareholders. For each share of their stock, Texas Commerce shareholders would receive $7 in cash; .09 of a share of Chemical common stock, valued at about $4; one share of a new series of Chemical adjustable-rate preferred stock valued at about $12; and one share of new Chemical Class B common stock, based on Texas Commerce's future earnings, which company officials valued at $9–$10 per share.

The innovative element of the structure called for Texas Commerce to spin out $300 million of their $840 million in nonperforming assets into a new company to be owned by the existing Texas Commerce shareholders. They would receive one share in the "bad bank," or workout bank, for each share of Texas Commerce they owned. Estimates of the value of the workout shares were $3 per share.

Company officials valued the entire deal in the $35.00 to $36.00 per-share range. Sandra J. Flannigan, a banking analyst at Paine Webber, Inc., in Houston, estimated that after adjusting for projected loan losses, Texas Commerce's book value was closer to $20.00 than the stated $35.83 as of September 30, 1986. "The shareholders have gotten a good deal," she said. "Without a takeover, their stock would have traded at about $20.00 per share."[11]

Mark Alpert, a banking analyst at Bear, Stearns & Company, observed, "It's a risky acquisition that's part of Chemical's expansion strategy, but it's not as desirable in our opinion as expansion in the Northeast. . . . If Texas Commerce thought they had identified most of their problems and the worst was behind them, selling out at book value would be a low price."[12]

In a follow-up article on December 17 on the proposed acquisition, the *Wall Street Journal* proclaimed that, "The economic difficulties of the Southwest–combined with structural changes toward national markets in the banking industry–have brought an end to the era in which Texas controlled its own capital and, ultimately, its own economic destiny."[13] Francis Tuggle, dean of the graduate business school at Rice University, agreed. "There is a strong symbolic message in this," he said. The notion of the Republic of Texas and the idea that we can do everything all by ourselves have gone by the boards, and this merger is going to force people to face up to it. Given the economics in the state, it's inevitable that we just can't go it alone any longer."[14]

Yet a rush by the other major Texas banks, or their would-be out-of-state suitors, to enter into similar deals wasn't expected. The Texas economy was considered to be high risk, and contingent deals, based upon future earnings and the collection of bad loans, were considered hard to value. According to James McDermott, analyst at Keefe, Bruyette & Woods, Inc., Chemical's offer "is not good news for Texas bank shareholders. . . . Texas Commerce was considered one of the better banks in the state."[15]

Analysts speculated that candidates ripe for the taking included TAB, NBC, and Allied Bancshares; the stocks of these banks were trading close to book value, making them attractive to a prospective purchaser. MCorp intended to remain independent, as did RepublicBank Corporation, which also intended to acquire weaker Texas neighbors. Analysts believed that the financial fortunes of InterFirst and of First City had deteriorated to the extent that they were more likely to be restructured, on less favorable terms than their peers.[16]

Although I fully expected there to be acquisitions under the new law, I didn't expect a deal to be announced so early, given that the law wouldn't become effective until January 1, 1987. I certainly didn't expect one of the strongest of Texas's major banks, Texas Commerce, to be the first.

RepublicBank Corporation/InterFirst

As astonishing as the Texas Commerce sale to Chemical Bank was, the blockbuster announcement the following day was even more astonishing: the proposed merger of RepublicBank Corporation of Dallas and InterFirst Corporation of Dallas to create First RepublicBank Corporation, the twelfth-largest banking organization in the nation.[17]

In a move designed to ensure that there would be at least one major Texas bank independent of out-of-state control, Republic, the nation's eighteenth-largest banking organization, with $22.5 billion in assets, and InterFirst, the nation's twenty fifth largest with $19.2 billion in assets, put aside their bitter cross-town rivalry with a merger plan involving a stock transaction valued at $1.17 billion. Billed as "a company made by Texans for Texans," the combined company would have $35 billion in assets (after eliminations) and 109 banks located in all of the major markets in Texas. Consolidation of duplicate offices and of functions would result in the layoff of some three thousand of the combined company's nearly seventeen thousand employees.[18]

Although advertised as a merger, it was apparent that Republic was acquiring InterFirst. Gerald W. "Jerry" Fronterhouse, chairman and CEO of Republic, at age fifty, would become CEO of the new company. Robert H. "Bobby" Stewart III, chairman and CEO of InterFirst, at age sixty-one, would become chairman.

For each of sixty-seven million shares outstanding, Republic would pay shareholders of InterFirst eight-hundredths of a share of common stock in the new company, one-tenth of a share of Class A convertible common stock, whose dividend would depend upon future earnings, and two-hundredths of a share of $100-value preferred stock in First RepublicBank Corporation. At the end of five years, the Class A common would convert into common stock of the new company.[19]

According to officials of the two companies, the transaction was valued at $580 million to the shareholders of InterFirst, versus a book value of $890 million. On a per-share basis, the deal was valued at $8.10 to $8.60 per share, compared to a book value of $13.29 per share and a market price of $5.00 per share at the close of business on Tuesday, December 16. The discount of the purchase price from book value was attributed to the poor performance of InterFirst and the poor quality of its assets.

InterFirst had yet to recover from the hangover resulting from its large exposure to oil and gas loans and its participation in energy credits with the defunct First National Bank of Midland. As a consequence, the Dallas company had lost $172 million in 1983 and had been in the black in 1984 only because of the sale of its downtown Dallas headquarters buildings. In 1985, the company earned $61 million, primarily as a result of a weak recovery in the Texas economy and of layoffs and other cost control measures. But, through the first nine months of 1986, ended September 30, InterFirst had chalked up losses of $279 million. Republic, in comparison, had earnings of $36.3 million for the same period.[20]

Whereas Ben Love could proclaim that the acquisition of Texas Commerce by Chemical wasn't a bailout, Bobby Stewart could make no such claim with regard to InterFirst's sale to Republic. It had been rumored that InterFirst was on the block for quite some time. And, aside from Love, the principal champion of interstate banking was Bobby Stewart, who openly acknowledged that he was looking for refuge for his beleaguered company. According to sources close to the company, it had been very close to inking a deal with the Los Angeles–based Security Pacific Corporation, the nation's seventh-largest banking organization, but Security Pacific got cold feet because of the rapidly deteriorating Texas economy.

For Republic, the chance to acquire archrival InterFirst was compelling. It would eliminate a fierce competitor, which had been a thorn in the company's side for years; it would insulate itself from acquisition by an external source by creating a company that would probably be too big to acquire; it would create a dominant force in Texas by virtue of its geographic reach and its size; and it would position itself to compete effectively with such interlopers as Chemical through its intended acquisition of Texas Commerce. Banking analyst Judah Kraushaar with Merrill Lynch observed, "I think it really has the potential to give them a dominant position in the Dallas market and make it difficult for non-Texas banks to crack open that market."[21]

On the other hand, Republic would put its future at risk by taking on a weak partner. Some pundits believed that the end result would be to merge two weak organizations into a larger, weaker organization. Unlike the Texas Commerce/Chemical plan, the two companies decided not to spin off a workout bank, or "bad bank," to contain problem loans. In an effort to explain why such a structure wasn't used, Bobby Stewart said, "We looked at that kind of arrangement. . . . But when you create an entity to handle bad loans, you have to provide capital for it."[22]

The risks and rewards of the two strategies were enormous. Texas Commerce chose to take the safe, conservative approach, in its intended combination with Chemical.

In contrast, Republic chose a higher-risk approach in electing to merge with InterFirst, one of the weakest of the major Texas banking companies. Republic virtually would push all their chips into the middle of the table by choosing to take on InterFirst's liabilities. If it didn't work, the entire ship could sink, wiping out Republic's capital and its shareholders.

In a bad economy, access to capital may mean the difference between survival and failure. In that respect, Texas Commerce's strategy could be far superior to that of Republic's.

TAB's Strategy in the Interstate Banking Environment

With the announced Texas Commerce/Chemical and Republic/InterFirst transactions, three of the largest seven bank holding companies in Texas, the field of available acquisition candidates in Texas was vastly reduced. This thrust TAB, the smallest of the seven, into the spotlight. It was obvious that TAB, with its attractive Dallas/Fort Worth franchise and its relatively low market price, was an especially appealing acquisition candidate.

TAB's public reaction to the Texas Commerce/Chemical and the RepublicBank Corporation/InterFirst announcements was carefully framed to leave TAB's doors open to any offer. Hopefully waiting for a proposal, management expected the phone to ring, and was disappointed when it didn't.

With the arrival of interstate banking, TAB hired the prestigious New York investment banking firm of Goldman Sachs to evaluate its position and to represent the company in the event an offer was received. The conclusion they reached, which was confirmed by the TAB board of directors, was to wait for better times and a higher price than might be expected in the current environment.

Anticipating this result, the TAB management had already asked Goldman to explore other capital alternatives that might be available. From the outset, it was apparent that the normal sources of financing were not available to a Texas bank. Consequently, the best alternative was a private placement with either an individual or an institutional investor, which now could include out-of-state banks. Accordingly, TAB began quietly to explore these possibilities in fall of 1986.

Deals So Near

RICHARD RAINWATER

Richard Rainwater, the former chief investment officer for the ultra-wealthy Bass family of Fort Worth, was intimately familiar with the banking business and the challenges it faced in Texas. In the early 1980s, the Bass family had purchased a very large ownership position in InterFirst Corporation, the Dallas banking giant.

Even prior to TAB's hiring of Goldman Sachs, Richard Rainwater had approached the company with the idea of buying its TAB headquarters building. While this never progressed beyond the conceptual stage, it led to an ongoing dialogue about TAB.

It is not surprising, then, that one of the first people we approached in late fall of 1986 about a private placement was Rainwater. He had a brilliant mind, was extremely creative, and was absolutely consumed by business and the ever-elusive "home-run deal." There would, however, be problems in selling him to the TAB board.

The TAB board was comprised of a mixture of old-line Fort Worth aristocracy, the blue bloods of the city, and a handful of successful executives who were CEOs of their companies. They were traditional, conservative, and very careful as to whom they would accept into their ranks. In order to be considered, any candidate had to have the "right" image and had to pass muster with Lewis Bond, who, having relinquished his position as CEO, was still chairman of TAB's executive committee and a person of great influence.

Rainwater, on the other hand, came from a middle-class background, had worked his way to the top as the deal man for the Bass family, and was regarded as a wheeler-dealer. He had a vastly overstated and largely undeserved reputation for turning transactions quickly for a profit. In any case, I knew I would have a hard time selling Richard Rainwater to Lewis Bond.

After several weeks of negotiations, a tentative agreement was reached. Rainwater would invest $50 million in TAB convertible preferred stock.

Both Gary Cage and I felt very good about the structure and believed it to be fair for all parties. We also were enthusiastic about Rainwater's potential involvement. To hear him talk about his plans for the bank made our adrenaline surge. But we had to convince the other members of our senior policy committee, consisting of the five top executives of the company. For this purpose, we met in Rainwater's offices on the twentieth floor of the Bass Brothers' First City Tower in downtown Fort Worth, where Rainwater put on a dazzling performance.

"I want to help make TAB the most profitable and admired bank in the Southwest," Rainwater said. "It is a great organization, with a great reputation, and you all are great bankers. But, with this affiliation, you'll have opportunities you've never had before. We'll accelerate your growth and improve your profitability."

The whole time Rainwater spoke, he stalked back and forth across the room like a panther hunting its prey. When he wasn't gesturing with his hands, he wrote on the erasable walls, creating images of TAB, illustrating the growth possibilities, and calculating with the precision of a computer the possible return to investors of an invigorated TAB. He was evangelistic in his enthusiasm.

"This will be a partnership, modeled after the partnership we forged between the Basses and Mike Eisner and his team at Disney." Rainwater's voice rose with excitement as he spoke. "I believe that the people who make things happen, who achieve the results, should share in the benefits. I want to increase the stock ownership plans so all of you have a greater stake in the results, so if the company wins, management wins.

"We'll eventually bring new young directors to the organization. We'll energize and revitalize TAB. My role will be to bring new opportunities and to act as a catalyst to make things happen. But you guys will run the organization. It will be fantastic! I promise you it will be fun and it will be exciting." Rainwater reminded me of a coach exhorting his team before an important game. All we needed were "high fives" and cheers to complete the scene. It was a virtuoso performance that completely wowed the TAB group.

While working with Rainwater, we had been actively soliciting other interests, recognizing that consummating a transaction with Rainwater was far from being accomplished. One such call was placed on January 9, 1987, to John LaWare, CEO of Shawmut Corporation and later a member of the Federal Reserve Board. Shawmut had been our joint venture partner in American AgCredit Corporation, a firm based in Denver, Colorado, that specialized in financing the agriculture industry and that had been liquidated a few years earlier. LaWare expressed keen interest in making us a proposal for the injection of $50 million.

We also had opened discussions with Duncan, Cook & Company, a private investment banking firm in Houston, whose principals were Charles W. Duncan, Jr., former president of Coca Cola and former secretary of defense, and John H. Duncan, former president and founding stockholder of Gulf & Western Industries. Duncan, Cook believed there was a good chance of getting American General Life Insurance Company of Houston interested in investing $50 million in TAB.

With three possible deals in the hopper, we asked Goldman Sachs to evaluate each and to brief our board on January 29, 1987. By that time, we had received a preliminary proposal from Rainwater and Shawmut. It was my hope that we might be able to marry Rainwater and American General in a joint venture, which I believed would be the best of all worlds–and more acceptable to our board. Goldman concluded that the Shawmut proposal was "totally unacceptable" due to the exercise price of warrants and to a "poison pill" feature, which would have given Shawmut the ability effectively to block the purchase of TAB by a third party–or at least make it far less attractive. Based on Goldman's findings and recommendations, the board asked management to continue to pursue the Rainwater and American General possibilities.

During the course of these discussions, I kept Lewis Bond advised of our progress, inasmuch as his endorsement would be necessary to get any deal approved by the TAB board of directors. During our meetings, he repeatedly expressed his reservations about Rainwater and said on a number of occasions, "I just don't know if we can live with this guy," and "I don't think we can ever make a deal with Rainwater; his pencil is just too sharp."

Meanwhile, we had heard from Duncan, Cook that American General wasn't interested at this time; they wanted to "keep their powder dry," presumably to help with the recapitalization of First City Bancorporation in Houston.

Rainwater was, thus, the only viable option left. Accordingly, he was invited to meet with TAB's executive committee on February 11. As I was preparing for the meeting late in the afternoon of the 10th, I received an urgent call from Jack McSpadden at Goldman Sachs.

"Jody, we've just finished reviewing Rainwater's term sheet, and we've got some real problems with the deal," he said haltingly. "We think the variable interest rate on the convertible preferred stock would be too expensive, and the conversion would cause too much dilution to the existing common stock. Additionally, we strongly believe the sale of such a large block of stock might put the company in the control of speculative or undesirable investors."

Goldman's objections had effectively scuttled Rainwater's chances. In lieu of presenting Rainwater's deal, we presented alternative, "go-it-alone" proposals that we had been working on as a contingency. Although some of the strategies were speculative, the executive committee received them enthusiastically.

TANDY CORPORATION

After the executive committee meeting of February 11, John Roach, chairman and CEO of Tandy Corporation and a TAB director, asked if he could visit with me.

"Well, Jody," he began slowly, in his deep West Texas accent, "it looks like you've run up against a brick wall. This bank is important to this city and it's important to Tandy. I've been thinking about ways we might be able to help. Maybe Tandy could recapitalize the bank. Call Charlie Tindall. I've already spoken to him about it, and he's expecting to hear from you."

This was music to my ears after the Rainwater disappointment, as Tandy clearly had the muscle to do whatever they wanted, and Roach could pretty well call the shots.

On the day following the executive committee meeting, Gary Cage and I had our first appointment with the Tandy chief financial officer, Charlie Tindall. Before we could even sit down, Tindall began telling us of his deep affection for TAB.

"When Charles Tandy was struggling to get this company off the ground, when none of the big city banks would touch us, the Fort Worth National Bank stood by us. I remember Pete Peterson and Al Cosby really sticking their necks out. Hell, there were times when we didn't know if we could meet the next payroll. But, no matter how tough it got, the bank was always there to help. We've got a debt to repay. We owe it to you, and I'm going to do everything I can to help."

Within a few weeks, Tindall, Cage, and I had the framework of a deal mapped out. Although we weren't ready to take the terms to the TAB board of directors, we had made enough progress to give an interim report to the executive committee at its regular meeting of March 10, 1987.

Gary Cage and I came in early that morning to review our progress and prepare for the 10:00 A.M. meeting. We were confident and enthusiastic, as we were very close to having a deal that would work. Then I received a telephone call from John Roach. As I picked up the phone, I said, "John, we've made a lot of progress. Let me briefly tell you where we are."

"Well, that's what I wanted to talk to you about," said Roach. "The

Vantage Company and Nash Phillips/Copus announcements are pretty disturbing. We've had to take another look at this whole thing. We think things are just going to get worse. We can't go on. I wish we could, but we just can't commit the company at this time."

Once again my day was shattered by an unexpected phone call. I couldn't blame Roach. Nash Phillips/Copus, of Austin, the nation's largest, closely held home builder, which owed TAB $21.5 million, had just declared bankruptcy. The Vantage Company of Dallas, one of the nation's top-ten commercial real estate developers, was restructuring its debt. The newspapers were filled with horror stories every day, which did nothing to build confidence.

On April 1, Charlie Tindall died of a massive stroke. With his demise, any hope of reviving Tandy's interest in assisting TAB was lost.

By this time, worry was beginning to turn into desperation.

BEN FORTSON/ANNE WINDFOHR (NOW MARION)

During the spring months of 1987, I had relied more and more on the TAB director Ben Fortson for advice and counsel. He had been eminently successful in the oil and gas business and had built a substantial net worth in the process. He is married to Kay Kimbell Carter, niece of grocery-store magnate Kay Kimbell, who endowed the renowned Kimbell Museum of Fort Worth. While Kimbell left the vast majority of his fortune–today estimated in the hundreds of millions of dollars–in endowment for the benefit of the museum, he also left a substantial amount to Kay Fortson. As a consequence of Ben Fortson's success and Kay Fortson's inheritance, the Fortsons were considered to be among Fort Worth's wealthiest citizens.

In his business interests and investments, Fortson would frequently team with the wealthy Fort Worth heiress Anne Windfohr, whose family is legendary in Texas. Her great-grandfather was Burk Burnett, who was a trail boss at age eighteen, a friend of the famed Comanche chief Quanah Parker, and founder of the rich Burkburnett Oil Field in West Texas. According to legend, Burnett won the 237,000-acre 6666 Ranch in a poker game. Anne Windfohr's mother was married to Charles Tandy, founder of Tandy Corporation; upon their deaths, they left much of their respective wealth to the Anne Burnett and Charles Tandy Foundation with assets of about $190 million.[23]

According to the 1987 edition of *Forbes* magazine's "The Richest People in America," Anne Windfohr's net worth was at least $450 million. At that time, she owned five ranches with over 500,000 acres; a Fifth Avenue apartment worth $10.5 million; a home in Fort Worth designed by I. M. Pei, the only residence he has designed; and condominiums in Santa Fe and Palm Springs.[24]

On Saturday, June 27, I received a telephone call from Ben Fortson, asking me to meet him at Anne Windfohr's house. He explained that they wanted to talk to me about the bank. When I arrived, Ben and Anne greeted me enthusiastically. After we had settled in, Ben said, "Anne and I want to help recapitalize the bank. We would do this together as partners, putting $50 million into the deal, with each of us contributing $25 million. My thought is we would do it like I've done some of my oil financing, where we would put up half the money, borrow the rest without recourse [with no personal liability], pledging the stock as collateral."

I was elated. There was no question in my mind that they had the resources to pull it off, and I couldn't think of two better partners. They were Fort Worth natives, well respected in the city and the state, and would pull business to the organization like magnets. Moreover, I thought we could have a lot of fun dreaming about what could be, planning it, and turning it into reality.

Unfortunately, we weren't able to get the deal financed: no lender was willing to do the deal with no recourse to the individuals. One of my greatest disappointments was informing the TAB board at its meeting on August 27 that we were unable to arrange the financing. At this point, our alternatives were few, and I sensed a somber and worried attitude among the board members.

ALLIED BANCSHARES

After the effort with Rainwater failed, TAB president L. O. "Buzz" Brightbill and I traveled to Houston on April 9 to visit with Gerald Smith, chairman and CEO of Allied Bancshares, and Kent Anderson, president of Allied Bancshares. Allied Bancshares was the fifth-largest banking company in Texas, with about $9 billion in assets. We had found it useful, if not therapeutic, to visit with our counterparts at the other Texas holding companies to share information about common problems and to see if there were ways we could help each other.

Allied's new fifty-story tower in downtown Houston was awesome, with its richly grained, polished-marble facade. The interior was as sumptuous as the exterior, with lavish traditional furnishings and a priceless collection of western art adorning the walls. In these elegant surroundings, it wasn't surprising that coffee was served by a white-jacketed butler.

Indeed, it seemed that no expense was spared. It was paradoxical that Smith and Anderson were sitting in the lap of luxury while their bank was deteriorating around them.

In the early 1980s, Lewis Bond had held several conversations with Smith about the feasibility of merging our companies. Although those discussions never led to anything serious, we had thought a merger with Allied was possible ever since. During the course of our visit with Smith and Anderson, we again brought up the idea of putting the companies together. We discussed the pros and cons, and all agreed it was worth exploring. We thought we might be able to attract new capital to the combined companies, whereas neither company could independently.

Although we recognized that any deal with Allied was a long shot, our spirits were nonetheless buoyed over having another prospect to work on, no matter how remote. We were, therefore, totally shocked when less than thirty days later, on May 21, Allied announced its intention to merge with First Interstate Bancorp of Los Angeles in a transaction valued at $415 million to $450 million. First Interstate, with $52 billion in assets, was the nation's ninth-largest bank. The combination with Allied would create the seventh-largest banking company, with about $65 billion in assets.

In making the announcement, First Interstate officials said that Allied was a strongly managed bank, that its emphasis on the lower end of the middle market fit with their own market strategy, and that the move into Texas was a natural extension of their market territory. When asked if they were aware of the risks in the state's depressed economy, Frederick J. Elsea, senior vice president, said, "the rewards were worth the risks."[25]

Unlike the Texas Commerce deal, Allied would adopt the First Interstate name, but it was expected that management would stay in place. Otherwise, the transaction was structured similar to the Texas Commerce acquisition, with the value determined by future performance and First Interstate protected by the spin out of $250 million of Allied's nonperforming loans into a workout bank for the benefit of Allied's shareholders. Allied also expected to receive a capital infusion of $250 million to $350 million in cash from First Interstate.

Was this a rescue?

We could only surmise that, since our visit, Smith and Anderson must have looked down the tunnel and seen a train headed toward them.

However, in media reports of the transaction, Jay C. Crager, Allied chief financial officer, said, "We feel Allied definitely had the independent option. The board had as its primary function to enhance shareholder value and enhance the financial strength of the company."[26] But, at the same time, the company announced that it would report a $100 million operating loss in the second quarter of the year.

The transaction called for Allied's shareholders to receive a package of securities valued at between $10.00 per share and $10.85 per share, substantially below Allied's book value at March 31, 1987, of $14.29. Commenting on the transaction, Sandra J. Flannigan, an analyst at Paine Webber in Houston, said, "Based on the valuations of the investment bankers, this is coming in at the low end of what we had expected."[27]

To gain more insight into their motivation, Buzz Brightbill and I met with Gerald Smith and Kent Anderson at the Fairmont Hotel in Dallas on Wednesday, June 24. According to Smith, they were very concerned about the continued deterioration of the Houston market, where their assets were concentrated. They had hired J. P. Morgan as an advisor on the deal. Morgan had convinced them that on a present-value basis, they couldn't expect to do any better than the First Interstate deal for many years. The risk in waiting for the markets to recover was too great.

In recognition of the continued deterioration in the Texas and Houston economies, the transaction closing was postponed while the deal was retraded. As part of the new terms, the total value to the Allied shareholders was reduced to $337 million from the original value of $415 to $450 million. For 1987, Allied reported a loss of $317.96 million, after suffering a deficit of $77 million in the fourth quarter.[28]

With the acquisition of Allied by First Interstate, Texas lost its second major banking organization to out-of-state interests.

First City Sold to Abboud

In addition to the Texas Commerce/Chemical, Republic/InterFirst, and Allied/First Interstate deals, there was one other blockbuster transaction in 1987. On September 9, the FDIC announced that it would assist former Chicago banker A. Robert Abboud in his acquisition of First City Bancorporation of Houston by contributing $970 million in new capital to the company.

The rescue of First City had been widely anticipated. An early casualty of the oil depression that ravaged Houston, First City, with $12.2 billion in assets and 61 banks, had been fighting a losing battle for survival. It was once heralded as *the* energy lender in Houston, with a portfolio consisting of the most prominent Houston energy borrowers and growing in excess of 20 percent per year. Unwisely, however, First City concentrated over one-third of its energy loans in the risky service and drilling sector, sustaining huge losses in the process. In an attempt to reverse its fortunes, the company turned its attention to the hyperactive real estate lending market, increasing its concentration in that sector to over 35 percent of its loan portfolio. But, disaster followed disaster, as the Houston real estate market sank with the city's energy economy and First City drowned in a sea of red ink. For 1986, the company lost $406.1 million; it was expected to lose as much as $1.1 billion for 1987, an amount that would have rendered the company insolvent.

Given the staggering losses of 1986, First City's senior chairman, James A. Elkins Jr., scion of the bank's founder, put the company up for sale. After months without a successful sale, the FDIC apparently assumed the role of auctioneer and chose to make a deal with Abboud. The transaction, the second-largest bailout in history and the second-largest "open bank" bailout (the rescue of Continental being the largest in both categories), would all but wipe out the shareholders. In commenting on the deal, FDIC chairman L. William Seidman said, "In terms of the stockholders and management the bank has failed."[29]

The structure of the deal called for the FDIC to contribute $970 million in new capital in the form of a promissory note. Private investors would invest an additional $500 million, of which $275 million would be in common equity and $225 million in preferred stock, with half of the preferred convertible into common. Following the Texas Commerce/Chemical model, all of First City's $1.9 billion in nonperforming and 90-day past due loans would be spunoff into a "bad bank" to be managed by First City. In return, First City's banking units would receive $550 million in senior notes in the "bad bank," to be repaid from loan collections. The FDIC in return for its $970 million note would receive junior notes in the "bad bank," to be repaid by whatever was left after payment of senior notes.

With the passage of First City into the hands of Abboud, backed by the Wall Street investment banking firm of Donaldson, Lufkin & Jenrette Securities Corporation, three of the five largest Texas banks were controlled by out-of-state interests. Although Abboud moved to Texas, only a small part of the $500 million in new capital was raised from Texas investors.

Proposed Merger

Our lack of success in attracting new capital was depressing, demoralizing, and frightening. TAB was all alone, adrift without a lifeline on a giant, turbulent sea.

With disappointment after disappointment behind us, we decided to turn our efforts in a different direction. On September 30, 1987, Buzz Brightbill and I went to San Antonio to call on Richard Calvert, chairman and CEO, and Mark Johnson, president, of National Bancshares of Texas (NBC). There were many common ties between our companies. Moreover, San Antonio and Fort Worth were similar in terms of lifestyle, social structure, and business climate.

In June 1978, representatives of TAB and NBC had met in San Antonio to discuss the possibility of merging. Unfortunately, NBC wasn't interested at that time. Nine years later, in fall of 1987, circumstances had changed: TAB and NBC were both beleaguered and in need of additional capital.

In both appearance and demeanor, Calvert and Johnson are cut out of the same cloth. Each is tall, slim, and good looking. Calvert, approaching sixty, has medium dark hair, patrician features, deep-set eyes, and an easy smile. Educated at eastern prep schools and at Princeton, he possesses an aristocratic air of sophistication but not snobbery: he was always warm and friendly.

Johnson, on the other hand, is much more a Texan. In his early forties, his hair is darker than Calvert's, and he has softer, less sculptured features. When he speaks, it is with a Texas accent that is very much in keeping with his San Antonio origins.

At NBC, we appreciated the absence of rich "trappings," which had been so visible at Allied. Coffee and soft drinks were served by Calvert's secretary, and the "service" consisted of plastic cups.

Our discussions focused on our respective attempts to raise capital. In talking about NBC's situation, Richard Calvert disclosed that one of their existing shareholders was considering the investment of $50 million in new capital, and that his representatives were presently engaged in due diligence in connection with that effort.

NBC's investor was Mohammed al-Fayed, an Egyptian-born investor living in London, who already owned 10 percent of their outstanding stock. The scion of Egyptian cotton growers, Al-Fayed made his money in construction, oil exploration, and cargo brokering, and is the owner of one of the most famous department stores in the world, Harrods in London, and of the renowned Ritz Hotel in Paris.

When the two companies had talked about merging before, the timing wasn't right. But much had changed since then, and we agreed that we could accomplish more together than we could separately. From the standpoint of geography and market coverage, the two franchises complemented each other beautifully. Philosophically, and in terms of management style, there was little difference. Additionally, the chances of raising capital to merge the organizations would be much easier than it would be to recapitalize each separately. We believed that if Al-Fayed committed $50 million, we could leverage off that and a proposed merger, and raise another $100 million from TAB's shareholders.

A merger of TAB and NBC would produce a banking organization with $8.5 billion in assets, about the same size as Allied and the sixth-largest in Texas. With sixty-four banking offices, the combined company would be represented in every major market. NBC's shareholders would benefit from their entry into the attractive Dallas/Fort Worth markets through TAB, and, likewise, TAB's shareholders would benefit from entry into the similarly attractive San Antonio market through NBC. Additionally, the merged companies would enjoy efficiency in corporate administration, data processing, and bank operations, producing savings of millions of dollars per year.

On November 16, after receiving approval from the respective boards to proceed, Richard Calvert, Mark Johnson, Buzz Brightbill, Gary Cage, and I presented the concept to the regional Dallas offices of the OCC, FDIC, and Federal Reserve. We left each with a merger proposal. All three agencies were enthusiastic about the concept and asked to be kept advised of our progress.

Our optimism was tempered soon thereafter, however, when, in the first week of December, First Republic announced that it expected to lose as much as $350 million in the fourth quarter of 1987. We had counted on the enthusiasm over the First Republic deal to provide momentum to our plans. If the First Republic merger began to sour, it could, likewise, scuttle a TAB/NBC combination.

Several weeks later, on December 22, Richard Calvert called. From the tone of his voice, I could tell he didn't have good news. Without mincing words, Richard said, "Jody, we have just heard from Al-Fayed's representatives. They have decided to pass."

This was even a bigger blow than the loss of the Rainwater deal had been, as a merger with NBC would have made us a major regional player. It was also the last viable hope I could see for raising capital. Calvert explained that the due diligence loan portfolio review had not been encouraging, but, perhaps as important, Al-Fayed had seen a lot of his liquidity eroding with the stock market plunge on October 19, 1987, known as "Black Monday."

The prospects of moving forward without a lead investor like Al-Fayed weren't promising, and there were no other prospects for that position. The TAB board was advised at its meeting on December 23 that the proposal had been placed on hold due to the poor investment climate and First Republic's announcement.

We also reported to the board that TAB had sustained a loss of $24 million through November, compared to $110 million for the same period the previous year. Although this represented a significant improvement, we indicated we were contemplating an extraordinary addition to the loan-loss reserve prior to year-end in anticipation of continued weakness in 1988.

On the last day of 1987, TAB took a special charge to earnings, adding $56 million to the reserve and producing a loss of $54 million in the fourth quarter. With the swift stroke of a pen, we had wiped out $56 million of equity, more than the equity infusion we had worked so hard to obtain. In retrospect, it was fortunate that we weren't successful in our efforts, since $50 million would have fallen far short of our needs. Our investor would have been faced with contributing more capital, being significantly diluted if we had raised capital from another source, or, in a worst-case scenario, losing it all. The prominent Midland businessman Clarence Scharbauer had reportedly lost $80 million trying to save the First National Bank of Midland.

The year's loss of $78 million was substantially below that of $115 million for 1986, but nonperforming assets now totaled 12.3 percent compared to 6.9 percent in 1986. At this level, TAB could no longer make money on an operating basis, and, as each month passed, the losses would diminish our equity. If this trend couldn't be reversed, the company would eventually no longer be viable–a horrifying prospect.

TAB was being swept along by a series of events over which we had no control. The Texas real estate markets were cratering, and TAB's real estate loan portfolio was depreciating daily.

SEVEN

THE BEGINNING OF THE END

On February 16, 1988, Bill Isaac, Richard Calvert, and Mark Johnson visited TAB's offices to keep a previously scheduled appointment with Buzz Brightbill and me. Given the cast of characters–Isaac, former chairman of the FDIC, and Calvert and Johnson, the top executive officers of NBC–Buzz and I concluded that the reason for the visit had to do with merging the companies.

They arrived promptly at 9:00 A.M. After everybody exchanged greetings and helped themselves to coffee, Bill Isaac got right to the point. Isaac was now CEO of his own bank consulting firm based in Washington, D.C., The Secura Group, 25 percent owned by the prestigious law firm of Arnold & Porter.

"I've been working with Richard and Mark to help them find a solution to their Houston problem," Bill explained. "We went to the FDIC with a proposal which we thought would work. It's still on the table, but something else came up during our discussions that may have greater possibilities. That's what we want to talk to you about."

Calvert elaborated that their $400 million Houston bank was facing imminent insolvency due to bad real estate loans. As we well knew, the Houston real estate market was in shambles, and NBC's bank in Houston was reflective of the market: it had approximately $75 million of foreclosed real estate.

"We have a buyer for our Houston banks," Calvert continued. "But only with financial assistance from the FDIC. Without assistance it can't be accomplished: the buyer just won't take the risk. If we can't sell the Houston banks, they will be insolvent, probably by March 31, 1988, or June 30, 1988, at the latest. If that should happen, we don't know what we would face. It could trigger a run and a liquidity crisis at the other banks: in the worst case, it could take the entire company down."

At that point, Isaac broke in, speaking in rapid-fire, staccato sentences:

> Frankly, they didn't think much of our plan to jettison Houston. It was their third choice. The second is to aid NBC in its entirety. By far, though, their preference is to assist in a merger of TAB and NBC.
>
> You guys must have done a hell of a job in selling the regulators in the logic of putting the companies together when you visited their Dallas offices last fall. Evidently your proposal was passed up to Washington, and they liked the idea.
>
> Why do they want to do this? For three reasons. First and foremost, they want to encourage troubled institutions to come in earlier than they normally do. They believe that if a company in threat of failure requests and receives assistance before its franchise begins to deteriorate, the agency would materially reduce its cost of assistance. Second, they believe that by facilitating a merger of the companies, they could solve two problems at once. Finally, they want to attract private capital to assisted transactions, and they feel that this deal would be attractive.
>
> To induce you to come in early, they are willing to make concessions. Normally in an assisted transaction, they insist that the management and directors be replaced and that shareholders and creditors be virtually wiped out. This has been almost a religious principle with them. But, in this case, they are willing to temporize.
>
> They're willing to make an exception to their policy statement of December 8, 1986. They'll allow management and the directors to stay; they'll treat creditors fairly, paying them an equitable return; and they'll allow the shareholders to retain ownership based on a pre-agreed formula. We wouldn't do a deal unless we had concessions. I'm confident they'll keep their word on this.

After the NBC group left, TAB's senior policy committee convened to evaluate the risks. This committee, which I chaired, met weekly to consider all policy or other major decisions of TAB and TAB/Fort Worth. Its other members were Buzz Brightbill, president of TAB; Gary Cage, chief financial officer of TAB and TAB/Fort Worth; Gene Gray, senior credit officer of TAB and president of TAB/Fort Worth; and Bob Herchert, executive vice president of TAB and head of the human resources function.

Buzz Brightbill, at age fifty-one, was the elder of the group. He was conservative in both manner and dress, had spent most of his career with the organization, and had never been known for taking risks, either personally or on behalf of the company. Quiet and reserved, he was a deliberate thinker and didn't formulate opinions or positions quickly.

Like Brightbill, Gene Gray, age forty-five, had spent his entire career with TAB. A star football player from Albany in West Texas, he had attended Rice University on an athletic scholarship. As head of lending at TAB/Fort Worth, he exercised good credit judgment. He was known for holding strong opinions and for being outspoken in those opinions. It was said that Gene was often wrong, but never in doubt. He was bright and quick to form judgments or opinions, but he would sometimes speak without considering the consequences. Because of his intelligence, I wanted his opinion.

I had hired Bob Herchert, age forty-five, in February 1985 to run TAB's human resources function and eventually to head all administrative non-banking activities. He had been city manager of Fort Worth for about eight years and in that capacity had earned high marks for good judgment and a cool head. In the short time he had been at TAB, I had found his judgment to be sound, and I would often use him as a sounding board before advancing an idea or embarking on a course of action.

Gary Cage, at age forty-three, was the youngest of the group. He had an accountant's mentality, with a bent toward quantitative analysis, but he was practical as well. Cage also tended to be conservative and cautious, and more pessimistic than optimistic. From Gary, I could always count on an honest, carefully analyzed, if not somewhat gloomy, appraisal.

After I finished briefing the committee on the meeting with the NBC representatives, Gene Gray was, not surprisingly, the first to speak up. Referring to the FDIC, he said grimly, "Once we get in their web, it's all over; we'll never get out. I don't trust them."

"We'll end up there in any event," added Cage. "And I would darn sure rather go in under these circumstances, at their invitation, than be drug in involuntarily. Everybody comes out better under this scenario."

"In spite of the fact I don't trust 'em, we need capital and there is no place else to get it," Gray said dryly. "We've got a much better chance of surviving this thing with early help from the FDIC. I would rather roll the dice with Isaac and NBC than stay the course we're now on."

Herchert, who had been customarily quiet, carefully analyzing what everyone else thought, pointed out that the advantages of merging with NBC were at least as attractive now as they had been previously.

Cage then reminded us of the condition of our own Houston bank. "TAB/Houston is about to drain us dry," he said. "It's hemorrhaging, and if we can't put a permanent tourniquet on it, we're likely to find ourselves in the same shape as NBC. We've already contributed over $25 million in new capital, it needs that much more again, and we can't afford to do it without putting the entire organization at risk."

In summary, it seemed there was a reasonable probability TAB would ultimately end up seeking FDIC assistance in any event, and the shareholders and creditors would probably fare better by our going in under the umbrella of the NBC merger and thereby attempting to obtain the concessions the FDIC seemed willing to offer.

Under the Garn-St. Germain act passed in 1982, the FDIC was authorized to enter into various transactions, including making loans, purchasing assets, assuming liabilities, or making contributions to an insured bank to prevent its failure. An assistance proposal must adhere to the FDIC's policy statement of December 8, 1986, the major provisions of which include the following:

1. The proposal must be the lowest cost alternative.
2. It must provide for adequate management and capital.
3. There must be a significant capital infusion from non-FDIC sources.
4. The financial impact on common and preferred shareholders and on subordinated debt holders must approximate the effect had the bank failed.
5. It is preferable that the FDIC not be provided with an equity interest in the bank.
6. It is preferable that the proposal provide the FDIC with repayment in whole or in part.
7. If the assisted bank is a subsidiary of a holding company, the transaction should be structured so that (a) assistance is not given to the holding company except when compelling reasons require it; (b) the impact on directors, management, shareholders, and creditors of the holding company approximates what would be expected had the assisted subsidiary bank failed; and (c) available resources from the holding company and its other banks and/or non-bank subsidiaries are contributed.

Isaac had given his assurance that the FDIC was willing to make an exception to the foregoing policy to induce our cooperation. Clearly, that had to be a prerequisite to any deal.

FDIC—The First Visit

Gary Cage accompanied me to Washington, D.C., for our first meeting with the FDIC on Friday, February 19. With Richard Calvert, Mark Johnson, and Bill Isaac, we arrived at the FDIC building and were directed to a rather austere conference room. We were cordially greeted by a contingent of FDIC officials headed by Stanley J. Poling, director, Division of Accounting and Corporate Services, who had been assigned to our case.

Perhaps appropriately, they sat on one side of the table and we sat on the other. Bill Isaac looked and acted comfortable and at home in the offices he had occupied as chairman for over five years. He opened the discussion, stating why we were there. He then asked Stan Poling to reiterate to us what he had told them on their initial visit concerning the agency's desire to assist a merger of TAB and NBC and the conditions upon which the assistance would be provided.

Poling reconfirmed Isaac's comments of two days earlier in Fort Worth. He explained that they liked the idea of a merger between TAB and NBC, and they wanted to use us in a pilot project to test their belief that early intervention to prevent failures would be much more cost effective to the insurance fund. Further, he emphasized that as an incentive they were willing to consider altering their policies related to their treatment of shareholders, officers, and directors.

We were startled by what Poling said next: "It's just as well that you all are here now, because both TAB and NBC were on our list of companies to address in 1988, anyhow."

No one said anything in response. It seemed clear: TAB and NBC were in jeopardy in any event, since the FDIC had already prejudged each of us to be in need of assistance. Without a merger, a capital infusion, or some other type of aid, each company would come under intense scrutiny by the regulators. Given the FDIC's power and influence over the other regulators, the demise of one or both of us might become a self-fulfilling prophecy. As I struggled to regain my equanimity, I wondered if Poling was being unusually forthcoming or if this was subtle intimidation designed to encourage us to accept the FDIC's proposal. In either event, I was sure he had gotten the attention of both Calvert and Johnson, as he had my own. Before the meeting ended, we agreed to further discussions and to reconvene after we developed a plan to present to the FDIC.

Before leaving, we had the opportunity for a brief stand-up meeting with the FDIC chairman, L. William Seidman, outside his office. His curt manner lived up to its reputation. After introductions, he said coolly,

"Well, good luck." Then he turned on his heels and abruptly went into his office. His reception left us puzzled and even more apprehensive than we were after Poling's comment.

Negotiating the Deal

Coincidentally, TAB and NBC both used Goldman Sachs as their investment banker. It was obvious to us that the same firm could not issue a "fairness opinion" to both companies. Accordingly, NBC decided to use Shearson Lehman, and we would use Goldman. Goldman assigned Chris Flowers to the project, who was made a partner in the firm the following fall. Jack McSpadden, who had been assigned to our account for the past several years, continued in that capacity as a principal contact.

We felt fortunate to have Bill Isaac working with us and would have suggested he be hired if NBC hadn't already done so. Bill had the initial conversations with the FDIC and knew the inner workings of the agency.

Both a concern and an advantage was that Bill had a stable of investors, one or more of whom he thought might be interested in the transactions. These included Carl R. Pohlad of Minneapolis, who was among the nation's wealthiest individuals and who already had significant banking interests. We later learned that Pohlad had looked at NBC the previous fall and had expressed keen interest in investing in the company.

We had felt very strongly ever since interstate banking had been authorized in August 1986 that banking organizations owned, based, and managed in Texas needed to be preserved to serve the interests of the state. We hoped TAB would be one of the survivors.

On Thursday, February 25, Bill Isaac and Christie A. Sciacca, who had been Bill's assistant when he was chairman of the FDIC and had joined Bill as a principal in The Secura Group, had adjourned from our meeting to go to the FDIC to visit with Stan Poling in order to discuss the rationale for the deal. Poling was to ascertain the feelings of the FDIC board members about the parameters of the transaction and to call Isaac and Sciacca the following day.

It was Monday afternoon, February 29, before we heard the report of Stan Poling's efforts. Bill Isaac convened the TAB and NBC contingents, as he would many times in the future, by conference call. Buzz Brightbill and Gary Cage joined me on our end, while Richard Calvert, Mark Johnson, and NBC's attorney, James R. "Jamie" Smith, represented NBC.

Bill Isaac opened the call with disturbing news, in his usual rapid-fire way. "Well, we've got a problem. According to Poling, the board hasn't bought into the 'come in early' concept. They are concerned that it would be in contradiction with their policy statement on 'open bank' transactions. The policy statement, passed December 8, 1986, is in the Federal Register and sets forth all the criteria for 'open bank' transactions."

"It basically says that the impact on shareholders and creditors and on management and directors has to be the same as if the bank had failed," added Christie Sciacca.

After a moment's pause, Isaac, in a much more deliberate manner, explained, "Look, the board can't deal with concepts or issues in the abstract. We have to show them a specific transaction. I think they'll come around once we have agreed with the staff on a structure, and they'll fall all over themselves to do a deal once we have the money."

The ABC Plan

Before leaving Washington on February 26, we developed the framework of a plan to present to the FDIC for their consideration.

The ABC plan was by far the simplest plan we considered. It called for three classes of stock. The first, Class A, would consist of the old shareholders, who would absorb 100 percent of the losses until their equity was exhausted. The second, Class B, would consist of the FDIC, which would absorb 90 percent of the losses until their equity was consumed. The third, Class C, would consist of the new investors, who would absorb 10 percent of the losses until the FDIC's equity was exhausted, and then all subsequent losses.

At the conclusion of a five-year period, the equity would be divided between the old and new shareholders and the FDIC. It was contemplated that the old shareholders would end up with a minimum of 5 percent and a maximum of 25 percent, the FDIC a minimum of 5 percent and a maximum of 10 percent, and the new shareholders would have a minimum of 70 percent and a maximum of 85 percent.

This plan was submitted to the FDIC, and we learned on March 30 that the staff liked the concept. They asked that it be refined for submission to the board. Work began immediately, and we eagerly set our next meeting for March 14 and 15.

First Republic Asks for Assistance

When we convened in the offices of Ernst & Whinney in Dallas on the morning of March 14 to refine the plan, the first topic of discussion–and the one that occupied much of the morning–was the article in the *Wall Street Journal* reporting that the board of First Republic Bancorporation of Dallas–the result of a merger of InterFirst Bancorporation and Republic Bancorporation–would meet that afternoon to consider asking the FDIC for assistance.[1] This actually came as no surprise to anyone. As early as December 9, 1987, First Republic had reported that it would sustain a $350 million loss for the fourth quarter, and its mounting problems had been continuously chronicled in the press since then.[2]

At TAB, we had been skeptical of Republic's success prior to the merger. We knew they had always been one of the largest real estate lenders in the country, and we shared a large number of borrowers. In fact, we were aware that some of our most troubled relationships were also their borrowers. Whereas we had recognized those relationships as problems and were treating them accordingly, Republic had not.

This skepticism was later confirmed. On January 19, 1988, First Republic reported a loss of $658.8 million for 1987, and nonperforming assets of $3.9 billion, an alarmingly high 15.9 percent of loans and foreclosed assets.[3] Shortly thereafter, on February 1, the *Wall Street Journal* revealed that First Republic was "privately forecasting an estimated $450 million loss" for 1988 and was launching a major cost-cutting effort. This was more than four times the loss expected by analysts.

The same February 1 article cited an analysis by Keefe, Bruyette & Woods, Inc., a New York investment house specializing in bank stocks. The article stated that First Republic's efforts to build capital through cost-cutting efforts and efficiencies just hadn't worked.

It was further reported that Robert L. Crandall, chairman and CEO of American Airlines–a First Republic director and a man with a reputation for "tight-fisted budget management"–was invited to speak at a weekend meeting of top executives to exhort them to renew their efforts at cost cutting. He was said to have told them that the survival of the company depended on their success. Clearly, the situation was urgent, and management was turning up the heat on the First Republic senior personnel.

On February 19, the *Wall Street Journal* reported that federal bank examiners were poring over First Republic's books and that the FDIC had drawn up a $4.5 billion rescue plan for the company as a precautionary measure.[4] Coincidentally, February 19 was the day of our initial meeting with the FDIC. At the outset of that meeting there was considerable discussion about the article, and we were assured that the FDIC had no such plan.

Funding and liquidity were, of course, major concerns of all the troubled banks in Texas. The first hint of a funding problem at First Republic appeared in the February 19 article, which disclosed that deposit withdrawals were taking place on the part of some customers, and other large commercial customers were taking steps to limit their deposits to no more than the $100,000 covered by FDIC insurance. General Motors Corporation was named as a company that had switched some of its accounts to other banks.[5] In an article appearing several days later on February 22, the *Wall Street Journal* reported that withdrawals were accelerating and that the bank had lost a total of $1.14 billion in average deposits since December.[6]

We were aware of First Republic's tenuous liquidity through our own monitoring of reports of weekly average deposits published and distributed by the Federal Reserve Bank of Dallas. We had been astonished to see week after week that First Republic Bank of Dallas had a loan/deposit ratio consistently over 150 percent; that is, its loans exceeded its deposits by over one-half. Conservative banking would dictate that the loan/deposit ratio not exceed 100 percent.

The most damaging information, which probably hastened the demise of First Republic, appeared in the February 22 article in the *Wall Street Journal*. The newspaper related that, in the fall of 1987, a team of InterFirst officers conducting due diligence on Republic before the merger were "shocked" at what they saw. It was acknowledged that InterFirst was in trouble, but Republic's public statements had not hinted of similar problems. An InterFirst executive who participated in the review reportedly said, "It was hard to say which bank was worse." Moreover, when Robert H. "Bobby" Stewart III, InterFirst's chairman and CEO, recommended the transaction to his board, he commented that "Republic's loan portfolio wasn't in as good a shape as its public reports had led outsiders to believe."[7]

The same February 22 article in the *Wall Street Journal* related that, in the fall of 1987, the First Republic loan review committee was "stunned" by the deterioration in property values, as reflected by current appraisals. The article further stated that the company had been "besieged with rumors about a possible failure or takeover," and depositors were withdrawing deposits following a downgrade of its certificates of deposit by Keefe, Bruyette & Woods to their lowest rating. Further corroborating the story were rumors that the examination under way by federal bank examiners was not going well.[8]

The February 22 article also questioned the concept of the merger itself. It was alleged that other major banking companies wouldn't consider InterFirst without FDIC assistance. Security Pacific Corporation, Los

Angeles, was specifically named as an interested party willing to make a bid for InterFirst with an assistance package amounting to $2 billion. A source close to the negotiations was quoted as saying he was "dumbfounded" that Republic was willing to take InterFirst without assistance. It was also rumored that the Federal Reserve Bank of Dallas had been opposed to the merger on the grounds that two weak institutions were being combined, and that they had conveyed their opposition to the Federal Reserve Board in Washington, D.C., which had final authority and ultimately approved the ill-fated transaction.

Many people close to the scene in Texas had questioned the wisdom of the merger from the outset, primarily due to the bitter rivalry that existed between the two cross-town competitors. Almost immediately, rumors of internecine warfare were rampant. For example, Republic directors became chairmen of all board committees, with InterFirst directors in subordinate roles, and most of the key management positions were awarded to Republic officers. Shortly after the merger became effective on June 6, 1987, Bobby Stewart, chairman, announced his retirement. Gerald W. Fronterhouse was named chairman, replacing Stewart on July 21. Stewart's departure began a long succession of resignations of InterFirst executives until none were left among the top six executives of the company.[9]

It was no surprise, then, when we convened on March 14 and learned of Republic's decision to consider seeking assistance. Bill Isaac excused himself from our meeting to have lunch with the top executives at First Republic prior to the First Republic board meeting.

On Tuesday, March 15, the company announced it was holding preliminary discussions with federal bank regulators for a program to "rescue, restructure, and recapitalize the company."[10] On March 17, the company disclosed it had resorted to borrowing at the Federal Reserve discount window the previous Tuesday, and it would receive a $1 billion loan from the FDIC to infuse into its subsidiary banks. As collateral for the loan, First Republic pledged the stock in twenty-nine of its largest banks, representing 8 percent of its total assets.[11]

We later learned from Bill Isaac that he had strongly advised the First Republic management and directors not to accept the note and not to pledge the stock due to the control it would give the FDIC over the company. The significance of this would become very clear to us later on and would help guide us in devising our own defensive strategy. Isaac also told us the FDIC had been "unmerciful" in its treatment of the company and its management.

On April 12, almost a month after receipt of the $1 billion loan, First Republic made a foreboding and terse announcement that it expected a loss of $1.5 billion for the first quarter, and that Jerry Fronterhouse had announced his resignation. His replacement, handpicked by FDIC chairman L. William Seidman, was Albert V. Casey, the former chairman of American Airlines and former postmaster general of the United States.[12]

Jerry Fronterhouse's tenure at the helm was short lived: he was elected CEO of Republic on January 15, 1985, and was forced to resign just over three years later on April 12, 1988. He was proclaimed a hero on December 16, 1986, upon the announcement of the merger of InterFirst and Republic, and he was declared the scapegoat upon the merged company's demise. Had it worked, he would have, indeed, been a hero. The fact that it didn't was mostly the fault of the economy, not the fault of Fronterhouse. Actually, the bank's fate was sealed years before its failure, due to its real estate concentration.

On May 2, shortly after the resignation of Jerry Fronterhouse, First Republic announced that seventeen of its thirty-three directors would not stand for reelection. Among them were H. R. "Bum" Bright, a mentor of Jerry Fronterhouse and an avid proponent of the merger, and James D. Berry, who picked Fronterhouse to succeed him as chairman and CEO.[13] I was later told by Al Casey that the FDIC had given him a list of officers and directors whom they wanted fired, as a condition of further assistance.

The rescue of First Republic brought unwanted attention to the woes of Texas financial institutions and created additional problems for those of us still struggling for survival. Part of the First Republic rescue package included a blanket guarantee of all uninsured deposits (amounts over $100,000) by the FDIC, a move that halted the run on First Republic but that put all their competitors at a disadvantage. In response, the Independent Bankers Association threatened to sue the FDIC on behalf of its members.

The First Republic problem raised more questions about the viability of TAB and of Dallas-based MCorp. We did our best to dispel these questions by calling our good customers to reassure them of the safety of their deposits.

From the perspective of TAB and NBC, the timing of the First Republic problems couldn't have been worse. Certainly, the FDIC would be preoccupied, and the handling of that case might set precedents for our transaction. It appeared that time was running out, and we needed to pull out all the stops to expedite a solution to our situation.

A Contingency Plan

Throughout the fall of 1987, we had continued to work on remedies to our problems. One approach was to organize an effort for a solution for all troubled Texas banks modeled after the Reconstruction Finance Corporation (RFC), which was created in 1932 to make long-term loans and to provide capital to banks.

It was evident that today's problem was economic, and that the solution was an infusion of capital from external sources, without which there would be a large number of additional bank failures at a considerable cost to the FDIC. Additionally, with no capital to meet legitimate loan needs, the recovery of the economy would be impaired. A vicious cycle would continue, wherein a lack of capital would further weaken the economy, creating continued deterioration. The ripple effect would become a tidal wave, resulting in more bank failures. Moreover, the floundering Texas economy was a considerable drag on the national economy.

There were precedents for government intervention in the successful bailouts of Chrysler and Lockheed. Likewise, the experience of the RFC during its existence was very encouraging. From 1932 to 1950, the RFC made $1.1 billion in loans and invested $1.2 billion in new capital in open banks. It was credited with preventing the failure of the whole financial system, and it was done with no loss to the government or to the taxpayers. In fact, a profit accrued through the return of interest and dividends, which covered the overhead of the RFC.

The concept of our plan was simple. It provided that:

1. The FDIC would invest in preferred stock in qualifying banks in economically depressed areas utilizing funds from the insurance reserve.
2. The stock would have a maturity of twenty years but would be callable on demand to prevent imprudent and unsound use of the funds.
3. The dividend rate would be low in the initial years to allow the bank to rebuild capital, but it would escalate to a premium or penalty rate in later years to encourage prepayment. The dividends would have a preference over all other dividends.
4. To qualify, a bank would have to be in an economically depressed area, have capital below the minimum guidelines, have capable management and directors, and have exhausted all other reasonable alternatives to raising capital.
5. A bank applying for eligibility would submit to a rigorous qualifying exam.

While the foregoing represented the framework of a workable plan, my purpose was to put something on the table, with the hope that it would stimulate an effort to devise a solution to the problem. I wanted to stimulate a dialogue with federal regulators on the merits of an industry solution, as opposed to an individual bank solution.

I did not delude myself into thinking that selling this, or any other concept, would be easy. In Texas, there was a lack of leadership in relation to doing something about the banking problem, and mustering such leadership would be a considerable chore. In Washington, D.C., Texas was well represented in high places, but that could do as much harm as good. Jim Wright, the Speaker of the House, had compromised himself by becoming identified with unsavory individuals in the savings and loan industry in Texas, and it was unlikely that other Texas politicians such as Vice President George Bush or Secretary of the Treasury James Baker would get involved in an election year. Nonetheless, it seemed worth a try, and we really had nothing to lose.

I recruited a blue-ribbon group of supporters, including Bayard Friedman; Bill Isaac; Rodgin Cohen, an extremely well-regarded attorney with Sullivan & Cromwell in New York specializing in bank regulatory work; Charlie Pistor, vice chairman of First Republic and president of the powerful American Bankers Association; and James L. Sexton, former deputy director of the FDIC and commissioner of banking in Texas, who was now associated with the prestigious Houston law firm Bracewell & Patterson, the firm with which Comptroller of the Currency Robert L. Clarke had been associated.

The efforts of this group were monumental. Bayard Friedman took our case to both Washington and to the Texas state capital in Austin. Unfortunately, he got no encouragement from Deputy Secretary of the Treasury George Gould, whom he had met while heading up a task force on the S&L problems in Texas for Governor Bill Clements. Gould believed the only person in Washington who understood the Texas problem was Federal Reserve Board Chairman Alan Greenspan, and since he wasn't on the FDIC board, he probably couldn't help.

Friedman's efforts with Governor Clements were even less encouraging. According to Friedman, the governor said that the banks were broke, they deserved to be broke, and he wasn't going to do a damned thing to help them.

The governor's attitude was shocking and appalling: it was incomprehensible that the chief executive of the state had so little understanding of the economic fallout that would result from the banks' crippled status, or of the significance of the FDIC's piecemeal dealings with them–auctioning banks off to the highest bidder. Texas would be left with no home-based and locally managed large banks to handle the needs of the state's business and industry.

Through Rodgin Cohen, I introduced the rescue plan to John Stone, assistant director, Failing Banks and Assistance Programs Division of the FDIC. Stone expressed interest but, in the final analysis, did nothing to advance the concept.

I also called Comptroller of the Currency Bob Clarke to discuss the idea with him. Subsequently, I sent him a draft of the proposal, but that was the last I heard of it.

Charlie Pistor pushed the concept inside First Republic, as I needed the support of the state's largest and most prestigious bank. In particular, I needed Pistor's help, and he needed the backing of his chairman, Jerry Fronterhouse, to aggressively support the proposal. But Fronterhouse wasn't interested because he didn't think First Republic would need such help. This was on December 17, 1987, just four months before the FDIC took over the bank and fired Fronterhouse.

Bill Isaac was able to win over Gene Bishop, chairman and CEO of MCorp, the second-largest banking organization in Texas. Additionally, Isaac managed to have his own plan promulgated by Charles Lord, a former deputy comptroller of the currency, in an article on the op-ed page of the *New York Times* on March 25.

The proposal was a simple one. It basically called for the FDIC to swap notes with troubled banks, thus infusing capital; provide an interest rate subsidy to help the troubled banks carry their problem loans; and receive warrants to purchase common stock in return for the assistance. In 1982, a similar plan had been used by the FDIC, under Isaac, with favorable results to help troubled mutual savings banks in the East.

After four months of effort, it was patently clear: the plan was dead. The reasons were threefold. First, there was a general distaste for bailouts. In this case, however, it seemed like the least-cost alternative. Second, there was, in the opinion of a lot of people, a bias against Texas and Texans. The popular television series *Dallas* had done much to stereotype Texans, and we had not helped ourselves with bumper stickers during the energy crisis that said "FREEZE A YANKEE." Third, there was probably a tendency to indict the entire state for the sins of the fraudulent S&L operators. Thus, a bailout of Texas financial institutions wouldn't have been politically popular.

My efforts were diverted toward trying to bring political pressure on the FDIC to act quickly in dealing with the Texas banks. It occurred to me that after the FDIC had taken control of First Republic, Governor Clements's attitude about getting involved might change. I visited with Bayard Friedman and was relieved that he agreed with me. He made an appointment to see Governor Clements on April 8, along with Jim Sexton; Peter O'Donnell, an influential Dallas oilman and a former chairman of the Texas Republican Party; and Ron Steinhart, former vice chairman of First Republic. Fortunately, this meeting had a different tone, and the governor agreed to go to Washington and speak to the regulators, which he did several weeks later.

Public Disclosure

On Monday, April 6, Alan Whitney, an FDIC spokesman, disclosed in a press conference that two more Texas banks would be receiving assistance in the near future. This was an untimely reference to two Texas banks other than TAB and NBC. However, rumors had been circulating that the two companies were working on a merger proposal with FDIC assistance, and, with this coincidental remark, the *Dallas Times Herald* irresponsibly reported that the banks Mr. Whitney referred to were, in fact, TAB and NBC. Even though Whitney publicly denied that he was talking about our companies, and the denial was carried in the *Fort Worth Star-Telegram* on February 7, we felt compelled to disclose our efforts in view of the news reports and the speculation.[14]

On Thursday, April 8, the entire city of Fort Worth was greeted with the following front-page headline in the *Fort Worth Star-Telegram*: "Texas American Exploring Merger." The accompanying articles carried a complete chronology of the company's problems over the previous two years.

"Go Find the Money"

On April 13, I traveled to Washington to meet with President Ronald Reagan and with a contingent of leaders from the Young Presidents' Organization, of which I was the immediate, past international president. This seemed like an ideal time to see Seidman as well, and, accordingly, an appointment was made for 9:00 that morning.

Upon arriving, I was shown into Seidman's rather austere offices, which I found to be in keeping with the role of the chairman of the FDIC. After greeting me and exchanging some small talk, he led the way to a conference table.

After being seated, I immediately got down to business. "Chairman Seidman, in spite of our recent financial results, TAB and NBC are good companies. Each is the leading financial institution in its community, and each has existed for over a hundred years. The franchises of the organizations are very attractive, and if you put them together, they constitute one of the best banking networks in Texas. We think the merger makes a lot of sense, and it's the best alternative."

To this, Seidman responded coldly, "We're a lousy partner. My advice to you is to go home, run your company, and let your friends in San Antonio fail."

After recovering from shock, I said, "Mr. Chairman, let's hope that isn't what happens. All I am asking at this point, however, is for a prompt response once we present a firm proposal."

"That you'll get," Seidman allowed.

My report of the meeting to the TAB/NBC working group was received with mixed emotions. It was comforting to know we would receive a prompt hearing, but Seidman's other comments were alarming.

On April 19, Seidman gave a speech in Boston at The Morin Center for Banking Law Studies, which gave us further cause for concern. He started the speech by saying, "Look to your left, look to your right–by the end of the year one of you will be gone from sight! Come to think of it, that sounds a bit like Texas bankers at their 1988 Convention." Not only was this remark tasteless and unnecessary, but it was also a clear indication of his disdainful attitude toward Texas bankers.[15]

Early the following week, we received word that the ABC plan had been tentatively approved, and Seidman had given approval to "go find the money."

EIGHT

LOOKING FOR DADDY WARBUCKS

With the charge from Chairman Seidman to find an investor, our work began immediately. Bill Isaac was asked to arrange appointments with his investors who might be interested, and Goldman and Shearson were requested to contact all of their clients and others to determine their interest.

This broad solicitation was not in keeping with TAB's preference for a Texas investor. With Texas Commerce and Allied merged with out-of-state banks, First City awarded to Chicago banker Bob Abboud, and First Republic's destiny uncertain in the hands of the FDIC, I was becoming more and more convinced of the necessity to preserve TAB and NBC as a company based and managed in Texas.

Out-of-state ownership, in all likelihood, meant eliminating the Texas headquarters operation, with a considerable loss of jobs to the state. The local boards of directors would be left powerless. Loan decision-making authority would be greatly reduced, making it much more difficult to make loans to entrepreneurs and emerging businesses, which had been the engine of growth in Texas. There would not be as much incentive and interest on the part of out-of-state control in financing the growth of local municipalities by purchasing much of their new debt in the bank investment portfolios. Charitable contributions would be dictated out-of-state. Most importantly, the institutional structure, which was the spawning ground for many of the state's leaders and the focal point for many of the critical decisions affecting their communities, would be lost or altered significantly.

Three of the state's bank holding companies had already passed into out-of-state hands, and I didn't want to see it happen to any of the rest. If the state's major banks were all owned externally, I believed the impact on the state's future would be significant.

In spite of my concerns, we had been convinced by our investment bankers that we had to solicit all potentially interested parties or we could be subject to a shareholder suit, claiming we had not obtained the highest value possible. The investment bankers also had to issue a "fairness opinion," attesting that the shareholders had gotten the best deal they could.

Besides, by this time we were becoming more and more anxious about an examination of TAB by the OCC that had commenced on March 31. Additionally, we had just learned on April 12 that First Republic expected a $1.5 billion loss following the completion of their exam, and the same examiners who had evaluated First Republic's real estate portfolio were to examine TAB's. We were also concerned that the examiners might take an exceptionally hard line due to our negotiations with the FDIC. If we were brought to our knees, our negotiating posture would be weakened considerably, and the FDIC could dictate the terms of the transaction.

It was obvious that we had to develop as many options as possible.

The Players

Bill Isaac promptly lined up a meeting with Carl Pohlad in Minneapolis on Monday, April 25. Our assignment was to contact Richard Rainwater; the Bass Brothers, Sid and Lee Bass; Bob Bass who was doing deals on his own account, separate and apart from his brothers; and H. Ross Perot in Dallas. Rainwater and the Basses were all in Fort Worth.

RICHARD E. RAINWATER

In view of Richard Rainwater's previous attempts to acquire a major position in the bank, and his continued expressions of interest, we felt him to be the best prospect among the potential investors we had identified. Thus, my first call and appointment was with him.

On April 19, I went to see Rainwater in his office on the twentieth floor of the First City Center Tower, the Basses' ultramodern office complex in downtown Fort Worth. Rainwater greeted me in his usual effusive manner and escorted me to a conference room near his office. The room was designed for work, utilitarian in every sense of the word, void of decorations, with a single, white, Formica-top conference table. Similar to the rest of the Rainwater offices, there was nothing to distract anyone from the business at hand.

I opened the conversation by bringing Rainwater up to date on the TAB/NBC opportunity, beginning with Isaac's initial visit to TAB on February 16 and concluding with Seidman's charge to "go find the money."

"Richard," I continued, "the way this deal has been structured, it is going to be a hell of an opportunity for whoever gets it. We think that it's critical that it be someone from Fort Worth, someone who knows the city, the bank, and its customers. You are the one who can do this. You know this bank better than any other investor we can think of, and more importantly, you can do more for it than anyone else."

This was the opportunity Rainwater had been waiting for, and I could almost see his eyes light up at the thought of rescuing and owning TAB. Excitedly, he said, "I really want to do this; I just hope the FDIC is ready to do a market deal. So far, all they have done is screw up First City. Let's hope this will be different. Jody, you need to review the deal with Peter Joost. If he likes it, we'll take it from there."

Before leaving, we stepped next door to see Peter Joost, Rainwater's right-hand man. When Rainwater left the Basses to go into business for himself, he chose the brightest person in the Bass camp to go with him. That person was Peter Joost. Peter and I arranged to get together the next day to review the particulars of the deal.

My initial reaction to Rainwater when we first met in 1975 was that he was an extremely intelligent, well-informed businessman. He had started working for the Bass family in 1970, and their successes were still in front of them. So Rainwater had not yet received any of the recognition he would later receive in such abundance. In addition, although a native of Fort Worth, he was principally of Lebanese descent, with some Cherokee heritage. He came from a middle-class background and, from childhood, had dreamed of being rich: he wanted to be a millionaire by the time he was thirty.

Rainwater attended the University of Texas where he majored in math and physics. He then went to Stanford University Graduate School of Business on an academic scholarship, where he met Sid Bass. Upon graduation, Rainwater went to work for Goldman Sachs as an institutional salesman in their Dallas office. Shortly thereafter, Perry Bass turned over the running of the business to his oldest son Sid, who needed assistance in managing the family fortune, estimated to be in the neighborhood of $50 million at that time. To help with this task, he enticed Rainwater back to his roots in Fort Worth.

For Rainwater and the Basses, success begot success. In 1981, the Basses began accumulating stock in Marathon Oil Corporation at the height of the oil boom. Mobil Oil Corporation and U.S. Steel also were accumulating the stock and, in late 1981, were locked in mortal combat to acquire the company. Ultimately, U.S. Steel won, although from the Basses' point of view it didn't matter who prevailed. They were going to make a handsome profit regardless: a $160 million gain on an investment of $165 million.

After the Marathon transaction, the next big winner was Texaco, in which the Basses had acquired a 10 percent interest. Texaco, in turn, was attempting to buy Getty Oil, a move the Basses didn't favor. Fearing that the Basses might acquire a larger and perhaps even a controlling interest in Texaco, CEO John K. McKinley bought out the Basses for a profit of $450 million.

The last, and most profitable, big winner before the split up of the Bass/Rainwater team was the Arvida-Disney transaction. Disney was an underperforming company that was under attack by the takeover specialist Saul P. Steinberg, and the Basses had previously purchased a controlling interest in Arvida Corporation, a large Florida land-development company. With Disney being aggressively pursued, Richard proposed that Disney purchase Arvida, thereby making the Bass group 25 percent owners of Disney and putting it out of the reach of Steinberg, as well as of Irwin Jacobs and Ivan Boesky, who had joined the fray.

This proved to be an attractive transaction for a number of reasons. First, it established the Basses as "white knights" in a squeaky-clean deal. Second, it provided a logical marriage for Arvida, with its real estate development know-how, and Disney, with its vast holdings of Florida real estate. Third, it gave the Basses access to the untapped potential of Disney, which they maximized by bringing in the world-class managers Michael Eisner, chairman, and Frank Wells, president. Finally, based on a December 31, 1994, value of Disney, the Bass group's original investment of $400 million would be worth about $8 billion, if all the shares had been held.

It was a unique experience to visit Rainwater's offices. There was electricity in the air, an atmosphere of hyperactivity, created by Rainwater, who was in perpetual motion. It was not uncommon for him to have two or three meetings going simultaneously, moving from one to the other, providing input and giving directions, with no apparent loss of continuity. If he wasn't roving from meeting to meeting, he was most likely on the speakerphone, concurrently tending to an important business matter and dictating notes to his secretary.

The offices were modern, in keeping with the building, and extremely functional to maximize productivity. The walls were metal with see-through glass, all equipped with felt-tip markers and erasers. Deals were scribbled on practically all available wall space, the graffiti of a world-class deal maker. The furniture was modern and plain, and each desk was equipped with a computer, providing the latest data from Wall Street.

Lunch was catered from the kitchens of the adjacent Bass-owned Worthington Hotel, so the business day wasn't interrupted with a luncheon break. There was also an exercise room, with the most up-to-date equipment and a full-time trainer to program and monitor training routines. Everyone in the office was encouraged to take advantage of the facilities, and frequently Richard would take calls while on the stationary bike or treadmill. It was also customary to find him at his desk in his training gear or in an open-neck shirt.

Few people enjoy their work more than Rainwater. Over dinner one evening, Bill Isaac asked Rainwater why he didn't just pack it in and "go to the ranch."

Rainwater responded, "This is my ranch, it's my beach, it's my Riviera. My work is my hobby and my vacation. It's what I enjoy doing and I wouldn't be happy doing anything else."

Richard E. Rainwater, at the youthful age of forty-four, had definitely arrived in the world of high finance. He had been the subject of a cover story in *Business Week* in its October 20, 1986, edition. In commenting on Rainwater in that article, Brian F. Wurble, an executive vice president of Equitable Life Assurance Society, said, "He suddenly appears, asks the five most penetrating questions right away, and then disappears. A few minutes later the deal's been done. I have never known anyone so biased toward quick action."[1]

Rainwater was described by his peers as "awesome," "the best-kept secret in high finance," "a certified legend," and "one of the financial greats of the age."[2] In 1975, Richard's net worth was about $200,000; in 1988, it was estimated in "The Forbes Four Hundred" to be $225 million. Rainwater was also given a large part of the credit for multiplying the Bass fortune from the estimated $50 million to between $4 and $5 billion.[3]

After the initial meeting on April 19, Gary Cage and I met several days later with Peter Joost. We unrolled the ABC plan for Joost, along with our financial projections for the merged company. Joost's initial reaction was, "This is really a good deal–it makes a lot of sense." This was the first hurdle, one we were delighted to clear, as now TAB had an interested investor from Texas.

CARL R. POHLAD

Carl Pohlad, age seventy-three, the son of an Iowa Railroad brakeman, sold cars repossessed by banks to work his way through Gonzaga University, in Spokane, Washington, where he played football. After being in the service during World War II and earning two purple hearts, he joined his brother-in-law in taking over a small bank holding company in Minnesota called Bank Shares, Inc. Following the death of his brother-in-law, he assumed the presidency of Bank Shares in 1955.

In February 1982, Pohlad purchased a failed savings bank, Farmers and Mechanics Savings Bank, and merged it into Marquette Bank Minneapolis to form the city's third-largest bank. This transaction was consummated with assistance from the FDIC, when Bill Isaac was chairman of the agency. His ability to turn around Farmers and Mechanics through the merger impressed the regulators and the Minnesota banking community. One of his Minneapolis competitors was quoted as saying, "He's probably the best banker in Minnesota." In 1988, Marquette Bank was Pohlad's flagship bank and was the principal asset of Bank Shares, comprising $1.4 billion of its $1.8 billion in assets. In aggregate, Pohlad owned approximately forty banks in eight states with some $4 billion in assets.

Pohlad is perhaps better known, however, as a bottler of Pepsi Cola. In 1986, he sold the nation's third-largest Pepsi bottling operation to PepsiCo, Inc., for $590 million. Thereafter he reentered the business by buying a large Pepsi bottling operation, Mid-South Bottling Company, with sales approximating $180 million. "The Forbes Four Hundred" listed Pohlad's net worth in 1988 to be "at least $670 million," mostly centered in Bank Shares, of which Pohlad owned about 90 percent; in MEI Diversified, Inc., a processor and distributor of candy, nuts, raisins, dried fruits, and other bulk food products, of which Pohlad owned about 60 percent; in his other banking interests; and in his ownership of the Minnesota Twins baseball team and the Vikings football team.[4]

For many years, Pohlad had maintained a very low profile in Minneapolis, and, according to the *Wall Street Journal*, wasn't well known by his fellow citizens. All that ended in 1984, however, when Harvey MacKay, author of the best-seller, *Swim with the Sharks–Without Being Eaten Alive* (1988), and of *Beware the Naked Man Who Offers You His Shirt* (1990) and *Sharkproof* (1993), recruited Pohlad to buy the Minnesota Twins.[5] Pohlad's interest in our banks was not his first interest in Texas or Texas-based companies. In 1963, he bought Central Air Lines in Fort Worth, which was subsequently merged into Frontier Airlines, and later he acquired controlling interest in Texas International Airways, the predecessor of Texas Air. Pohlad was on the board and was chairman of the executive committee of Texas Air when it was run by Frank Lorenzo.

Our greatest concern about Pohlad was his close association with the controversial financier, Irwin Jacobs, sometimes referred to in financial circles as "Irv the Liquidator" because of his practice of stripping a company to its barest elements once he took control. To get a read on Jacobs, we called James R. Campbell, president of Norwest Bank in Minneapolis, which was where Jacobs did his local banking business. According to Campbell, Pohlad was Jacobs's mentor and father figure. They had done a lot together; they were business partners in a number of ventures, including a 51 percent interest in the Minnesota Vikings. Jacobs was also a member of the board of directors of MEI Diversified, Inc., a company Pohlad controlled. "I wouldn't be concerned about Jacobs being an investor," Campbell said reassuringly. "We have had a long relationship with Jacobs, and it's been excellent. He's lived up to every promise and commitment he's ever made, and we believe he's a man of high integrity and moral fiber."

Jacobs only would be an indirect owner in our deal through his directorship in MEI Diversified, Inc., thus, we weren't dissuaded from soliciting Pohlad as an investor. Bill Isaac thought very highly of Pohlad, and Richard Calvert and Mark Johnson were very impressed from their contact with Pohlad and his people the previous fall.

Upon arrival at the Marquette Bank building in Minneapolis, our first impression of Pohlad's offices was that they were very conservatively decorated, with muted colors, plain but functional office furniture, and appointments that were very much in keeping with our expectations of an upper Midwest business operation. Unlike a lot of very wealthy, powerful men, Carl Pohlad didn't need a luxurious office to define his identity.

We were met by Jim Pohlad, the youngest of Carl's three sons, who worked in the banking side of the business; Donald E. Benson, president of MEI and executive vice president of Bank Shares; Thomas A. Herbst, executive vice president of Bank Shares; and Albert J. Colianni, vice president of Bank Shares. Most of the meeting was spent informing our hosts of the merger plans of the companies–why the merger made sense, the catalytic role of the FDIC in getting the proposed transaction to this point–and generally trying to sell them on Texas and the deal.

Don Benson, who had listened intently, framed their initial response.

"As you are all aware," he said, "we spent some time with National Bancshares last fall, and we're interested in Texas. The combination of the two companies makes sense from what you've told us, but it's too big for us. We would prefer to purchase National Bancshares alone, but we'll give it some thought." Benson did not offer much encouragement either in words or in tone.

We had started our meeting at about 11:00 A.M. and Carl Pohlad joined us just before lunch. As a head of state is usually the last to join an official function, top executives are often the last to join a meeting.

Pohlad was a very attractive, distinguished-looking gentleman, with a slight build, a handsome countenance, and thinning grey hair. He dressed conservatively and was extremely cordial and engaging. It was evident at the outset that, when he was in the room, he dominated the scene.

Carl Pohlad enjoyed fielding questions about sports and was particularly effusive about the Twins. He also spent considerable time discussing the Bank Shares philosophy of community banking. Then he described his vision for a banking empire stretching from Minnesota to Texas.

"I want to put together a banking organization that spans the Midwest, stretching from north to south, with the weight, like a barbell, on each end, in Minnesota and in Texas," Pohlad waxed enthusiastically. "I've always wanted to create a large regional banking company. If we could bid for both companies, National Bancshares and Texas American, the Texas franchise would be the anchor of the holding company."

We left Minneapolis late in the day feeling extremely uncertain about where we were with the Pohlad group. Benson had made it clear that they would have a continuing interest in NBC but that both companies in a merger might be too big for them. Pohlad, to the contrary, seemed enamored with the idea of having the merged banks as his anchor in Texas.

SID R. BASS/LEE M. BASS

At the time of our search for capital to recapitalize and restructure TAB and NBC, Sid Bass was involved in divorce proceedings and was spending virtually no time in Fort Worth. He handed the reins of the company to Lee during this period, and accordingly, I decided we would present our proposal to Lee. Besides, Lee's father-in-law, Arthur Seligson, was one of the seven outside directors of NBC. As a result, Lee was familiar with both banks, their franchises, and their problems.

I wasn't sure whether or not the Basses would have any interest in our situation. They had been burned badly with their investment in First Republic, losing an estimated $25 to $30 million.

After listening to my pitch on TAB and NBC, Lee talked about the agony his father-in-law was suffering as a director of NBC. Then he said, "We are just too heavily invested in Texas with our West Texas oil and our investment in downtown Fort Worth real estate [estimated at $300 million]. If we did the TAB/NBC deal, we would have too many eggs in one basket. We can't afford to have that heavy a concentration in Texas at a time when the Texas economy is continuing to slide."

This response was puzzling since their largest investment by far was in Disney stock, not remotely connected to Texas. It was possible, of course, that Lee's insight into NBC's problems through his father-in-law and his vantage point to observe the rapidly deteriorating health of TAB and the Texas banks hurt us. Actually, it is probable that the primary reason was Sid Bass's pending divorce. I'm sure they needed to keep their powder dry, expecting a settlement in the neighborhood of hundreds of millions of dollars, and, strategically, I believe they wanted to maintain a low profile.

In any event, it was a major disappointment but not a disaster, since Richard Rainwater seemed to have a genuine interest.

ROBERT M. BASS

On April 19, the same day of the initial meeting with Richard Rainwater, I also called Bob Bass and explained that I wanted to visit with him about investing in TAB. Shortly thereafter, Gary Cage and I had a meeting with Bob and his chief financial advisor, Jay Crandall.

At this time, Bob Bass had the greatest capacity of all the brothers to do the deal. Bob had enjoyed great success in his investment activities. He had participated in the early successes of Sid Bass and Richard Rainwater through Bass Brothers Enterprises, the investment partnership of the four brothers, prior to splitting out his assets to form Robert M. Bass Group. Bob liquidated his Disney holdings and shrewdly invested the proceeds in a series of winners, including effective control of Alexander's, Inc., a large position in Taft Broadcasting; Westin Hotels, from which he carved out and sold the Plaza Hotel in New York City to Donald J. Trump for a profit of $200 million; and the $702 million buy out of Bell & Howell. In 1988, "The Forbes Four Hundred" estimated Bob to be the richest of the brothers, with a net worth of "at least $1.6 billion."[6]

When Gary and I presented the TAB and NBC deal to Bob, we had no way of knowing he was already committed to what would be his most widely publicized investment, the purchase of Financial Corporation of America (FCA), the highly sought, parent company of the giant insolvent American Savings & Loan of California. For an investment of $550 million, he would acquire $29 billion in assets, versus an outlay of $200 million to acquire $8 billion in our case.

Due to the attractiveness of the FCA deal and recognizing that he only had the manpower resources to do one transaction of this nature at a time, it is no wonder Bob Bass had no interest in our proposal.

H. ROSS PEROT

The next person on my list of potential investors to contact was H. Ross Perot. There was some reason to believe that Perot might have an interest, as we had been told that he was extremely distressed over the crippled condition of the large Dallas-based banks and had considered putting up $200 million to capitalize a new bank to serve local Dallas needs. There was no question about his financial capacity. According to "The Forbes Four Hundred," his net worth was estimated to be close to $3 billion, placing him among the three wealthiest people in the country in 1988.[7]

Additionally, Perot knew TAB well, since Electronic Data Systems (EDS), the company he founded in 1962 and sold to General Motors in 1984, did our data processing from 1975 to 1983. We thought an investment in a company with a strong data processing subsidiary might have some added appeal to Perot since he had sold his interest in EDS.

Perot was unavailable when I placed the call, but, not unexpectedly, he returned the call promptly. I explained to him the nature of my call and gave him the strongest pitch I could as to why he should be interested in the deal.

"Jody, I just can't invest in a Fort Worth bank, when every major Dallas-based banking organization is asking me to help them recapitalize their banks. It would be difficult for me to select one over the other," he said apologetically.

With Dallas and Fort Worth only thirty miles apart, I understood that it would be especially awkward for Perot to invest in a company based in Fort Worth instead of a Dallas company.

THE REST

While we were busy contacting the Texas prospects, Bill Isaac, Goldman Sachs, and Shearson Lehman were scouring their list of clients and contacts, none of whom were interested at this time, each for different reasons. At the end of the process, we were satisfied that every logical prospective investor had been solicited.

NINE

BIDDING THE DEAL

By the end of April 1988, we had completed the process of finding potential investors. After an extensive search, we had two parties: Carl Pohlad and Richard Rainwater had the capacity and preliminary interest in the transaction. Now the difficult task began: soliciting bids, selecting an investor, and presenting the deal to the FDIC.

Following the trip to Minneapolis to meet Pohlad, we arranged a meeting to introduce Richard Calvert and Mark Johnson to Richard Rainwater. We met in the early afternoon on Tuesday, April 26, in Rainwater's office, where we exchanged the usual cordialities and discussed the deal and our merger plans. Rainwater then talked at some length about his philosophy of doing a deal.

"Neither the FDIC nor the FSLIC have done market deals!" he exclaimed. "And that's why they haven't been successful in attracting interest from investors. That's the reason they are having trouble completing First City. This is a chance to do a really smart deal."

While we all agreed with Rainwater philosophically, we questioned whether the FDIC was ready to sign off on his notion of what constituted a "good deal." We believed that if he gave the same speech to the FDIC, it would fall on deaf ears, and he would shoot himself in the foot.

Calvert and Johnson were extremely impressed with Rainwater's intellect but were apprehensive about him as an investor because of the rate of return they believed he sought. This was a significant problem, and we realized that it was going to be difficult to get them into the Rainwater camp.

The Bidding Begins

With Pohlad and Rainwater in the fold, we decided to set a deadline of Friday, May 20, for the bids to be in. Management would choose the winning bid on Saturday. The respective boards would meet the following Monday and Thursday, May 23 and 26, to review and approve the bid, and we would present the bid and the winner to the FDIC on Tuesday, May 31, which was the deadline the FDIC had previously given us.

On Saturday, May 21, the TAB/NBC working group met as scheduled at the Hilton Hotel at Dallas/Fort Worth Airport to review and select the winning bid. Both Rainwater and Pohlad had submitted their proposals the previous day. Jack McSpadden of Goldman Sachs and Frederick "Rick" Wolff of Shearson Lehman were charged with reviewing the bids and making a recommendation. The management teams would then caucus and make a decision.

At mid-morning, the investment bankers gave us their report. Calvert and Johnson were on one side of the table with their attorney, Jamie Smith, of the San Antonio firm of Cox & Smith, while Cage and I were on the other side with Christie Sciacca of the Secura Group. Bill Isaac had another commitment and couldn't be with us, although he was available by phone. McSpadden sat down at the end of the table; Wolff pulled up a chair beside him. As McSpadden spoke, a hush fell over the room.

"It's Rainwater–it's no contest," McSpadden said assuredly. "His bid is better than Pohlad's in every way, particularly in the sharing formula. There is no way we could recommend Pohlad's deal. There's at least a $50 million difference to the shareholders at the end of the five-year period."

I yelled a silent hooray, as I'm sure Cage did. We wanted our hometown investor, not because we didn't want Pohlad–we admired him greatly–but we believed a Texas bank owned by a Texan was important for the state, the bank, and its customers, particularly since Texas Commerce and Allied had already been acquired, and it appeared likely that the same would happen to First Republic and First City. Of the major banks, only MCorp, Cullen Frost, NBC, and TAB remained.

We knew Isaac and Sciacca would have preferred Pohlad because they believed Pohlad would sell better with the FDIC, but even they found the Rainwater bid to be overwhelmingly more favorable.

Generally, everything was beginning to fall into place, and we were feeling good about our progress and prospects. Unfortunately, those feelings were shattered when Christie Sciacca dropped a bombshell in the meeting.

"Of course, the FDIC will want to see the Pohlad bid, as well as Rainwater's," he said almost nonchalantly.

With these simple words, the rug was virtually yanked out from under Rainwater, and our game plan. We were stunned. We suddenly realized that we could very well be at cross-purposes with the FDIC: our goal was to obtain the best deal we could for our shareholders by maximizing the amount of FDIC assistance and the percentage of shareholder equity ownership, whereas the FDIC would want to minimize their assistance and maximize their own equity participation or profit sharing.

The fact of the matter was that the Pohlad proposal was more favorable to the FDIC but less favorable to our shareholders. With this knowledge, the FDIC would prefer the Pohlad proposal over Rainwater's, regardless of the preferences of the companies. In any event, Pohlad's proposal most certainly had become the standard against which Rainwater's would be judged. Even if the FDIC accepted Rainwater, they would probably impose on him Pohlad's sharing schedule.

This turn of events was a real blow.

Board Meetings—May 23

On Monday, May 23, both boards met to consider the proposals submitted by Pohlad and Rainwater. We had decided the appropriate procedure was to present both bids, with management's recommendations. Representatives of Secura and respective investment bankers were present at each meeting to provide advice and counsel and to answer questions.

Before we were able to present either bid, our meeting was sidetracked by several of our directors who strongly felt we should back out now and go it alone. However, the decision had actually been made for us on the previous Friday, May 20. On that afternoon, Gary Cage, Buzz Brightbill, Gene Gray, and I had an appointment in Dallas with representatives from the OCC.

A month earlier, the OCC examiners conducting the exam of TAB's banks had been recalled to Dallas for new instructions and had returned with a much harsher attitude. The tone of the examiners in discussing loans with our officers was much more aggressive and questioning. Whereas before they had taken the appraisals in our files and our valuations at face value, they were now challenging all the underlying assumptions. It was clear they were going to hammer us with huge additions to the loan loss reserve and large write-downs on foreclosed real estate. We had requested the meeting with the OCC because, even though our relationship had always been excellent, we were concerned that their harsher stance in looking at our loans had been brought on by our discussions with the FDIC.

It was a fact that the OCC had been terribly embarrassed in the case of First Republic: they had recommended the merger. Less than a year later, the FDIC ordered large additions to reserves and write-downs on real estate, ultimately causing the lead bank's insolvency and repudiating the OCC's previous recommendation. As a result of this black eye to the OCC, it was likely that there was a lot of self-protection motivating the OCC in our case.

On this visit, they assured us it was business as usual and that all Texas banks were being judged by the same standards. Our negotiations with the FDIC wouldn't bias the results, but we would receive no official regulatory forbearance. In the context of the OCC, regulatory forbearance meant allowing banks to operate with capital ratios below the minimum standards or permitting banks to delay charging off recognized loan losses, thereby temporarily overstating capital.

In spite of the OCC's assurances, we expected the exam to get even tougher. It seemed as if their purpose was annihilation. We now knew how Gerald Smith must have felt when he agreed to sell Allied to First Interstate. We, too, were afraid that the light at the end of the tunnel was a freight train, driven by federal regulators, headed toward TAB. We had known survival would be difficult, and everything had to fall into place under the best of circumstances for us to have a chance.

The one thing we had not anticipated was the attitude of the examiners. We had hoped they would allow us to set up adequate reserves and to realize losses over several years. Many people believed real estate values were only temporarily impaired, and there was still hope the markets would stabilize and begin a slow and gradual recovery, thus improving values.

With enough time, we might be able to survive. It was evident at this point, however, the examiners were not going to give us the time we needed. They were not going to provide any forbearance: they were showing no mercy. As a consequence, the outlook for TAB had turned decidedly negative.

On Saturday, May 21, we saw for the first time financial projections for TAB using partial results from the examination; these results included only the work completed prior to the recall of the examiners to Dallas.

We were stunned. Seeing projections that validated our worst fears was shattering. We now knew we couldn't make it alone. Based on these partial results–which represented the most favorable scenario–we would finish the year with only $75 million in equity. We also knew it was likely to be much worse once we incorporated the results from the full exam. In only three short months after our initial meeting with the FDIC, the outlook for TAB had deteriorated markedly. We now *had* to have the merger and the accompanying FDIC assistance; there were no other viable alternatives. To me, the thought was suffocating, as if a noose was tightening around my neck.

But we had to listen to the objections of the two TAB directors who were opposed to the merger and who wanted TAB to steer its own course. They just couldn't believe TAB was in as bad shape as NBC, nor could they differentiate between our merger and that of InterFirst and Republic.

The truth was that TAB and NBC were in about the same condition. This had been verified through due diligence TAB's loan review staff had performed on NBC's loan portfolio during the previous two weeks. With that information, and the sobering facts from the meeting with the OCC and from the projections we had run, the board rejected the recommendations of the two minority directors and voted to pursue the merger with NBC without further debate.

Bill Isaac then explained that the up-front assistance from the FDIC made our transaction much more attractive than the merger of InterFirst and Republic, and that the TAB/NBC merger was something the FDIC wanted to facilitate. He did a marvelous job in giving the background and presenting the alternatives, which were few.

Next we disclosed that Governor Clements had had a meeting in Washington, D.C., with the respective chairmen of the three bank regulatory agencies and with representatives of the U.S. Treasury. It was related to me through Bayard Friedman that Seidman, the FDIC chairman, told Clements that both TAB and NBC would "be fixed" this year, but they didn't know what they were going to do about MCorp.

Then we played our hand. I said:

> Gentlemen, we have no choice. There is only one option available to us, and that's the merger with NBC. On Friday, we received the preliminary results from the OCC's exam. I'm afraid the news is bad. They are going to require additions to the loan loss reserve of at least $70 million. And that is based on the work they did prior to being

> recalled to Dallas. The final number could be substantially larger. We had asked Bob Scott [TAB's treasurer] to do some new projections over the weekend using the best-case scenario. The result–and remember, this is the best case–is that TAB will have only $75 million in equity left at the end of the year.
>
> I'm sorry, we can't make it on our own. We have to have the merger or FDIC assistance.

With this disclosure, a deathly silence fell over the room, although it is likely that no one was really surprised.

Both the Pohlad and the Rainwater proposals were then presented and the merits of each discussed. The meeting adjourned with an endorsement of the merger concept but without a decision between Pohlad and Rainwater. That decision would be made at Thursday's meeting in accordance with the previously adopted schedule.

On Tuesday and Wednesday, May 24 and 25, the TAB/NBC working group continued to meet to prepare for Thursday's board meetings. Richard Calvert and Mark Johnson came to Fort Worth on Tuesday to meet with Rainwater. The meeting was much more satisfactory than their first meeting, because this time Rainwater dealt with specific issues. Calvert and Johnson were particularly impressed with his vision of a Texas-based holding company, owned and managed by Texans for the benefit of Texans.

While we continued our work on Wednesday, we received an alarming report on the FDIC board meeting of the previous afternoon. Christie Sciacca confirmed our worst fears: the FDIC wanted to see all the bids submitted to the companies.

Gary Cage's reaction expressed what we all felt: "They've finally proven what we've known all along: you can't trust 'em."

This was a major change in the ground rules by the FDIC. We were assured it was standard operating procedure; but it was news to us, and we might have followed a different plan had we known about it before. We felt betrayed and compromised.

It was curious that the FDIC hadn't told us the ground rules when we were instructed to "go find the money"–or maybe they just made the rules up as they went along. We concluded that once they knew that Pohlad had submitted a proposal, they had no choice but to adopt the position of seeing the bid. Rainwater's negotiating power had been severely damaged, if not nullified altogether, since the FDIC knew there was another deal available. And it was also very clear that the authority of the TAB board of directors had been usurped by the FDIC: the FDIC was going to decide who the new owner would be, rather than take the recommendation of the board.

Board Meetings—May 26 and 27: Pohlad Sends a Missile

Thursday, May 26, began with great anticipation and expectation. It appeared that the NBC board would meet and approve Rainwater, and I was hopeful our board would meet on Friday and follow suit–we had postponed our meeting from Thursday to Friday due to quorum problems. Not surprisingly, the events of the day were to be the unexpected rather than the script we would have written.

My day began with Lewis Bond in my office, lobbying for Pohlad. "You can't go with Rainwater–he's in for the short run, will drive too hard a bargain with the FDIC, and we'll never get a deal done," he said, with little emotion but great deliberation.

NBC's meeting had started at 9:00 A.M. and at mid-morning the unexpected happened. We received an emergency call from Richard Calvert and Mark Johnson, along with their investment bankers and attorney.

Calvert, usually calm and collected, was extremely shaken. His voice quivered as he spoke: "We can't believe what's happened. Our entire game plan has to be redrawn. We've just received a new bid by fax from Pohlad that changes this whole thing. He's beaten Rainwater, and we've suspended our board meeting until tomorrow. We don't know what to do."

I had put the call on the speakerphone so that Gary Cage and Jack McSpadden could listen in. None of us, however, were prepared for what we were hearing. We were speechless, exchanging looks of bewilderment as Calvert spoke.

Pohlad had rewritten the rules of the game by submitting a revised late bid and had taken the initiative away from the companies. We had to hand it to him, he was a master strategist. Even though we were dismayed over his actions, we felt admiration for him.

The San Antonio group was looking to us for leadership. If Rainwater was going to get back into the game, we would have to figure out how to get him there.

After pausing for a few moments, I responded. "This isn't the last shot that's going to be fired; this ball game is far from over. Richard, reschedule your board meeting for 9:00 tomorrow morning, and we'll schedule ours for 11:00. In the meantime, we'll talk to Rainwater to see if we can get him to increase his bid. Our job is to get the best deal we can for our shareholders."

Since Pohlad had submitted a revised late bid, it was only fair that Rainwater should be allowed to submit a late bid as well. We were obligated to solicit another bid from Rainwater, who until now had followed precisely the bidding guidelines.

Before hanging up we reaffirmed that, if Rainwater could put a competitive bid on the table, he was our first choice because of the Texas ownership issue. We were to try to reach Rainwater immediately and get back to Calvert and Johnson as soon as possible.

Upon reaching Rainwater to explain the circumstances, we learned that Pohlad had called him to try to make a deal to join forces. Pohlad was covering all the bases. It was obvious he was as cunning as a fox, didn't like losing, and was willing to play hardball to win.

Richard informed us, "I'm not willing to change without Peter Joost signing off on the deal. He did most of the work in structuring it, and he's on his way to Massachusetts to attend his fiancée's graduation from college. Besides, it's impossible–I'm tied up all day and can't visit until tomorrow."

We were dismayed at how nonchalant Rainwater was after he had worked so hard to win. Clearly he wasn't as concerned about the deal as we were; however, *our* survival was at stake.

I said, "Richard, you don't understand–you are in second place. Pohlad has a new bid in, and our investment bankers advise us we can't ignore it. The rules of the game have changed."

We agreed to meet at his house at 7:30 A.M. the next morning, just one and a half hours before the NBC board would convene–not much time to accomplish a major change and incorporate it into a bid. I decided not to tell him at this time that the FDIC wanted to see all bids, as I felt it would serve no useful purpose. In fact, we weren't optimistic Rainwater would change his bid, and we didn't need any additional obstacles.

During the remainder of the day we burned up the long distance lines between Fort Worth, San Antonio, Washington, D.C., and New York, trying to devise new strategies.

I arrived at Rainwater's home promptly at the appointed time. He met me in shorts and a T-shirt, offered me a cup of coffee, and ushered me into the living room. We sat together on the sofa, and I explained that the companies would very much like to have him as their investor and urged him to improve his bid.

"Jody, trust me," he responded emphatically. "I want to talk to both boards, National Bancshares' by teleconference and Texas American's in person. We'll get it done."

I left Rainwater's home somewhat relieved but with no notion of what he was going to do. It did seem, though, that the winds were shifting in our direction.

As I arrived at the office at about 8:30 A.M., Peter Joost was calling from a telephone booth at a filling station in Massachusetts. He said, "We'll go back to the old sharing schedule for ownership with the shareholder." This was a schedule that had previously been put on the table but was later discarded by Rainwater as too generous to the shareholders.

I responded, "Okay, you need to get with our respective investment bankers to get that quantified and incorporated into your bid." Peter agreed, and we patched him into Jack McSpadden in Fort Worth and Rick Wolff, who was in San Antonio.

At 8:50 A.M., the new bid was relayed to San Antonio. At 9:30 it was submitted to the NBC board, and at 10:00 the NBC board, Rainwater, and Mort Meyerson, Rainwater's partner in this transaction, were teleconferenced into the board meeting. We were told later that Rainwater did a masterful job selling a group of people he hadn't met and wasn't addressing in person. One big plus was Meyerson, who knew two of NBC's directors. One of them, Martin Goland, president of Southwest Research Institute in San Antonio, served on the Governor's Committee to obtain the $4 billion Superconducting Supercollider for Texas, which Meyerson chaired. At the conclusion of their teleconference, the board voted unanimously for Rainwater.

The first hour of the TAB board meeting was spent reviewing the events of the last several days and the quantitative and qualitative elements of both bids. It was clear that Rainwater's bid was superior in most categories; most importantly, it was superior in the critical aspect of the shareholders' share of the deal.

At noon, Rainwater and Meyerson arrived. While Rainwater needed no introduction, I introduced Meyerson, whose credentials were impressive to say the least. He had enjoyed a brilliant business career: he had been an employee of Electronic Data Systems (EDS); Ross Perot's handpicked CEO to fix DuPont Glore Florgan, which was beyond help when Meyerson arrived; president of EDS; and Perot's closest confidant. As a measure of his esteem, Perot had recently donated $10 million to build a new symphony hall in Dallas, with the provision it be named after Meyerson. Meyerson's appointment by the governor on the supercollider project gave him some additional cachet. Further, he was a native of Fort Worth.

Rainwater did an artful job of explaining why the board should select him. He elaborated on his vision for the companies and Texas. "I'm a native of Fort Worth, my family is here, my business is here, and this is where I'm going to stay. I've had an interest in doing something with this bank and have been talking to Jody about it for the last two years. This is a great institution, with a great management team, and what has happened is nobody's fault–and it's not yours either, Gene [turning to Gene Gray, TAB's senior credit officer]. Texas will be back. The oil business will improve, and real estate will come back."

Rainwater paused, looking each director in the eye, then continued with the easy confidence of a highly successful deal maker, a man in his element in a situation of this sort.

"This bank is uniquely positioned to take advantage of the rebound. There aren't going to be too many banks that are Texas owned, based, and managed, and those that are will have a significant advantage. My plan is to offer stock, on the same basis that I'm buying it, to every significant customer or potential customer in your markets. I want all the existing shareholders to invest, and I hope all of you will invest as well. I think it would be a great partnership, and I really want this deal."

Meyerson followed with a few words, they adjourned, and we voted unanimously in favor of Rainwater's bid. I felt extremely gratified about the events of the day. However, the next few weeks would produce more surprises.

TEN

RAINWATER MEETS THE FDIC

I felt a huge sense of relief after Rainwater was selected the winner. It was the outcome I had wanted and had worked so feverishly for during the previous three months. Even those few members of the TAB board who had been doubters seemed satisfied: our effort to seek an FDIC-assisted merger with NBC was going according to plan.

First FDIC Encounter

The next order of business was to introduce Rainwater and the structure of the deal to the FDIC. A meeting was arranged for Wednesday, June 1, 1988, in Washington, D.C., for that purpose. Gary Cage and I left on Tuesday, May 31, on the 7:00 A.M. flight for Washington to meet with Bill Isaac, Christie Sciacca, and the NBC representatives prior to Richard Rainwater joining us later in the day.

The meetings in the Secura offices had by this time become predictable: Isaac drifting in and out, taking care of other business in the interim, with Sciacca basically presiding and running the meetings. When Isaac was in the room, he would cradle a diet Coke in one hand while he ate popcorn–an Isaac staple–with the other. In the interest of time, a working lunch of sandwiches and cookies would be served. There was always a lot of milling around, as people called their offices, consulted with their advisers, or took a break. Even so, we seemed to accomplish our work.

Tuesday night, Richard Rainwater joined us. Isaac, knowing of Rainwater's love of Lebanese food, took us to his favorite Lebanese restaurant. Spirits were high, and the wine flowed freely. Toward the end of the evening, Isaac toasted Rainwater's victory.

Rainwater responded exuberantly. "Bill, this deal is going to put your firm on the map. And we're going to make a lot of money–I mean a whole lot of money–and we're going to have fun doing it. This is a really good deal."

On Wednesday morning our entire group met with Stan Poling and his associates at the FDIC offices to discuss the parameters of the deal approved by both bank boards. The FDIC representatives listened intently to our presentation, taking copious notes. When we had finished, Poling, speaking slowly and deliberately so that no one could misunderstand him, said, "We have a problem with the old shareholders receiving 5 percent to 25 percent, and the FDIC ending up with 5 percent to 10 percent of the company. It just doesn't seem equitable, since the FDIC is providing the assistance, which we believe will be close to $500 million. We need to study it further."

We agreed we would take their comments under advisement, and we set a tentative date to meet again on Friday, June 3. Unfortunately, that meeting was postponed. To everyone's dismay, Rainwater decided he wanted to become more familiar with the loan portfolios of the banks before meeting with the FDIC and agreeing to the amount of assistance. Thus, Thursday and Friday were spent in Rainwater's offices going through loans. Although Rainwater cut through the portfolios of both banks like the grim reaper, he finally agreed that $500 million was the right amount.

Second FDIC Encounter

The cast of characters for Tuesday morning's meeting with the FDIC was the same as the previous Wednesday: Rainwater, Isaac, Sciacca, Calvert, Johnson, Cage, Poling for the FDIC, and me. The meeting was a memorable one.

I had never seen Rainwater in better form than on this occasion. He began with unbridled panache. "I personally went through $800 million of Texas American's loans. The commercial and oil and gas loans have virtually no loss. This is a real estate problem–the bottom fell out of the market. These managements are not to blame–they are good, and they did their jobs responsibly."

We then presented new sharing schedules equating the FDIC's ownership in the merged bank with that of the old shareholders, which seemed acceptable to the FDIC.

Then Poling shifted the conversation to one of the thorniest issues with which we would have to deal: the creditors. He looked almost apologetic as he asked, "Would you be willing to merge all your banks into one bank? That would give us the lever we need: it would set the stage for a bridge bank."

A bank is bridged when the FDIC declares it insolvent, organizes a new bank to take its place, owns the new bank, and runs it themselves until new ownership can be arranged. In the event that a bank holding company owns the bank, the act of declaring the bank insolvent by the FDIC leaves the holding company with a worthless asset, the stock of the failed bank. Thus the shareholders and the creditors of the holding company have been cut off and have nothing of value, while the FDIC owns the new bank.

I knew that dealing with the creditors would be one of the biggest hurdles we would have to overcome. The FDIC had been terribly embarrassed by their inability to deal effectively with the arbitrageurs in closing the First City transaction. The target had been for at least 90 percent of First City's bonds to be tendered for a new security worth $.55 to $.65 for each dollar of bonds tendered. At the closing on April 20, 1988, less than 70 percent had been tendered, leaving the holders of the untendered securities with an opportunity to collect 100 percent on maturity (assuming the FDIC accepted the tendered shares and went ahead with the transaction, which they did).

In his inimitable way, Rainwater leaped in, exclaiming, "What we need is big-time larceny to deal with these guys! We need a tall fence with a big sign that says BEWARE OF DOG, and behind the fence is the dog–the FDIC–with a backup plan that would wipe out the creditors if they don't cooperate."

After this moment of levity, Poling forced a chuckle, then turned deadly serious. "You realize, of course, that we will have to take your proposal, as well as those of others, to the board."

I watched Rainwater as Poling spoke. He remained cool, and his expression didn't change, although I knew he was seething over what he was hearing. Then he asked Poling point-blank, "Would you do a deal with one of the groups which has an unsolicited offer on the shelf [an obvious reference to Pohlad], without approval of the management or the boards of the companies, and after all our effort?"

Poling replied coolly, "Yes, we would."

In complete dismay, Rainwater dropped the pen that he had been cradling in his hand. He fixed his eyes on the pen, which he was now twirling on the table. The stark reality was that the FDIC was pulling the rug out from under us. But they were clearly in the driver's seat, and there wasn't anything we could do about it.

After our meeting with the staff, we had a good meeting with Chairman Seidman. Rainwater had met Seidman and Bob Clarke in Nantucket the previous summer, which gave them mutual ground for conversation. At the end of the session Seidman said, "We want a quick fix on Texas banks. Write a check, and let's do a deal."

Seidman's response gave us all, and Rainwater in particular, a sense of security. We had heard from the chairman that he wanted to do a deal and do it quickly. There was no reason to believe he wasn't sincere, or that he wouldn't make it happen.

We returned to Texas from our session with the FDIC with confidence that progress had been made. But we knew time was our worst enemy. As the respective situations of each company worsened, we were afraid that events would overtake us.

A New Arena

The next day, the tough negotiations with the FDIC began. Rainwater's proposal specified a guaranteed rate of a 12 percent dividend on the $200 million of investor capital and a conversion to common after ten years. Poling wanted 10 percent on the dividend and five years on the conversion, and he was non-negotiable on these points. On Thursday afternoon, Rainwater countered with 11 percent and seven and a half years.

On Friday morning, Poling formally rejected Rainwater's counter and again emphasized they were non-negotiable. In a conference call later that day, Rainwater explained to Poling and me that he couldn't change his proposal because he, Peter Joost, and Mort Meyerson had agreed on these numbers and, since they were out of town and couldn't be reached, he couldn't change.

Rainwater was finding himself in a new arena, where the rules of the game were totally different than any he had faced before. He had never attempted to negotiate a deal with an agency of the federal government, with whom gentlemen's agreements, handshakes, and verbal commitments meant little and could be abrogated by a higher authority. He was dealing with a different mentality, one in which decisions were not driven by profit but by politics. The compromise counteroffer Rainwater had proposed to Poling would have been a normal negotiating gambit on Wall Street, but at the FDIC it fell on deaf ears.

Rainwater was livid: he couldn't believe that the FDIC was non-negotiable, and I began to sense his growing frustration. Did Rainwater have the patience and perseverance to negotiate his way through this morass? That was the real question, and a very worrisome one.

Bill Isaac, upon hearing of Richard's response to Poling, placed a call to Fort Worth and San Antonio. He was furious. Irritation and frustration evident in his voice, he said,

> Richard is being greedy. Hell, his yield on the deal is going to be obscene. Poling is non-negotiable. He'll take all proposals to the board with no recommendation. Listen, there's another complication. The board has received a letter from Jerry Ford [Gerald J. Ford, an investor from Dallas, who had been trying to get a foot in the door], claiming that he has been unfairly excluded from bidding. They don't know how they are going to respond, but they might decide to open up the whole process again. Rainwater's got a chance to win by agreeing to the FDIC's terms; if he doesn't, he's jeopardizing the entire transaction.

Tuesday, June 14, seemed endless, but it was to be just one of many long days to follow. Most of the morning was spent trying to maneuver Rainwater into sweetening his bid, but to no avail. Finally, late in the day, Christie Sciacca called. "Look, First Republic is a nightmare. The board never even considered or discussed our deal; they were too preoccupied with First Republic."

We felt sick. We had worked and worried ourselves into a frenzy under the false illusion that TAB and NBC were of the highest priority to the FDIC.

Upon arriving at work on Wednesday, I allowed impulse to override good judgment and called Poling to get a firsthand update on the status of our situation.

"Stan, we're on a tightrope. Time is running out for both companies!" I exclaimed in a strained voice that betrayed the stress I was under.

Poling was candid. "Jody, I'm not negotiating. Pohlad has a deal on the table with a significantly lower cost to the FDIC than Rainwater's, although the sharing schedule is the same."

On learning this new information about Pohlad, I once again could feel the deal slipping away from us. With a renewed sense of urgency, I walked the short distance to Rainwater's office in double-time in order to explain the situation. I arrived at 11:00 A.M. and compared the two deals for Rainwater as I perceived them. After some gentle but persuasive arm twisting, I was able to get Rainwater to agree to the compromise we had been seeking for the last week: a lower dividend on the preferred stock and a conversion to common stock after five years.

Thursday, June 16, would prove to be unforgettable. It opened on an extremely bullish note as I was certain, with the compromises reached the previous day, the FDIC would surely award the deal to Rainwater. But before the day would end, we would nearly lose it all.

Rainwater called me after lunch to report that he had spoken with Poling but never reached closure on the issues we discussed the day before. My heart plummeted: once again, the deal was slipping away.

Back in my office, I called Isaac, and he agreed to try to mediate between Rainwater and Poling. At 4:40 P.M., Rainwater and Poling's conversation from earlier in the day was repeated in a conference call, including Isaac. I was in Rainwater's office for the call.

After Poling terminated his part in the call, Rainwater asked Isaac why Pohlad had been invited back into the deal. Isaac responded nonchalantly, "This is a high-profile deal. Congressional hearings are likely."

Rainwater leaped up, kicking his chair back, and excitedly paced the room, gesturing wildly with his hands. He shouted, "Congressional hearings! I knew dealing with the government was a mistake. Why did I ever get into this? I apologize to you, Jody, and I apologize to you, Bill. I've had it." He then glanced at his watch and said, "Gene Bishop is waiting. I need to go."

Wondering what Isaac thought of the abrupt dismissal, I followed Rainwater into his conference room where Bishop, CEO of MCorp, was waiting. Bishop or no Bishop, I decided that I needed to make one more run at Richard to see if I could bring him around, as time was running out. For the next half hour, I used the wall to illustrate our proposal and the changes necessary to make us competitive. After a lengthy monologue, my voice becoming hoarse, I saw Rainwater begin to relax slightly. Heartened, I continued my cajoling. He nodded and agreed when he realized he was out of it if he didn't meet Poling's demands with his best and final offer.

Once again, our irons were pulled out of the fire, as Rainwater bought into the changes. We called Isaac, who relayed this information to Poling, who confirmed that Rainwater's bid wouldn't have been considered otherwise.

Bishop sat quietly, incredulous over what he was witnessing. But given the exigencies involved, confidentiality was not a principal consideration. Besides, I figured MCorp was headed in the same direction as we were, and they might benefit from the experience and even contribute something.

On Friday, June 17, Christie Sciacca called late in the day to report that the board had a briefing that afternoon, most of which was spent talking about Jerry Ford. He said our deal was to be approved at the board meeting the following Tuesday. Totally frustrated and exhausted by now, I only expected the unexpected.

Monday and then Tuesday morning passed uneventfully, except for the anticipation of waiting for the results of the FDIC board meeting on Tuesday afternoon. The call from Isaac and Sciacca came at 3:15 P.M., immediately after they had spoken with Stan Poling.

"Bad news!" Isaac began, his voice incredulous. "The FDIC is ordering a thirty-day delay before considering the bids. They received a letter earlier today from Jerry Ford that got their attention. It requested that Ford be provided forty-five days to conduct due diligence, after which definitive bid proposals would be submitted and acted upon."

As I responded, I was wondering what else could go wrong. "Bill, neither company can stand the delay. Pohlad has conducted no due diligence, and Rainwater has done very little. Why does Ford need to? Why don't we just agree to give Ford access to our projections and require that all parties have their bids in by the next Monday, in time for the board meeting on Tuesday, June 28?"

Isaac agreed with my idea, then called back fifteen minutes later with more bad news. The FDIC didn't buy into our suggestion and instead gave all parties two weeks for due diligence, with all offers to be in by July 6 at 6:00 P.M.

During his conversations with Poling, Bill Isaac gleaned that the FDIC liked our deal and really wanted to do it, but Ford was the problem. It appeared that politics were now driving the FDIC–and the deal. How tragic for both companies, because every minute the deal was delayed, the franchises deteriorated and the cost of the recapitalization increased.

A Shocking Number

By the middle of June, both companies knew their examinations had gone very poorly, resulting in large losses and similar reductions in capital, which might require immediate public disclosure. Such disclosure could precipitate massive deposit withdrawals, thereby damaging both franchises beyond repair, and perhaps even jeopardizing our deal with the FDIC. Thus, we decided to wait in hope that we could announce earnings in conjunction with a transaction with the FDIC, which we believed offered the greatest protection to the shareholders.

On Friday afternoon, June 24, we were notified that we were to be at the OCC offices in Dallas on June 30 to discuss their preliminary recommendation with regard to the appropriate level of the loan loss reserve. NBC received notice of a similar meeting to be held on the same day. In the meantime, both companies were attempting to come up with their own reserve computations to try to refute the OCC's numbers.

The June 30 meeting began promptly at 8:30 A.M. and concluded about an hour later. The FDIC had a full complement of brass, including Jimmy F. Barton, acting director from the Washington office, and Peter Kraft, deputy comptroller for the Dallas region. On our side, I was accompanied by Buzz Brightbill, Gene Gray, and Gary Cage.

The fact that Barton was there was an ominous sign. They would only bring the Washington hierarchy in for a very special situation.

Jimmy Barton opened the meeting and quickly passed the baton to the local staff. As John Foucault, examiner in charge, began speaking and thumbing through his papers, you could have heard a pin drop. After what seemed like forever, he finally got to the bottom-line number.

It was as if Foucault had shot the number from a cannon, and it had ricocheted repeatedly from wall to wall. The impact was deafening.

Foucault was requiring an increase in TAB's loan loss reserve from $220 million to $250 million. It was a shocking increase of $150 million to $180 million over the preliminary number of $70 million we had previously received. This would leave us with negative equity capital of $17 million to $47 million.

This result left us absolutely defenseless. Whatever negotiating power we once had with the FDIC was gone. We were now at their mercy. They did grant us a chance to respond and appeal, however, with a deadline of July 11. They would share their methodology with us but wouldn't let us see their work papers.

I can't remember leaving any session as deflated and disheartened as I was on this occasion. Buzz, Gene, Gary, and I could say little as we took the elevator to the lower lobby level where we were to meet Richard Calvert and Mark Johnson. When they saw us, they must have thought they were seeing four people coming from a funeral, and that is exactly how we felt. The funeral was that of TAB.

As TAB's situation had gone from bad to worse, I had become so totally consumed by the company's problems and our inability to solve or control them that I could think of little else. I was not sleeping well or long, probably four to five hours a night. On Saturday night, June 25, I did not sleep at all. As far as I can remember, that is the only time this ever happened to me. A thousand thoughts raced through my mind, all related to how Rainwater's proposal could be improved to assure a winning deal. The more I thought, the more fertile my mind seemed to be. These were productive hours, and I believe if some of the suggestions I made thereafter had been adopted, the chances of winning would have been enhanced materially.

After our meeting with the OCC on Thursday, June 30, we had a TAB board meeting at which we disclosed the results of the morning conference. The board was extremely understanding and supportive, and Lewis Bond said some exceptionally flattering remarks about management's efforts. I knew Lewis was suffering with us, and that he felt a deep sense of responsibility for what had happened to the company. He had built it, and now he was watching it come apart before his very eyes. It had to be extremely tough, and yet Lewis, being the stoic he was, never showed emotion or grief.

That night I did what I had often done after a tough day: I jogged on the Shady Oaks Country Club golf course near our home, one of my favorite places. The smell of freshly mowed grass from the meticulously manicured fairways accented the air. The sun was sinking behind the century-old oak trees, and a light breeze from the south made it seem much cooler than the ninety-five-degree temperature. Although I was in the city, the vastness of the golf course, with its wooded areas and ravines, made it seem like the country. On several occasions I had seen a fox on the course, and I hoped on this run I might see the beaver who had recently adopted the golf course as his habitat. But he was nowhere in sight; perhaps he had been trapped and returned to the country before he could cut down any of the native trees.

I allowed my thoughts to run free, back to simpler, more carefree times. I purged my mind of anything associated with the bank or the decline in the value of TAB's stock. Instead, I concentrated on the grass, the trees, the birds, the ripples on the lake, the squirrels gathering acorns, and the rabbits running across the fairways. The physical and emotional relief was something I needed and found salubrious.

The Final Countdown Begins

With the bids due on July 6, the decision would be made shortly thereafter; thus, the final countdown had begun. Accordingly, the companies and our advisors were busy planning last-minute strategy. On advice of Rodgin Cohen, our legal advisor on the deal from Sullivan & Cromwell in New York, Richard Calvert and I arranged for appointments on July 6 with Chairman Seidman, Bob Clarke, and C. C. Hope, the third FDIC board member.

In an effort to support Rainwater, the companies each sent similar letters dated June 30 from their boards to the FDIC urging his selection. The letters emphasized the "value added" a Texan could bring to the transaction, highlighting Rainwater's experience in dealing with creditors and his following in the investment community. The letters also pointed out that Mort Meyerson could be of great assistance to the companies in data processing.

Richard Calvert and I arrived in Washington, D.C., on July 5 in time for separate meetings with C. C. Hope and Chairman Seidman, and the next morning we had breakfast with Bob Clarke. We brought each of them up to date with regard to the status of the proposal and spent considerable time answering their questions.

Seidman commented on a study the OCC had recently released, which maintained that banks fail because of poor management. He said, "I disagree with Bob on this point. All you have to do is look at the failures west of the Mississippi, and eight out of ten of the largest banks are in Texas. It's an economic problem. Banks fail for reasons other than bad management."

After our breakfast with Clarke, Calvert and I went to Bill Isaac's office to work on our proposal, which was due at 6:00 P.M. Christie Sciacca actually had the responsibility of submitting the bid, and thus material was being faxed in from Fort Worth and New York.

Before leaving Washington that evening, we had a session to evaluate Rainwater's chance of prevailing. Bill Isaac felt that Rainwater was a cinch to get the deal, even though there were objectionable features in his proposal.

On the plane on the way home I had a long visit with Al Casey, chairman of First Republic, who had been in Washington on his own mission–the restructuring of his bank. Instead of spending all his time with the FDIC board, however, he was involved in heavy lobbying on Capitol Hill to sell his program, which had been characterized as "management's plan." We discussed the pros and cons of playing politics to influence a decision, and agreed he had a lot less at risk since he had been appointed to the post by Seidman in April. TAB and NBC were totally in the hands of the FDIC, which seemed unable to make a decision.

I had been concerned that Pohlad would submit a sweetener to his bid at the last minute. Christie called us early on July 7 and related that Pohlad had, indeed, come in with a very attractive late bid, and that it was a "horse race." Bill Isaac gave the nod to Rainwater, and Christie was betting that Pohlad would get it in a squeaker. A decision was to be rendered on Friday, July 8.

ELEVEN

THE FDIC SELECTS A WINNER

I knew something was wrong the minute Gene Gray walked into my office on Friday morning, July 8. His expression was grim and he sounded unusually serious as he spoke. "We've got a problem, Chief. Earlier this morning John Foucault [OCC examiner for TAB] gave me a copy of a $50,000 letter of credit issued by TAB/Austin to Caldwell National Bank on behalf of Don Cockerham [chairman and CEO of TAB/Austin]."

Hearing these words, I intuitively knew Cockerham was in dire trouble. Evidently, Foucault had gone to the collateral files of the Caldwell bank after learning from the TAB/Austin board minutes that Cockerham was borrowing there.

Gray continued. "I talked to Lester Duncan [executive vice president and second-in-command to Cockerham]; the letter of credit isn't recorded on the bank's books, and it was issued out of sequence. The last entry in the bank's ledger is #1635 and the letter of credit is #2150. Lester said Don had asked him to sign it, and he hadn't questioned its validity."

As the story unfolded, I felt numb, weak with sorrow, and sick with disappointment. It was incredible to the point of being unbelievable. Don Cockerham was one of our outstanding CEOs.

Gene Gray and Gary Cage left for Austin that afternoon to terminate Cockerham. In addition, we decided to ask Lester Duncan to take a leave of absence until the matter could be fully investigated. We were all tremendously saddened by what we had learned. We liked Cockerham, and we never would have dreamed he could have done something like this.

Unfortunately, like many other professional people in Austin, Cockerham had been playing the Austin real estate market and had bet heavily on its future. His role model had been Eldon Beebe, who preceded Cockerham as president and served as chairman of the board until March 1988. Beebe also had invested extensively in real estate and had done quite well over the years, accumulating a net worth in excess of $4 million. For the last ten years, Cockerham, Beebe, and Lester Duncan had worked together, had developed a very close relationship, and had even invested in real estate together.

After Cockerham's termination, I became aware that he had over $3 million in debt, an amount far in excess of what his $110,000 salary would enable him to carry. Of this, $1 million was Cockerham's half of a partnership with Eldon Beebe, which had borrowed $2 million from Congress National Bank in Austin to invest in raw land in northwest Austin.

There is no way TAB's internal auditors could have discovered the violation of law involving the fraudulent letter of credit, since there was no record of its issuance. Only the OCC could have discovered it by looking in Cockerham's loan file at the Caldwell bank.

On September 20, 1988, the United States District Court in Austin returned a thirteen-count indictment against Don Cockerham for "misapplication of bank funds and credits, making false entries, and issuing unauthorized obligations."[1] Cockerham's actions and subsequent firing were a tragedy for the company, as it was just one more major reversal in a long sequence of depressing developments affecting employee morale. It was, in addition, exceedingly embarrassing, further eroding credibility at a time when credibility was being stretched to its limits as a result of asset deterioration.

On May 31, 1989, Cockerham pleaded guilty to fraud. He was subsequently sentenced to five years in prison and fined $5.3 million.[2] Lester Duncan was charged in September 1989 with seventeen counts of bank fraud. The government said that Duncan "approved the loans" to Cockerham and received half of his interest in various real estate ventures. On February 22, 1990, after pleading guilty, Duncan was sentenced to three years in prison and fined $5 million.[3]

The Final Hours

The stress associated with the Austin circumstances made waiting for a decision from the FDIC just that much more excruciating. Finally, on Monday, July 11, we were advised that a decision would be forthcoming on Tuesday afternoon.

Late in the day on Tuesday, we were told by Stan Poling that the companies would be informed by noon Wednesday. A decision had been made, but it needed to be reviewed by the Federal Reserve.

Wednesday was an excessively long day, mostly spent speculating about what the Federal Reserve was doing. Noon passed with no word. Later in the day we heard through Rainwater that Poling had advised them that the delay was due to a bank holding company regulatory matter, and we wouldn't get a decision until sometime Thursday.

As each deadline and hour of waiting passed, our tension level increased accordingly. It was difficult to concentrate on anything, as the question of who would win was always there.

Finally, on Thursday at about 2:30 P.M., we were asked to stand by for a conference call between Bill Isaac, representatives of NBC, and ourselves. Gary Cage and I took the call and listened silently as Isaac spoke without emotion.

"I've just heard from Poling. The board has decided. I know you're not going to like this, but their decision is final." Isaac then paused as if to catch his breath. "They've selected Pohlad. They want representatives from both companies to be in Washington for a meeting tomorrow morning. Then they'll tell us the terms."

While I didn't react outwardly, inwardly I was devastated. I could hardly speak and had a hard time accepting what I had heard. I could feel the veins in my temples pulsate with anger. I felt all of our hard work and all we had hoped to achieve for the company was lost. Our dreams of a Texas-owned-and-managed bank were shattered. After taking a few minutes to calm down and to reflect on what I had just learned, I called Rainwater in Nantucket to break the news to him in the event he hadn't heard.

"Richard, have you heard from Poling?" I asked.

"No. Have you?"

I dreaded giving him the news. "Yes," I said hesitatingly. "We lost–they awarded it to Pohlad. I don't understand it."

As I told him of the outcome, I heard Rusty Rose yell, "Oh, no!" Rose was one of Rainwater's close friends and an investor in many of his deals. He later would become partners with Rainwater and George W. Bush, President Bush's son, in the ownership of the Texas Rangers baseball franchise.

"Richard, you gave it all you had. No one could have asked for anything more than you and Peter put into this. I'm really sorry that it came out this way, but I want you to know how much I appreciate your friendship; it has meant a lot to me, and I'll always be grateful to you," I said, trying to be as upbeat as possible.

"It isn't over till it's over, Jody, and it isn't over yet. We'll see what happens now," he responded evenly.

We were surprised at Rainwater's never-say-die response, as we were sure he had had it with this deal, and with the FDIC.

No sooner had I hung up from my conversation with Rainwater than Pohlad called to express his pleasure at being selected the winning bidder. If the company wasn't going to be Texas owned, I couldn't think of anyone whose hands I would rather it be in than Pohlad's. He was highly regarded by Isaac and by the FDIC, and he was known to be a fine banker. "Carl," I responded, "we look forward to a long, pleasant, and mutually beneficial association." We then talked about the agenda going forward, and I agreed to convene our board to meet him and his associates as soon as we got back from visiting with the FDIC in Washington.

Before leaving that night for Washington, I went home to pack for the trip. I was dejected, but grateful that my wife Sheila–my confidante, best friend, and constant supporter–was waiting for me. She always had the ability to put things in the proper perspective and was constantly reassuring.

After the therapeutic relief of seeing Sheila, I went for a long run in our neighborhood. The sweet smell of the summer flowers perfumed the air, and their blooms painted a kaleidoscope of colors. In this setting, the problems of the day vanished. Mental anguish was replaced first by physical exertion, and finally by fatigue.

No Contest

The flight to Washington seemed exceedingly long. Gary and I sat together but said little as we were both dealing with our respective disappointment in our own way. Although Gary wasn't as wedded to the idea of a Texas-owned-and-managed bank as I was, he had to be concerned about the welfare of our employees and our customers under out-of-state ownership.

Friday morning we met at 8:00 A.M. in Secura's offices to discuss strategy prior to our meeting with the FDIC. Richard Calvert and Mark Johnson shared our disappointment over the FDIC's decision.

At 9:00, we met with Stan Poling and his associates to learn the details of the deal. As Poling revealed the parameters of Pohlad's bid, it became evident that Rainwater had been beaten, and beaten badly. We couldn't believe how aggressive Pohlad had been. A subsequent analysis of the two bids indicated that the Pohlad proposal was $122 million more costly to the company and less costly to the FDIC. Based upon the FDIC's mandate to select the least costly proposal, it was no contest.

Although we felt many emotions–remorse over Rainwater losing, anxiety over the prospect of losing the company to out-of-state interests, anger over having been sucked in by the FDIC in the first place–mostly, we felt betrayed by the FDIC. Their process had compromised Rainwater, who was honor bound not to change the sharing formula between the company and the FDIC, whereas Pohlad had been free to trade away the shareholders' interest to the FDIC. That, in fact, is exactly what he had done. Bill Isaac objected vehemently on behalf of the companies, and in a private visit with Poling was able to restore the shareholder's position so they shared the upside potential with the FDIC, each having a maximum 15 percent ownership in a best-case scenario.

While Isaac and Poling were out of the room, I wrote on a piece of scratch paper, "TAB/NBC exchange ratio, 60/40." I initialed it and passed it to Richard Calvert, who also initialed it and passed it to NBC's attorney, Jamie Smith, of the San Antonio law firm of Cox & Smith. Smith reminded us this agreement was subject to due diligence, in which each company would verify the assets and liabilities of the other, and to the approval of our respective boards. Thus, the exchange ratio between TAB and NBC was established. With this resolved, the meeting ended, and, after a short debriefing at the Secura offices, we left for Texas. During the trip I was preoccupied, thinking about the future of the company.

Although I had sensed the first hint of duplicity when the FDIC insisted on seeing both bids, this was the first time I actually had been confronted with the possibility of losing our strong Texas identity and our competitive advantage of being a company owned, based, and managed in Texas.

Pohlad Meets the Board

On Friday, both companies scheduled special board meetings for Monday to vote on the deal and to meet Carl Pohlad. He would visit with our board in the morning and with the board of NBC in the afternoon.

An hour before Pohlad was due to arrive, the TAB board convened to learn the details of Pohlad's deal and to discuss appropriate strategies and alternatives. Prior to the meeting, I called Poling to determine whether or not there were any alternatives.

"Stan, would the FDIC consider doing the deal approved for Pohlad, but with Rainwater?" I asked.

"Absolutely not," he responded. "We won't be a stalking horse for the company!"

I then asked, "What if we don't approve this deal?"

To this he replied, "You're then on your own, and we'll deal with you later under different circumstances."

Poling left no doubt as to our options–we had none. We had been swept into the vortex and were at the mercy of the FDIC. They would dictate who our new owner would be, as well as the terms of the deal. If we didn't like it, they would allow us to drift until we were sucked under and forced to deal with them under the most onerous terms, leaving nothing for the shareholders or creditors and replacing management and directors.

Upon learning this, the TAB board was angry, not with Pohlad but over the way in which the FDIC was ramming the decision down our throats. They were incredulous that the strong recommendations of the boards of both companies had been summarily dismissed by the FDIC. Additionally, they didn't like the deal Pohlad had cut. They felt he had given too much to the FDIC to the detriment of the shareholders. In the final analysis, they had no choice, as the FDIC had left us with no practical alternative. The board unanimously approved the Pohlad proposal.

Carl, Jim Pohlad, Don Benson, and Tom Herbst were greeted cordially when they entered our executive conference room, where we had elected to meet because of its less-formal atmosphere compared to the boardroom. I introduced Pohlad and his associates to our board and expressed our pleasure in having them as partners.

Then Pohlad addressed the board. "We're delighted to have been selected as the winning bidder," he said. "Being awarded TAB and NBC is a very important step in realizing my dream of establishing a major regional holding company stretching from Texas northward across the Midwest and joining our $4 billion in assets in Minnesota. Texas will be the anchor in this network, and I hope that I will have substantial Texas representation in the ownership of the company."

Our board's response was proper and appropriate under the circumstances. Lewis Bond, as chairman of the executive committee, was the spokesman. "Carl, I want to assure you on behalf of the board that you will have our utmost support and cooperation. We look forward to working with you and your associates and to assisting you any way possible. I'm sure it will be a long and mutually satisfactory relationship."

Wednesday, July 20: Press Conference

Since the meetings of June 30, when we received the OCC's preliminary reserve recommendations, TAB and NBC had been working with their respective OCC examiners in an attempt to reach an agreement on the required amount to add to the loan loss reserve. The OCC wanted to bring closure to this issue so that we could announce preliminary earnings simultaneously with the announcement of the deal with the FDIC and Pohlad. Accordingly, both companies had meetings scheduled with the OCC prior to the TAB/NBC/Pohlad press conference. NBC went first, and we followed at 11:30 A.M.

To our relief, we had been successful in convincing our OCC examiner, John Foucault, that the appropriate level of the reserve should be $195 million rather than the OCC's recommended range of $220 million to $250 million. As a result, our meeting, albeit somber, was routine. We felt that their acceptance of our numbers was a small victory.

As Gary Cage, Gene Gray, Buzz Brightbill, and I left the OCC offices and walked to the Secura offices to meet Richard Calvert and Mark Johnson, we agreed that it would have been a terrible feeling to have left that meeting without having a deal in place. Although we were all still adjusting to the shock of Pohlad's victory, at that moment Pohlad was being accepted as our new owner at a press conference conducted by the FDIC, and we were glad he was on board. After our recent experience with the regulators, we were beginning to look to Pohlad as our savior, our rescuer. However, although I was grateful for Pohlad, the new reserve figure would diminish our equity to the point where we had lost all our negotiating leverage. I felt sick, like I was going to a funeral instead of a press conference.

Unfortunately, Calvert and Johnson had not reconciled themselves to accept the reserve number the OCC had given them for NBC. Consequently, we were not able to release our earnings at the press conference. The important thing, however, was to have a deal announced prior to releasing earnings, which we now did.

The press conference began at about 4:00 P.M. at the Sheraton Hotel in downtown Dallas. It was well attended by the press, both television and newspapers. Carl Pohlad was the main attraction.

In his opening comments, Pohlad said, "This combined bank is going to create a new force in Texas. Just like in sports, a city or an economy can face adversity from time to time. But the real mark of a winner is how you react to adverse conditions and bounce back. I'm not interested in talking about yesterday. We're talking of today and what we're going to do tomorrow. And I'm putting my money where my mouth is."[4]

In response to questions from the media, Pohlad said he had not yet decided whether the merged bank would have a new name or a new headquarters. And no employee layoffs were planned, which was welcome news–if not, indeed, a gigantic relief–to everyone. He further stated, "I don't think you can blame individual managers for what has happened. The bank doesn't need new management; what it needs is new capital."[5]

What Pohlad was saying was music to our ears, and very reassuring. While events of the previous several months revealed him to be a tough and shrewd investor who didn't like to lose, he was also very cordial and engaging, although somewhat reserved.

Networking

Several weeks before the press conference, I had made appointments to see Al Casey, chairman and CEO of First Republic, and Gene Bishop, chairman and CEO of MCorp, on July 21.

I was greeted warmly by Al Casey, who talked enthusiastically about the restructuring plan that First Republic's management, under his leadership, had submitted to the FDIC. He believed he had a deal with Seidman and that they would win. The leading contenders, however, were considered to be Citicorp, the nation's largest holding company, and NCNB Corporation of Charlotte, North Carolina, the nation's eighteenth-largest holding company. A July 7 article in the *Wall Street Journal* reported that Citicorp had the edge over NCNB, and that First Republic officials were trying to hurry the process.[6]

During lunch with Bishop, I attempted to give him as much insight as possible about what I believed the future held for him and MCorp. His company was in the middle of an OCC examination conducted by the same individuals who had examined the real estate portfolios at First Republic and TAB. Gene didn't want to believe his company could be in the same condition and assured me that they had evaluated their real estate loans very conservatively.

Upon leaving, I said, "Gene, what's your loan loss reserve ratio?"

"It's about 3 percent," he responded.

"At the outset of our exam, ours was about the same as yours is now," I confirmed. "But, at the conclusion, we had to move it up to 6 percent. If you had to do that, what would that do to you?"

Gene winced as he heard our number, and then responded, "We'd have a lot to be worried about."

First Republic Is "Bridged"

Throughout July, the fate of First RepublicBank had been anxiously anticipated. As the date for a decision drew near, tension in First Republic and in the rest of the banking community mounted. There was keen interest in how the FDIC would handle the situation, as it would be a precursor of future assisted transactions, including that of TAB and NBC. On July 29, the question was answered, and the answer was not to our liking.

During the week of July 25, rumors were rampant. It was reported that FDIC and OCC examiners had checked in with each of First Republic's subsidiary banks in anticipation of taking them over. This usually occurs on a Friday, which gives the FDIC a weekend to determine the disposition of the bank and to liquidate it or sell it to the highest bidder. Liquidation (paying off all deposits of $100,000 or less) of First Republic was not an alternative, as it would be extremely costly, impractical, and precedent setting. It seemed inconceivable that the FDIC would have its liquidators at each bank, however, unless drastic action was contemplated.

After the close of business on Friday, July 29, the FDIC announced its most dramatic and expensive takeover ever: it had declared all of Republic's banks insolvent and announced that it would sell them to NCNB Corporation of Charlotte, North Carolina (now NationsBank Corporation). To facilitate the transaction, the FDIC would create a "bridge bank" to purchase all the assets and assume all liabilities of the insolvent banks. The bridge bank would then be sold to NCNB, leaving First Republic owning the corporate shells of the failed banks, which meant the shareholders and creditors would get essentially nothing.[7]

Bill Isaac had told the TAB/NBC working group at the meeting on March 14 that he had urged the First Republic management not to accept the FDIC's $1 billion loan and not to pledge the stock of all the solvent subsidiary banks as security for the loan. The disastrous consequence of their failure to follow his advice was now evident. Demanding payment on the $1 billion note, which was guaranteed by the solvent subsidiaries, was a critical element in the sequence of steps in the takeover by the FDIC, as it triggered the insolvency of all the subsidiaries.[8]

The significance of this transaction for TAB was frightening. First, it demonstrated that the threat of a bridge bank was not idle. Second, it highlighted the importance of maintaining liquidity and external funding sources, and of not being forced to borrow from the Federal Reserve discount window. Finally, it underlined the importance of not accepting a note from the FDIC to shore up our liquidity and of not pledging any assets to the FDIC.

TAB's directors were especially worried about their responsibility to the company's creditors not to encumber any of our assets. This fiduciary responsibility was further emphasized when the First Republic creditors filed suit against the First Republic directors and the FDIC for fraud and fraudulent conveyance of assets.[9] This further development regarding First Republic also stressed the importance of our having already announced a deal with the FDIC. On July 26, we had released our second-quarter results, which reflected a loss of $135 million, leaving us with equity of only $28 million.

Although our funding was holding up surprisingly well under the circumstances, it was possible that the First Republic failure could further destabilize our situation. We were particularly vulnerable with regard to funds purchased from correspondent banks, which we relied upon to the extent of about $100 million to meet our nearly $600 million borrowed funds requirement. These funds were sold to us under a one-day contract, subject to renewal at the end of each day. I was afraid they could evaporate overnight, forcing us to borrow from the Federal Reserve and leaving us at the mercy of the regulators. We would then be subject to the same forces that ultimately led to the FDIC's seizure of First Republic, in which event our shareholders would lose everything.

After hearing about how the FDIC had treated First Republic, I hoped we would be able to avoid a similar fate. Even if we did get into a liquidity bind, surely they would give us some consideration for "coming in early" in good faith. We had never tried to hide anything and had always been forthright and honest about the condition of the company. We had gone to the FDIC to avoid such an occurrence. Now our fate was in their hands.

Pohlad: "One of Us"

With Pohlad having been selected, the next step in bringing our recapitalization and restructuring to reality was for the Pohlad organization to conduct due diligence on both banks. In this exercise, Pohlad would send teams of people into TAB and NBC to verify the amount and value of the assets and of the liabilities in order to determine if they were properly reflected on the books of the banks. Major assets subject to verification would include banking quarters, investments, loans, and loan loss reserves;

liabilities to be verified or discovered would include deposits, short-term borrowings, loans against bank property and equipment, leases, contracts (for data processing and computer services or other major services supplied by outside vendors), and pending litigation. Deposits would be tested to determine volatility and reliability. Due diligence began on August 1 and was expected to last about a month.

On Thursday, August 11, Carl Pohlad came to Fort Worth to address our officers and employees. This was a major event for TAB, as Pohlad had received extensive publicity in the local press, all of which was quite favorable. Our employees were understandably anxious to meet him.

We met at 8:00 A.M. in the ballroom of the Worthington Hotel. I gave Pohlad a brief introduction, then it was his show. He said all the right things and was very reassuring to the employees. At the conclusion of his remarks, I presented him with a T-shirt that said on one side, "Texas American–That's My Bank," and on the other side said, "NBC–That's My Bank." "That's My Bank" had been a well-known TAB advertising slogan.

To my surprise, and that of everyone else, Pohlad peeled off his tie and dress shirt down to his undershirt and pulled on the T-shirt. This was totally unrehearsed and demonstrated Pohlad's charisma and showmanship instincts. We were deeply touched by his innate understanding of what our employees were feeling. He subsequently toured the bank wearing that T-shirt. Our employees absolutely loved it and, from that point on, regarded Pohlad as "one of us." Indeed, we regarded him as the man who would not only rescue us, but give us the opportunity to be a viable competitor in the Texas market again.

Due Diligence

The object of the due diligence was to reduce the book value of the assets to their market value–a process called "mark-to-market"–to be accomplished at the time the transaction was closed. In this manner, the amount of the FDIC assistance would be determined, which was the amount necessary to restore the capital of the bank to an acceptable level after the mark-to-market. The process involved a reevaluation of the underlying collateral behind each loan, using the latest information available, including sales of comparable properties and current appraisals.

Evaluating real estate was an inexact science at best. There was absolutely no demand in Texas from buyers for anything except income-producing property, and, as a result, there were no sales to base comparable values upon. Appraisals were based on intuition or on old information. In most instances worst-case scenarios were used, based upon extremely pessimistic views of the future.

At the outset of the due diligence, we convened all of our people who would be involved to brief them on the process. We urged them to be as honest as possible in evaluating the assets of the company, stressing that we did not want to overvalue the assets and, thus, undervalue the amount of assistance required.

We also explained that the due diligence process based on the approach of Arthur Anderson, the accounting firm Pohlad was using, was a "fire sale" approach. It was the difference between an orderly sale under a business-as-usual approach and a liquidation auction; each was guaranteed to produce far different results, with the auction producing the lowest possible values. We further explained that we had to keep this exercise separate and distinct from our ongoing business, which implied keeping two sets of books, based on two divergent thought processes. Otherwise, at the next reporting period, there could be a significant overstatement of our losses, resulting from larger than necessary additions to reserves for loan losses and write-downs of foreclosed real estate.

On Tuesday, September 6, Buzz Brightbill, Gene Gray, Gary Cage, and I went to Minneapolis, along with Richard Calvert and Mark Johnson, to receive the results of the due diligence. The total mark-to-market required for both companies was between $850 and $1,050 million, minus the $360 million in reserves on the books as of June 30. This implied a level of assistance of at least twice what had been previously estimated. We were extremely concerned over the FDIC's reaction: they might want to retrade the agreement we had reached with them, demanding a greater percentage of ownership for themselves and less for our shareholders.

After the FDIC finished their own due diligence on September 22, Poling confided to me that their evaluation had confirmed a number equivalent to approximately 75 percent of the Pohlad number. This meant that Pohlad and the FDIC could be hundreds of millions of dollars apart in their negotiations. With this gulf, they might never reach agreement on the amount of assistance, and the entire deal could fall apart.

Slowly but surely, I could feel the life being squeezed out of the company. We were adrift in a stormy sea without a sail or a rudder. I could only guess as to the ultimate outcome in relation to the shareholders, creditors, the board of directors, and management. My greatest fears were being realized, and I was powerless to change the course of events. I felt helpless and deeply discouraged.

TWELVE

POHLAD VERSUS RAINWATER: ROUND 2

With both the Pohlad and the FDIC due diligence completed, negotiations between Pohlad and the FDIC began in earnest during the last week in September. On Friday, September 9, Tom Herbst advised me that they would submit their final proposal to the FDIC the following Monday for presentation to the board on Tuesday. Then Herbst said almost nonchalantly, "Poling had said they would either accept the proposal or rebid the transaction."

REBID. The word hit like a thunderbolt. Neither company could afford a lengthy delay. This was a stunning and devastating revelation.

With urgency in my mind, I called Bill Isaac. Not even trying to hide my distress, I said, "Bill, you've got to talk to Stan Poling and find out what the devil is going on." I reported what Herbst had said. Then, without giving him a chance to speak, I added, "This is insanity. The FDIC couldn't be planning to rebid this again; we can't survive that long."

Isaac reached Poling and found him in a deeply pessimistic mood. Poling was upset because Pohlad was asking for very significant changes from their original bid: specifically, he wanted more assistance to cover potentially larger loan losses revealed in their "fire sale" due diligence approach. The FDIC, which had done its own due diligence using an orderly, business-as-usual liquidation approach, didn't believe this additional protection was needed, or justified.

Additionally, Poling felt that Pohlad had not put his best deal on the table. It was clear that Pohlad was trying to obtain as much assistance as possible to reduce his risk in this high-stakes game of poker, and Poling had concluded that Pohlad's intransigence might necessitate a rebid.

We were extremely fearful that the delays and disruption of another round of bidding would cause accelerated deterioration of the franchises, lessening the value to an investor and increasing the cost of the assistance to the FDIC. TAB had already experienced considerable deterioration in lost deposits and sources of funding. Although we were still able to meet our daily requirements from internal sources and from borrowing overnight funds from correspondent banks, funding had become more tenuous. We fully expected that the release of our third-quarter financial results, which would reflect a loss of $216 million, would bring on a funding crisis, forcing us to borrow from the Federal Reserve. We were slowly bleeding to death and in need of an immediate tourniquet.

The other major concern related to rebidding was the wear and tear on our people. Uncertainty was a pernicious enemy. The longer our fate was unresolved, the greater the uncertainty, which would undermine job security. Headhunters were contacting employees daily at all levels of the organization, and we were extremely vulnerable. TAB needed a decision *now*; a rebid would be a disaster.

Tuesday, October 4, was another day of anxious waiting, but with predictable results. The FDIC board met and discussed our transaction, but with no decision. They acknowledged that they had underestimated the potential losses in the companies and that the cost to the FDIC would be greater than originally anticipated, but they believed they could make a deal with Pohlad. We were told there also had been considerable discussion about the merits of rebidding or, to us, the unthinkable: declaring TAB insolvent and forming a bridge bank.

Preferring not to think about the "bridge bank" possibility, we felt our most immediate concern was to avoid a rebidding process. Accordingly, we decided to contact the under secretary of the U.S. Treasury, George Gould. Bayard Friedman had a close acquaintanceship with Gould and had visited with him previously about the proposal for a Reconstruction Finance Corporation look-alike solution to the Texas banking woes. At my request, Friedman contacted Gould on Wednesday, October 5, to ask him to encourage Seidman not to rebid the deal.

The following day, Friedman reported that Gould had visited with Seidman, that Seidman was aware of the risks of rebidding, and that they hoped a rebid could be avoided. This was good news in a spate of otherwise disastrous developments.

Further Delays

On Saturday, October 8, the FDIC board left for Hawaii for the American Bankers Association convention and subsequently went to Tokyo for meetings with regulators of other countries. We were advised that they intended to have a teleconference from Tokyo with the Washington, D.C., staff on Thursday, October 13, to further consider our situation. During the week of October 10, we had several conversations with Tom Herbst about the status of the deal and some of the particulars of their proposal.

"I'm totally frustrated," Herbst said. "And Carl is completely disgusted. They can't make up their minds. They tell us one thing one day and something else completely different the next. There is no consistency. Doing business with them is a disaster."

With his patience clearly tested to its limits, Herbst continued. "We've met every demand and condition they've imposed, but they've given us no idea of what it would take to make a deal. We're only told what isn't acceptable, not what is. We're holding Carl's hand, but if he gets the idea we're getting impatient and frustrated, he'll walk the deal." The reason for Pohlad's disgust was more than justified.

The next morning Bill Isaac called me. "Stan Poling has been instructed by his board not to negotiate with Pohlad because, if he does, he might have to negotiate with Rainwater and Ford. As a result, Pohlad is in the untenable position of having to negotiate with himself."

This was a ludicrous situation. Were all government agencies run in such a willy-nilly, irresponsible fashion?

As the week passed, our anxiety increased with the approach of Thursday's scheduled teleconference board meeting. Yet it was difficult for us to see how they could reach a decision by teleconference. In keeping with our fears, Poling called late Thursday morning and advised, "Chairman Seidman has decided that if it isn't absolutely urgent, the decision will be postponed until next Tuesday."

URGENT. The word rang like a loud bell. How could Seidman think our situation wasn't urgent? What rock was he living under? It appeared TAB had to have a liquidity crisis of the magnitude of First Republic to get his attention. We were furious.

On Monday, October 17, Christie Sciacca called late in the day. "I think I've presented a concept to Pohlad that should be acceptable to everybody," he began. "Pohlad would accept slightly more risk, but on a declining scale. This would limit his risk and put partial limits on the FDIC's exposure."

At that point, Bill Isaac, who was on the line with Sciacca, interrupted. "Poling says that there is a lot of resistance from the staff to the deal and a growing sentiment to put it out for rebid. It doesn't sound good."

Tuesday, October 18, was the day we were promised a decision would be made. At 4:45 P.M., Herbst called to give us a chronology of the day's events, sounding even more perturbed than usual:

> We received a call at noon from Poling. He asked if we would accept an arrangement which would effectively limit our losses to $75 million [15 percent of $500 million]. We agreed to do it.
>
> Then at 3:30 Poling called back to tell us that the FDIC still had a problem with the limit on the losses, and unless it were removed the deal might have to be rebid. Seidman subsequently called Pohlad to further explain the FDIC's position. Seidman said two of the three board members were strongly opposed to rebidding the deal, but some changes would have to be made. They postponed any further consideration until Thursday, October 20. There seems to be no end to this deal.

None of us could believe that Poling put a structure on the table, that Pohlad accepted it, and then Seidman took it away. This entire episode got more bizarre with each day. I was beginning to think Seidman had completely lost touch with reality.

Although we were getting used to waiting, Wednesday and Thursday were long and anxious days, like all the other days on which we had waited for a decision.

Rebid: Round 1

Finally, on Thursday, October 20, at 2:00 P.M., seventeen days after we had been promised a decision, we received the much-anticipated call from Stan Poling. By then, my anxiety had reached explosive heights. I was totally preoccupied, my nights had been sleepless, and my appetite had diminished. Even when jogging, which was my self-imposed therapy, I couldn't think about anything else. The FDIC had kept the Pohlad camp and us dangling on a string. All I had been able to think about for days was the decision and its meaning for TAB.

As I heard Poling's words, I was dazed by their significance: "The board's decided to rebid the deal," he said apologetically, but almost casually.

The conversation was short. Stan only added that the FDIC had problems with the Pohlad proposal. The staff would spend the weekend determining the procedures to be followed in the rebid, and he would get back to us on Monday with the details.

Gary Cage had joined me for the last part of the conversation. We looked at each other with horror and disbelief. We just couldn't believe that the FDIC was doing this to us, and to themselves. They had to realize that in all likelihood they had seen the lowest-cost proposal in Pohlad's last bid.

Reporting the delay, the *Wall Street Journal* said that "after a lengthy review of the books of both banking concerns, Mr. Pohlad found more troublesome loans and asked the FDIC to shoulder a greater share of any future losses the merged company might incur for the next several years. . . . The FDIC says it wants to be certain it undertakes a bailout with the least cost to the federal insurance fund."[1] The publicity accompanying the FDIC announcement was very disturbing because of the potential damage to the companies. The headline in the *New York Times* read, "Bank Rescue Deal Falters."[2] The *Fort Worth Star-Telegram* headline read, "Texas American Rescue Is Reopened–Minneapolis Banker's Deal with FDIC Fails."[3]

While we witnessed no significant loss of business on Monday, October 24, we fully expected continued, if not accelerated, attrition in the future, which was an extremely frightening prospect.

The Players

In addition to our fears about funding, we were extremely anxious that desirable parties participate in the rebidding process. We had been assured by Pohlad on the day of the announcement that they would rebid, which they affirmed in their press release of October 21.[4] We did not know, however, who else might be interested, and we could not be sure that Pohlad would be successful, since they had previously been unable to reach an agreement.

Consequently, on Friday afternoon, I called Richard Rainwater to advise him of the FDIC's decision. Almost before I got the words out, Rainwater yelled to Peter Joost in the next office, "Peter, they are going to rebid the TAB deal. We've got another shot at it." He then said to me, "Jody, I told you that it isn't over till its over, until the fat lady sings, and this deal isn't over yet."

Most of the week of October 24 was spent learning about the rebidding process. Any qualified party would be accepted as a bidder and would be allowed to conduct limited due diligence. Additionally, they would be given access to a "war room" in the FDIC's Washington, D.C., office containing the Pohlad due diligence, for which the FDIC had paid Pohlad $200,000. The final bids were to be submitted by November 16, and the FDIC would render a decision by November 22.

On Friday, October 28, we were told that eleven parties had expressed interest in our organizations: Pohlad; Rainwater; Bank of Scotland; Norwest Bank of Minneapolis; First Union Bank of Charlotte, North Carolina; Banc One of Columbus, Ohio; Wells Fargo of San Francisco; Equibank of Pittsburgh; Neil Griffin of Houston; Ron Steinhart of Dallas; and the investment banking firm of Donaldson, Lufkin & Jennrette for an undisclosed party.

On Wednesday, November 2, Bill Isaac learned through the Secura Group that Norwest Bank and First Union had dropped out and that Ron Steinhart, former president of InterFirst and vice chairman of First Republic, wanted to conduct limited due diligence.

On Friday, November 4, Carl Pohlad called to reassure us they intended to participate in the rebidding process. During the course of the conversation, Carl said, "Jody, what would you think if we teamed up with Rainwater?

"Of course, we have thought of that possibility, Carl," I answered, trying to mask my enthusiasm. "Goldman and Shearson believe the two of you bidding together would be an unbeatable combination. But we're really in no position to advise you. It's a decision you will have to make."

As I spoke, I thought to myself, "If only they would get together, it would be a dream come true." But I also knew that the chances of it happening were remote, if not impossible. Neither would want to play second fiddle to the other.

Rainwater's Bid

On Saturday, November 12, we learned the proposed structure of Rainwater's bid. They had completely abandoned the ABC plan in favor of a concept that was very similar to the FSLIC's much-maligned Southwest Plan for the S&L industry.

While this proposal was extremely attractive from the investors' point of view, it didn't have a chance. It looked like the Southwest Plan, smelled like the Southwest Plan, and even used the same terminology as the Southwest Plan. Peter Joost had gotten good advice from a technical point of view, but he had been sold a proposal that wouldn't fly. Apparently, on

Friday, November 11, Peter had spent the entire day in Dallas with attorneys and Arthur Young's banking "experts," who had sold Peter on its virtues.

I couldn't argue with its merits, but I knew how much Seidman hated the Southwest Plan because of its large tax incentives and minimal capital contributions. I also knew the board would never approve this structure. To do so would put Seidman right beside the FSLIC chairman Danny Wall in Congressional hearings, a circumstance Seidman would want to avoid at all costs.

Recognizing that I would be unable to dissuade Peter from presenting the bid structured as proposed, I urged him to submit an alternative bid based on the ABC plan.

This change in Rainwater's bid was a major setback. For a brief period, Rainwater's reentry had renewed my spirits; now they were shattered again.

Washington Meetings of November 17

On Wednesday afternoon, Richard Calvert and I left for Washington to join Rodgin Cohen for a meeting with Seidman. We also took the opportunity to make appointments with Bob Clarke and C. C. Hope, the other two members of the FDIC board. Clarke, the comptroller of the currency, was unfortunately not available, so instead we visited with the acting director, Jimmy Barton, who gratuitously opined that Pohlad would get the deal.

After lunch in Sullivan & Cromwell's Washington office, we traveled to the FDIC headquarters for our appointment with C. C. Hope, who was his usual warm and friendly self. Our discussions with C. C. were general in nature, not terribly incisive or penetrating, but very pleasant. There was no doubt that Seidman was both the power and the decision maker.

At 3:00, Seidman greeted us cordially, with Stan Poling at his side. After spending ten to fifteen minutes bringing Seidman up to date on the respective condition of each organization, we urged him to make a speedy decision in selecting the winning bidder.

"We will do everything we can to expedite the process," Seidman said. "We agreed upon a structure, and we will also do everything we can to do an 'open bank' transaction. You both came in early, and we feel a commitment to you. However, this will probably be the last 'open bank' deal we will ever do."

"Mr. Chairman, I don't understand. You did an 'open bank' deal with Bank of Oklahoma," I said quizzically.

"We did, and it was a terrible mistake," Seidman responded.

Now I was thoroughly puzzled. Only a short time ago, Seidman's people had invited us in to participate in an "open bank" experiment, which was believed to be a possible model for future deals. Just nine months later, Seidman had so soured on the "open bank" structure that he was vowing never to do another. Apparently, he was down on "open bank" deals because of the problems with the Bank of Oklahoma recapitalization, which it appeared would have to be redone.

"Now, in order to do an 'open bank' deal," Seidman added, "we may have to ask you to give us standing authority from your boards for a 'bridge bank.' The creditors are the problem, and we need a lever to force them to the table."

"As you know, Mr. Chairman," I responded cautiously, knowing that Rodgin would set the record straight if I said the wrong thing, "there are very serious liability implications for the boards of both companies, which would have to be considered."

Rodgin then observed, "If the 'bridge' authority were granted as part of a plan, which would give the shareholders and creditors value, we might be able to approve it."

Seidman then directed his comments to how we had portrayed our negotiations with the FDIC to the media: "At least you guys didn't broadcast to the media that you were going into bankruptcy." This comment was an obvious reference to Gene Bishop and MCorp.

As in the case of our previous meeting with Seidman, we felt reasonably positive about this meeting. While no commitments were made, we believed him to be sincere about doing an "open bank" deal and to be acting in good faith. Richard Calvert and I were both in fairly good spirits as we returned to Texas.

MCorp Seeks FDIC Assistance

While TAB had been suffering through the rebidding process, MCorp was experiencing its own problems. I had been following their situation closely through conversations with Gene Bishop and through newspaper reports. Shortly after having lunch with Bishop on July 20, Chairman Seidman reported to Congress that the examiners of the FDIC and the OCC were poring over the books of MCorp, which the *Fort Worth Star-Telegram* referred to as "the last big, sick Texas banking company."[5]

Slowly but surely, MCorp was drifting in the same direction as TAB and NBC; we were just a little further ahead in recognizing and addressing our problems. But, based on what I knew, I expected MCorp's condition increasingly to become a source of public scrutiny.

The examination of MCorp had begun in July after the OCC had concluded the exam of TAB, and, by the end of September, MCorp knew the preliminary results.

On Friday, October 7, the company issued a terse statement announcing that it would seek FDIC assistance.[6] Simultaneously, they disclosed that a loss of $525 million would be sustained in the third quarter prompted by the conclusion of the exam. This followed a loss of $169 million in the second quarter and $250 million in 1987.

Gene Bishop was noted for working hard on behalf of his shareholders. As MCorp's circumstances had worsened, Bishop had systematically sold assets and accumulated cash in the holding company. Now, in mid-1988, the company had approximately $400 million in its coffers, and ironically, this put Bishop and MCorp between the proverbial rock and a hard place. In this case, the "rock" was federal regulators and the "hard place" was shareholders and creditors. The regulators were demanding that the $400 million be used to recapitalize MCorp's banks, whereas the shareholders and creditors wanted those funds kept at the holding company, beyond the reach of the regulators.

Under increasing financial pressure, Bishop announced in late October that the company would suspend interest payments on approximately $470 million in debt and that there was a high probability that the company would seek protection under the bankruptcy laws to protect $400 million in cash in the holding company for the benefit of shareholders and creditors.[7]

With the tremendous amount of adverse publicity it was receiving, MCorp, like First Republic before it, began in late October to experience a severe runoff in deposits. Simultaneously, the Federal Reserve Bank of Dallas was reporting large increases in borrowings by member banks.[8]

On November 15, MCorp confirmed it had borrowed over $1 billion from the Federal Reserve, but that funding had stabilized after a standstill agreement between the company and the FDIC had been announced on November 6. By the terms of the agreement, MCorp would not voluntarily enter bankruptcy and the regulators would not require that the $400 million be used to recapitalize MCorp's banks.[9]

During this period, I hadn't talked to Bishop. I knew he couldn't disclose the results of the exam, and he must be under intense pressure.

When we did speak after the accord had been reached with the regulators, he told me that the mention of bankruptcy had really spooked their depositors, who assumed that it meant the company–and thus its banks–were broke. As a result, a run of massive proportions developed, necessitating the borrowings from the Federal Reserve. I felt a lot of sympathy for MCorp, but this was good intelligence for me to have, as it would help us avoid the mistake of taking TAB into Chapter 11 bankruptcy.

THIRTEEN 13

SHATTERED EXPECTATIONS

It had been our understanding, since first being advised that the transaction was being rebid, that the FDIC would select both the winning bidder and the terms of the transaction on November 22, 1988. To our knowledge, all the bids had been submitted by the November 16 deadline, but there was still no decision by December 1. As the days and then the hours passed waiting for the FDIC, everyone became more anxious. The TAB group and the NBC group spoke daily and sometimes two or three times a day. Additionally, we maintained close contact with Bill Isaac, Christie Sciacca, and our lead attorney, Rodgin Cohen, for progress reports.

We had expected some word on Tuesday, December 6, as the FDIC board usually met on Tuesdays. When Tuesday passed with still nothing, we became even more concerned. As we got closer to the holiday season, we realized that the chances we would get a decision grew less likely. It now looked like Tuesday, December 13, would be the last chance before January. Could TAB survive until January?

A Stunning Decision

Finally, on Friday, December 9, the long-awaited call came. In an unscheduled meeting, the FDIC had reached a decision.

Christie Sciacca broke the news to TAB and NBC in a joint conference call. On the TAB end of the call, complete silence enveloped the room, as we waited to learn of our fate.

"I just finished talking to Stan Poling," said Sciacca. "The board met to discuss only TAB and NBC. They had two bids, and only one of those was viable and received serious consideration."

As Christie was speaking, I wanted him to get to the bottom line. What *did* the board decide?

After discussing the procedure they went through and some of the obstacles, he finally said, "It's Pohlad–they have decided to negotiate exclusively with Pohlad."

Hearing the outcome, we felt an overwhelming sense of frustration. It was as if we had read the first half of a suspenseful novel, but were being denied the conclusion.

We were stunned, not because the FDIC had chosen Pohlad–we had assumed Rainwater was out of it when he selected the Southwest Plan look-alike bid–but because they still hadn't settled upon the terms of the deal. This was confirmed later that day by Rainwater, who said he had been asked by Poling to "stand by" in the event the FDIC was unable to negotiate acceptable terms with Pohlad. It was obvious there were significant issues still to be resolved.

We couldn't help but wonder about the FDIC's strategy: how did they expect to close a deal with Pohlad when he knew he had an exclusive?

Another Setback

The week of December 19 began with great expectations. We had been told by Stan Poling that a decision with regard to the terms of the deal would be reached at an FDIC board meeting on Monday morning. However, our hopes and expectations were dashed once again by an indecisive FDIC. After the meeting adjourned, Bill Isaac called to advise us that there was one unresolved issue, but that Poling had been given authority to negotiate the final terms without FDIC board ratification.

Having heard nothing further during the remainder of the day, I called Richard Calvert and Mark Johnson on Tuesday morning to see if they had any late news. Coincidentally, they had just talked to Stan Poling, who said, "It was in the hands of the chairman [Seidman]." We found this very disturbing; we didn't know what it meant, but we were apprehensive, fearing the worst. Next we decided to jointly call Tom Herbst, Pohlad's point man, to learn what he knew.

Tom Herbst is one of the easiest-going, most even-tempered, nicest people I have met. Normally he spoke softly, in an almost sing-song tone. But, on this occasion, he was fighting mad.

"Carl is thoroughly disgusted," he said, almost shouting. "We had a deal, and the FDIC reneged on it. Poling, Seidman, the entire board has lost all credibility with Pohlad. They have absolutely no integrity. But we're not going to give up. Carl is waiting for a call from Seidman."

With this bombshell having been dropped, Calvert and I decided to call Seidman to see what we could learn. We were surprised to be put right through; in the past, we often would have to wait for hours, if not days, for him to return a call.

Calvert opened the conversation by expressing our concern over the problems we were encountering, to which Seidman replied, "We're trying very hard to put a deal together, and I think we have made some progress. But you have to realize this transaction will be precedent setting, and, as a result, it has to meet our criteria. Frankly, there are several unresolved issues that we have to work our way through."

"We understand, Mr. Chairman," I responded. "Is there anything we can do to expedite the process?"

"What if this deal doesn't make?" asked Seidman.

"You have another bidder in the wings, Mr. Chairman, but we hope this deal *will* make," I answered.

"Well, the ball is in Pohlad's court."

Trying to keep my voice even, I said, "He is waiting for a call from you, Mr. Chairman."

"I have already made that call," answered Seidman, with a note of finality in his voice.

After this conversation, we called Herbst back to find out what had transpired when Seidman called Pohlad. To our astonishment, Herbst told us that they hadn't received a call from Seidman. Immediately, the Pohlad camp assumed duplicity on Seidman's part. They wondered what kind of game he was playing, and why he would have misrepresented the facts about the phone call.

Thus, the day ended with these disquieting developments. As unsettled as we were, though, it would get worse. Wednesday, December 21, began with another bombshell lobbed into the midst of the transaction.

Bill Isaac broke the news. "You're not going to like this: Poling is being pulled from our deal and being replaced by Bill Roelle." Although Isaac tried to sound under control, I could tell by the rapid staccato of his speech that he was upset. And why shouldn't he be? Our deal with the FDIC was based on mutual trust–a trust that had been forged between Isaac and Poling.

Once again the FDIC had broken faith. Little had gone right with this transaction from the outset, and our luck seemed just to get worse with time.

"Bill, this is a major setback," I said worriedly. "This could delay the transaction by months. What the hell is going on? Our deal was with Poling. He knows the history, he knows the companies, he knows all of us, and he had developed good rapport with the Pohlad camp. What happened? Why is he being replaced?" I did not even try to mask my growing anger and anxiety.

"I don't know–I haven't had a chance to talk to Stan. But either Seidman removed him because he hadn't been able to bring closure to the deal, or he quit out of frustration," Isaac responded, his growing impatience reflected in his voice.

It was obvious that Pohlad was a long way away from reaching an agreement with the FDIC on his proposal. With a new man on the transaction, who would be starting at ground zero, the prospect of finalizing a structure in the near future was remote.

Over the course of several weeks following Stan Poling's replacement, we learned that Poling had asked to be removed from the transaction. He believed that he had lost all credibility and effectiveness in dealing with the companies, and with Pohlad. We concluded that the FDIC board, by not supporting his decisions and commitments, had undermined his effectiveness.

We later learned that Poling was also a victim of internal politics. According to Herbst, he and Poling actually reached agreement on the structure of a transaction and received FDIC board approval. Incredibly, the board subsequently reversed its position due to second guessing on the part of the FDIC staff. Apparently, Poling had failed to brief the staff adequately before going to the board, and there was growing discontent among the staff with the "open bank" concept. Under the circumstances, it would have been difficult for Poling to continue.

We had come so close to getting the deal done, but we were shot down by petty bureaucratic politics. It was incredible. We were all terribly disheartened by this turn of events, and also disturbed because of our relationship with Bill Roelle, who refused to talk directly to anyone from TAB or NBC. We had enjoyed an open relationship with Stan Poling, and Roelle's attitude was extremely unsettling. We felt that our lines of communication with the FDIC had been severed.

Holding It Together

Since announcing the disastrous results of the second quarter of 1988, a loss of $135 million, a principal concern of TAB's management and board of directors was to control the damage and preserve the value of the franchise. This was becoming increasingly difficult as the company slid further and further toward a financial cataclysm.

There was no doubt that, with MCorp's announcement, the banking industry in Texas was in a crisis of confidence, and it was against this backdrop that we struggled to keep TAB from slipping into a funding and liquidity bind that would push us into the hands of the regulators. If a liquidity crisis were to develop, it would be at our lead bank, as had been the case with First Republic and MCorp. Accordingly, our efforts were focused on TAB/Fort Worth. It was imperative that public confidence in the bank be maintained.

The surfeit of bad news about Texas banks had created an environment in which any unfavorable event or rumor could precipitate a run on deposits. While we conscientiously attempted to manage the news about TAB, particularly in Fort Worth, there was little we could do to moderate the impact on the community of the problems of other banks.

This became a matter of increasing concern when four banks in succession failed in Fort Worth and in Arlington, a bedroom community between Fort Worth and Dallas. The first failure was the Lincoln National Bank in Arlington on May 5, 1988. This was followed by the closing of the Pioneer National Bank in Arlington on September 1. Both events were lead stories on the front page of the *Fort Worth Star-Telegram*'s business section.[1]

Several days later, on September 15, Capital National Bank in downtown Fort Worth failed. Liquidation by the FDIC, with depositors losing any amount over $100,000 of FDIC insurance coverage, was narrowly averted when another local bank stepped in at the last minute and bought the deposits for the princely sum of $1,000. Although the problems of Capital National had been widely known and publicized, its closing still came as a shock to the city because of the prominent and substantial people involved in its ownership and its board of directors.[2]

Downtown suffered another loss when, on October 6, Fidelity National Bank was closed.[3] Although all insured and uninsured deposits of Capital National Bank and Fidelity National Bank, as well as River Plaza National Bank–another Fort Worth bank that failed earlier in the year–had been fully protected, public confidence was being further eroded by these events.

The bad news on TAB accelerated in fall 1988. Early in September, we had decided that we couldn't make the interest and principal payments on several of our outstanding debt issues due September 15. Although this announcement came as no surprise to the investment community because of our previously announced second-quarter loss, it was additional bad publicity we didn't need.[4]

This was followed by successive adverse reports: Don Cockerham's indictment on September 20; a newspaper article on October 11 analyzing a 12.5 percent decline in deposits over twenty-one months at TAB banks; and the announcement of the rebidding of our transaction, which appeared on October 22.[5] But the most damaging news was that of our third-quarter loss, which was announced by the *Star-Telegram* with the following front page headline: "Texas American Reports $216.5 Million Loss."[6]

My greatest fear from the due diligence had been realized. Our efforts to keep two sets of books–one on a business-as-usual basis and another on a "fire sale" liquidation basis–had failed. It had become difficult to differentiate between liquidation values and reality.

As the due diligence process had progressed, its impact had become more pronounced. From the outset, the mission of the Pohlad team was clear: to assure that Pohlad obtained the maximum amount of financial assistance from the FDIC by valuing our loan portfolio as low as possible. Pohlad's people were on one side of the table attacking the values, and our people were on the other side with instructions to cooperate. This was unlike a regulatory examination in which we would vigorously defend the values. Instead our mission in this instance was to validate Pohlad's due diligence results. It was like a duel, with the Pohlad side using live ammunition to take potshots at our values and with the TAB side using blanks. Since we had effectively taken the "live" ammunition away from our people by instructing them to cooperate, the feeble shots they did return lacked firepower. It was a totally discouraging experience. At the end of the exercise, there was no fight left on our side–they had given up–and the liquidation values had become reality in their minds.

Toward the close of each quarter, we polled the banks to obtain the amount of the addition to their loan loss reserve, which, of course, was deducted from income and thus stockholder's equity. As the results came in this quarter, our anguish increased with each report. We couldn't believe that we had been unable to maintain the integrity of our ongoing business separate and apart from the due diligence results. Likewise, we couldn't believe that the examination that had concluded less than three months earlier could have been so far off the mark. The examination had produced a loss of $135.3 million for the second quarter, versus the loss of $216.5 million emanating from the due diligence in the third quarter.

In reality, no one could be sure of the validity of the due diligence or of our third-quarter earnings report. Estimating real estate values had become more than an inexact science–it had become impossible.

The article accompanying the October 29 *Star-Telegram* headline concerning our third-quarter loss elaborated that, while the loss for the quarter was $216.5 million, for the first nine months it was an astonishing $369.5 million and that nonperforming loans and foreclosed assets amounted to an alarming 19.3 percent of total loans and foreclosed assets. With the loss, stockholders' equity was now a deficit of $186.2 million, but primary capital, which included the reserve for loan losses, was still positive at $174.8 million. TAB was, thus, still solvent using the criteria of the OCC, which was primary capital.

The size of our loss and the extent of the deterioration in the quality of assets was shocking. Indeed, these results constituted the final nails in the coffin. How much longer could TAB continue?

Against this cacophony of unfavorable events and publicity, we were attempting to hold the franchise together. From the time I had taken over command of the company in April 1986, we had lost an aggregate $700 million, including the expected loss of $140 million in the fourth quarter of 1988, and the total assets of the company had declined by $2 billion from $6.4 billion to $4.4 billion.

Surprising to all of us, our funding had held up well under the circumstances, particularly in view of the experience of First Republic and MCorp. There had been no semblance of a run, and we had not had to borrow from the Federal Reserve since the May 1986 liquidity crisis. Nonetheless, this was a major concern to us and to the regulators, who were monitoring our liquidity on a daily basis.

A Tough Year

After a loss of $140 million in the fourth quarter, TAB's loss for the year was an unbelievable $510 million, which had reduced shareholders' equity to a deficit of $329 million. Primary capital (equity plus the reserve for loan losses) had slipped to a scant $38 million, leaving many of the company's banks barely solvent by OCC standards. Certainly, with normal operating losses and write-downs on foreclosed real estate, the largest banks, including TAB/Fort Worth, would be insolvent at the end of the first quarter and subject to closing by the OCC.

If there had been any doubt before, there was none now: we had lost the financial battle. TAB was left exhausted and incapacitated, incapable of adequately serving the needs of its customers. The company was "braindead," waiting only for the last rites to be performed by the OCC before the remains were turned over to the FDIC for burial.

When 1988 began, there was no way we could have anticipated the events of the year. Starting with our initial visit with the FDIC on February 19, the fortunes of TAB had disintegrated. It was ironic that we went to the FDIC at their invitation, that we had been told that they wanted to encourage banks to "come in early," and that because we had, we would be treated more favorably. Instead, our worst fears were becoming reality. It appeared that once the process of obtaining assistance had begun, events had swept TAB inexorably toward a disastrous destiny.

A Deal So Near

After tough negotiations with the FDIC for seven months, Pohlad's patience had nearly reached its limit. According to Herbst, dealing with the FDIC was especially frustrating: it was like negotiating with yourself in that the benchmark for any revision was the last deal you had presented to them.

Finally, in exasperation, Pohlad said, "No more! You tell us what it takes to make a deal and submit it in the form of a term sheet."

To everyone's surprise, the first FDIC term sheet was received on Friday, December 30.

Christie Sciacca, who was closer to Roelle than Isaac, had been keeping us advised of the progress of the negotiations since the assignment of Roelle. On Thursday, January 5, 1989, Sciacca called the companies with disturbing news. "I just talked to Herbst, he said. "The FDIC's term sheet is unacceptable. Carl has an appointment with Seidman on Monday. Herbst says this will be a showdown with guns blazing on both sides."

As bad as this news was, it wasn't as distressing as Sciacca's account of the mood within the FDIC: "We hear there has been a power struggle in the FDIC between the 'open bank,' 'come in early' advocates and the 'bridge bank,' or 'we'll deal with you when you're dead' crowd. It looks like the champions of the 'dead' approach are emerging with the upper hand. Apparently, the successful use of the 'bridge bank' approach in dealing with First Republic made converts of a lot of people who were on the fence. This isn't good news for us."

"There is no doubt," Christie continued, "there are advantages to the FDIC in declaring the bank insolvent and using a 'bridge bank.' All litigation, leases, and other contractual obligations are either abrogated or subject to renegotiation."

"Even so, Christie," I interrupted, "it isn't at all clear to me that the 'closed bank' approach is less costly than the 'open bank' approach. I think there is a significant cost associated with a 'closed bank.' They have to declare the banks insolvent and form a bridge bank. The bad publicity and the change in the identity is damaging in most cases and would be particularly damaging in the TAB and NBC cases. Then there's the change in ownership, management, and directors. All that change causes major disruptions. In TAB and NBC, a 'closed bank' solution would cost hundreds of millions of dollars more than an 'open bank' deal."

"We believe the FDIC doesn't want to incur the scrutiny of an 'open bank' deal," Sciacca continued, "and have to explain to Congress why the old shareholders are retaining ownership in the restructured bank. Believe me, the prevailing sentiment in Washington is that the shareholders should be wiped out because they hired the management–they are responsible for the problems, and they should be punished. Of course, we know that it's an unrealistic and erroneous assumption, but no one said these bureaucrats are mental giants."

I knew we couldn't change the views inside the FDIC as long as Seidman was there. If decisions were based on these moralistic and idealistic notions, it was going to cost the taxpayers billions of dollars. These ideas just weren't compatible with doing the lowest-cost deal.

Hearing of the mood within the FDIC and of the Pohlad/Seidman meeting worried Rodgin Cohen. "I don't want to be an alarmist," he said, "but if Pohlad decides to withdraw from negotiations, the FDIC might 'bridge' us as early as the following weekend. I think we should begin lining up backup merger partners just in case."

Bill Isaac discounted the possibility of a bridge bank. It wouldn't solve the problem because the FDIC would still have to find a merger partner for the companies. In any event, he agreed to contact Security Pacific to see if they might be interested.

On Tuesday, January 10, Bill Isaac called to report on the meeting between Pohlad and Seidman the previous afternoon. There was now only one unresolved issue left: the mandatory dividend on the preferred stock, which Pohlad regarded as a deal breaker.

According to Isaac, the reason for the concern about the dividend was due to the "heat Danny Wall was under." Wall, the chairman of the board of the Federal Home Loan Bank (FHLB) and the architect of the Southwest Plan, had approved a large number of bailouts at year-end to take advantage of tax benefits accruing to the purchasers of the defunct thrifts. Because these transactions were tax driven, with minimal equity being supplied by the purchasers, Congress had initiated a complete investigation of the deals. In a subsequent conversation, Bill Roelle admitted that the dividend question was a political, not a substantive, issue. Evidently, the FDIC was concerned that Congress might be critical of a deal that required a dividend be paid, especially if the dividend was unearned and had to be paid out of funds provided by the FDIC in the form of assistance.

That the TAB/NBC transaction might be aborted because of the politics of the Southwest Plan was beyond comprehension. But politics, more than anything else, seemed to be driving the deal at this point.

On Friday, January 13, I spoke to Herbst, who said that they had submitted a new proposal, which treated the preferred dividend as interest, and that "the ball is in the FDIC's court." Shortly thereafter, I spoke to Isaac, who said he was told by Roelle "the ball was in Pohlad's court."

What an unbelievable mess–as ludicrous as a Keystone Cops slapstick farce. It appeared that, the way this deal was being bungled, we didn't have a chance.

On Tuesday, January 17, the Pohlad camp and the FDIC again confirmed that the ball was in the court of the other. Actually, as it developed, there were issues in both courts. Our tension and anxiety continued to mount as we received updates on Wednesday and Thursday.

When I talked to Herbst late Thursday, he was totally frustrated. "This entire situation with the FDIC is insane, Jody. We realize this is a nightmare for you, Richard, and all your people, and we know how worried you all are, but it's a nightmare for us too." He paused, then added wearily, "On Monday, January 23rd, Carl is supposed to call Seidman, who is preoccupied with the [President Bush's] inauguration until then. I'll be in touch as soon as we know something."

Monday and Tuesday passed with no word from either side. Christie Sciacca broke the silence on Wednesday morning, January 25. He had just talked to Bill Roelle, who said the ball was *now* in the Pohlad court. This was becoming absurd. It would have been laughable if the stakes hadn't been so high.

On Thursday, the TAB board of directors was scheduled to meet. Prior to the meeting, I called Herbst for an update. Herbst was more subdued than ever. "We've submitted several alternatives: it isn't that they have said no–they haven't said anything. All of the publicity over the Southwest Plan year-end tax deals has absolutely paralyzed the FDIC. We don't know what to do. I'm busy working on some other deals." Then he paused and added emphatically, "Don't worry, Carl Pohlad won't walk. If the deal falls apart, he's not going to let the FDIC blame him."

At the request of the TAB board, I called Seidman on Friday, January 27, to request a meeting between representatives of the TAB and NBC boards. Seidman returned my call the following Wednesday afternoon. "We've been meeting with Pohlad, and we've made significant progress," Seidman reported. "I believe we'll be able to announce a deal within a week, and I think your people will be pleased."

With Seidman's call, we began waiting for what we hoped would be word of an agreement. But, just when our optimism was rising, the FDIC once again delivered another crushing blow, dashing our hopes for an immediate solution.

Seidman's Power Grab

In a headlong gallop to rescue as many troubled S&Ls as possible before tax benefits expired at year-end, Danny Wall concluded a large number of transactions before the deadline. As a consequence, the Southwest Plan came under Congressional and public scrutiny. Two deals in particular drew attention: Bob Bass's takeover of American Savings of Stockton, California, at an estimated cost of $1.7 billion to the FSLIC; and Ronald O. Perelman's acquisition with Gerald Ford of five failed Texas thrifts at a cost estimated at $5.1 billion.

In response to the furor over these deals and others, which provided $8 billion in tax breaks for all 205 transactions in 1988, the House Banking Committee began hearings in January 1989. Committee members unleashed vitriolic attacks challenging the terms of the transactions, the efficacy of the deals, the avarice of the buyers, and the acumen of the regulators. Representative Jim Leach (R) of Iowa described the buyers as "jackals picking over the bones of dead institutions," and said that "the Bank Board [FHLB] is itself bankrupt. It ought to go into immediate receivership of the U.S. Treasury."[7]

In the meantime, the Treasury Department was developing recommendations for the overhaul of the regulation of thrifts. On Sunday, January 15, Seidman said on NBC television's *Meet the Press* that between $30 billion and $40 billion was needed immediately to close insolvent thrifts, and the total cost of the bailout could be $85 billion to $100 billion.[8]

Seidman, according to knowledgeable sources, was fighting "vigorously" to have control of the FSLIC shifted to the FDIC. It was a widely held opinion that Seidman was a man with an oversized ego, who was politically motivated and wanted to expand his power base.

On February 6, Seidman got his wish when President George Bush announced his plan to restructure the regulation of thrifts. Under the plan, the FHLB, which charters thrifts, would be brought under control of the Treasury, the FDIC would take administrative control of the FSLIC, and the FDIC would regulate thrifts. In addition, a new agency, the Resolution Trust Corporation (RTC), was created to manage insolvent thrifts and to own and dispose of foreclosed real estate. The RTC would contract with the FDIC to manage the insolvent institutions.

In reporting on the restructuring, the *New York Times* stated that Seidman "deftly maneuvered his way through a maelstrom of competing interests and ended up insuring himself, his agency, and the industry he protects a place at the top of the heap. As a result, he has emerged as one of Washington's most powerful regulators and guaranteed himself a central position in the reshaping of the United States financial industry."[9]

TAB and NBC Play Second Fiddle

It was now patently clear to Pohlad and to us that, while the outcome of the restructuring of the regulatory agencies was in balance, no decision was going to be made on TAB and NBC. Seidman was not going to risk announcing a transaction that would be open to public scrutiny and criticism by his detractors. To delay a decision on TAB and NBC would be a small price to pay in this much larger game of "Washington Monopoly."

It had now been nearly a year since we first went to the FDIC to discuss the possibility of obtaining assistance, and it seemed we were no closer now to a resolution than we were then. We were consistently preempted by a more pressing problem or circumstance: the exigencies of First Republic and MCorp; the controversy over the Southwest Plan; the FDIC board's trip to Hawaii; Poling's resignation; and the inauguration of President Bush. At times our deal was relegated almost to obscurity.

Now on Monday, February 6, concurrent with the announcement of President Bush's reform plan for the S&L industry, we were informed by the FDIC of another change in the administration of our transaction.

Yet Another Reversal

Before President Bush's 3:00 P.M. press conference, I contacted Christie Sciacca to obtain an update on the negotiations, only to find he knew nothing. I then called Richard Calvert and Mark Johnson to learn what they knew.

"Jody, you're not going to believe this!" exclaimed Johnson, sounding completely exasperated. "We just tried to call Roelle, but were told by his secretary that he was no longer responsible for TAB and NBC."

For a moment, I was speechless. Surely, Roelle's secretary was mistaken. How could the FDIC do this to us? Removing Roelle, just as he was making progress in closing the gap between Pohlad and the FDIC, was an incredibly stupid thing to do.

But shortly thereafter Christie Sciacca called and confirmed that Roelle had, indeed, been reassigned to the Resolution Trust Corporation. There was no mistake. We were starting over with a new man. John Stone, associate director, Division of Supervision, had been assigned to TAB and NBC.

Our first reaction to Stone was favorable. Stone had a reputation for being tough but fair. He had been the point man on the First City transaction and had gotten high marks for his efforts. It had been an "open bank" deal, and this pleased us all, as we realized that Stone had experience with this structure.

On Wednesday February 8, Stone called to reintroduce himself. Given the lack of communication with Roelle, we felt that our relationship was off to a good start. After the usual formalities, Stone addressed the specifics of his assignment. "I'm not encumbered with any of the S&L problems," he said reassuringly. "My only existing assignments are the TAB and NBC transaction and MCorp. I'm not suggesting that this isn't a heavy load, but I want to assure you that I will see these situations through to their respective conclusions. The chairman has made this clear to me, and I am making it clear to you."

"With regard to structure," he said in response to my questioning about biases he might bring to the deal, "my preference is to do an 'open bank' transaction. I was responsible for the First City transaction and before that BancTexas, both of which were done on an 'open bank' basis. But I need to remind you that FDIC policy dictates that shareholders and creditors shouldn't get more in an 'open bank' resolution than they would if their bank were allowed to fail."

Stone's last point was nothing new, since that policy predated our initial visit to the FDIC. All things considered, I believed we were lucky to have John Stone. Only time would tell, however.

FOURTEEN

STARTING OVER

Only two days after President George Bush's announcement of his plan to restructure the regulation of thrifts, the FDIC's ability to handle the thrift crisis was questioned. On February 8, 1989, the prestigious daily newspaper, *American Banker*, pointed out that the FDIC's record in expeditiously completing rescues of larger banks wasn't good, as evidenced by the fact that TAB, NBC, and MCorp had been seeking federal assistance for almost a year.[1] Thus, our deal, along with MCorp's, had been showcased as evidence of the FDIC's ineptness.

We had been trying to maintain a low profile since our discussions with the FDIC had been first disclosed in April 1988. Now, ironically, we had been thrust into the spotlight because of a situation not remotely related to TAB and NBC. We knew this publicity would make it much more difficult for the FDIC to find a politically palatable solution to our problem.

The first indication that the FDIC might have a different agenda under John Stone for TAB and NBC came from Stone himself, when he told us on Tuesday, February 21, that he was sending in an FDIC team to examine TAB and NBC, ostensibly to determine the true condition of the banks. This seemed to be a classic case of overkill. Both TAB and NBC had been examined and reexamined since the first meeting with the FDIC in February 1988. Additionally, the FDIC had all the results of the Pohlad due diligence and had sent a team in to verify those results in September 1988.

We were both angry and perplexed at what was happening. Our funding was so fragile that news of another examination by the FDIC could bring on the run that we, so far, had avoided. It was unrealistic to think that in the intimate business community in Fort Worth we could keep the presence of the FDIC examining team at TAB a secret.

My mistrust of the FDIC grew with each successive breach of faith and change in agenda. I couldn't help but wonder if their real mission was to see if they could render all of our banks insolvent in anticipation of creating a "bridge bank" in a "closed bank" transaction.

It had now been over three weeks since Seidman had told me on February 1 that a deal might be approved "within a week." All of this seemed to have become history, however, with Seidman's preoccupation with the S&L crisis and with the assignment of John Stone. During this period, the feedback through the Pohlad camp and from Bill Isaac and Christie Sciacca wasn't encouraging.

On Thursday, February 23, Tom Herbst called TAB and NBC to brief us on a meeting they had had with John Stone the previous day at which Stone had issued an ultimatum: If the FDIC hadn't made a deal with Pohlad within the next week, they would begin to explore other options. Herbst also said that Stone had a new cast of characters from the FDIC at the table–presumably, his team–who we thought might have some very different ideas as to how our deal should be structured.

Herbst was decidedly pessimistic over these latest developments, and even seemed more downcast and frustrated with Stone in the picture than he had been with Roelle. With each successive development and revelation, I was beginning to conclude that I could have been wrong about Stone.

In view of the lack of progress between the FDIC and Pohlad, I had continued to pursue a meeting between Seidman and representatives of the TAB and NBC boards. We learned on Tuesday, February 28, that a meeting was confirmed for Friday, March 3.

The Boards Meet Seidman

The morning was cold and gray, and we were all subdued as we drove to the airport. I had picked up Lewis Bond and TAB director George Young, the other two members of the TAB contingent for the meeting with Seidman. We would join Richard Calvert and three of his directors on American Airlines, flight 804, for the trip to Washington.

Both on the way to the airport and during the flight I thought to myself how futile this trip would be. We had lost control of the process, if not our companies, months ago, and I didn't believe the FDIC cared what we thought. However, we had to keep trying to make something happen.

As usual, Seidman was late for our 3:45 appointment, and we waited with John Stone in a plain conference room across the hall from Seidman's office, furnished only with a long conference table. While waiting, we made small talk with Stone, whose incessant smoking had created a noxious blue haze in the room.

At about 4:00, Seidman came in. Without bothering to introduce himself to the individual members of our group, he immediately said, "The reason I'm late is that I've been talking to Carl Pohlad, who just finished telling me how disappointed he was with me and the FDIC, and I told him how disappointed I was with him." With this opening statement, a suffocating silence fell over the room.

Seidman continued: "I told Pohlad that his last deal was unacceptable. He didn't get rich leaving anything on the table. He wants guarantees: no risk and a guaranteed profit. He wants to put up $200 million in equity and have a guaranteed profit of $500 million. His deal is so costly that it can't be justified. I asked him if he wanted to submit a new bid, and he said no. I then told him that without a new bid, his period of exclusivity was over."

Richard Calvert and I, as spokesmen for our respective companies, had decided that we would divide our agenda between us. For my part, I stressed the urgency of the situation.

"Mr. Chairman," I said, "we have got to get a deal done, and we can't wait much longer. Both companies are losing large amounts of business. The value of each franchise is rapidly deteriorating. Liquidity and funding are tenuous–it's a struggle to meet our daily requirements–and our lead bank in Fort Worth will soon be unable to make loans or even approve overdrafts because of the depletion of capital resulting from loan charge-offs."

Richard Calvert then joined in. "At NBC our circumstances are essentially the same. Additionally, we are extremely concerned that the FDIC examination, which is about to begin, will only make matters worse. It couldn't come at a worse time. It could push both companies over the edge, and frankly, with all the examinations and due diligence that's already been done, we don't understand why it's needed. Is there any way it could be canceled?"

"Let me respond," Stone said abruptly. "The purpose of the exams is to evaluate assets for a 'closed bank' scenario, in the event we have no other alternative."

As soon as the words "closed bank" came out of Stone's mouth, Richard Calvert and I exchanged glances, each of us knowing what this could mean for our companies. What we had previously speculated about, and feared, had suddenly been thrown on the table. Was this really just a contingency in the event they didn't have a viable "open bank" bid, or was it Stone's "new agenda"? The possibility of a closed bank seemed to be increasing. The First Republic deal may have so whetted the FDIC's appetite that they now found it irresistible.

The directors then each had an opportunity to express their concerns.

Seidman closed the meeting by saying, "Bring us some 'open bank' bidders, and we'll do a deal."

Our group was even more somber on the flight back to Texas than they had been on the flight to Washington. The meeting had been a real disappointment. Unfortunately, no real progress had been made since the process began over a year ago, and it was clear to everyone that we were starting over.

New Rules/New Players

Our efforts to bring new players to the table were only partially successful. Bill Isaac had contacted Security Pacific and had received a preliminary indication of interest. Their representative was due to be in Fort Worth on Tuesday to begin gathering data. Christie Sciacca had also contacted Rainwater, who said that he would be interested in rebidding with the Southwest Plan look-alike proposal they had submitted the previous November. We still didn't believe this would work and, therefore, counted Rainwater out.

Herbst called on Tuesday, March 7, to update us on a meeting they had just concluded with Stone. I could feel Herbst's rage flow through the phone as he explained what had happened. To Herbst's astonishment, Stone had changed the rules of the game in complete disregard of the agreement we had with Poling. To Herbst, this was a complete breach of faith. I sympathized with him. With the change from Poling to Roelle to Stone, memories had become short, and commitments seemed irrelevant.

Stone had decided that he wanted to change the structure of the transaction from the ABC plan to a "good bank/bad bank" concept. This was the same structure that Stone had used in the First City transaction. In essence, it called for two separate banks: one in which all the good assets would reside and another that would contain all the bad assets. The "good bank" would be sold to an investor, and the "bad bank" would be owned by the FDIC, but would be managed by the "good bank" under its new ownership. According to Herbst, the good bank/bad bank structure would require $300 million in new capital instead of the $200 million required under the ABC plan. This would occur because all of the "reserve for loan losses," which was included as part of primary capital, would be transferred with the loans they supported to the "bad bank," leaving a bigger hole for the investor to fill with new capital.

Herbst seemed completely dejected, his voice lifeless. One obstacle after another had been thrown up against them. If Pohlad threw in the towel, no one would blame him.

We were even more discouraged than Herbst. We were not only no closer to doing a deal than we were a year ago, but we had actually lost ground. The capital requirement had increased, and the FDIC had completely taken over the process. And there were growing indications that the FDIC was gearing up for a "closed bank" solution. The FDIC had started examining our main banking units, and on Wednesday, March 8, both TAB and NBC received an urgent request for the addresses of our banks and branches. There could only be one reason for such a request: to prepare a plan to send regulators to all units in order to declare them insolvent.

In an effort to head off the worst, we decided, upon the advice of Rodgin Cohen, that we would propose a "Continental Bank" type transaction as a contingency in the event no "open bank" bidders were found. Under this scenario, the FDIC would assume ownership of the companies, with some token amount being retained by the old shareholders–probably less than 5 percent.

Christie Sciacca and Rodgin Cohen carried this proposal in person to Washington. The FDIC responded that they would only consider such a plan as a last resort under two conditions. The first was that we would agree to merge all our banks into one, thus setting the stage for a "bridge bank." The other was that the directors and management would resign. The FDIC, once again, had escalated the stakes and changed the rules of the game.

It was clear from this that any assurances we had received from Stan Poling the previous year had been discarded by Stone. Apparently, there was no honor within the hallowed halls of the FDIC. The FDIC had broken faith with us too many times to count. This was completely demoralizing and disheartening.

While we were negotiating a last-resort contingency plan with the FDIC, they were busy trying to line up potential bidders for the companies. We learned from some of those solicited that, in mid-March, Stone had begun seeking bidders by contacting banks, individuals, and investment bankers, and that three prospects were in Washington during the week of March 20. Based on previous contacts, or on information we already had, we guessed these were probably Security Pacific, which had by this time told Bill Isaac that they would bid; the Texas banker Ron Steinhart; and Equimark, the third-largest bank holding company in Pittsburgh with $3.4 billion in assets.

We were not only operating under new rules–but also with new players.

MCorp Seeks Protection

Although Gene Bishop and I had remained in close contact and had shared many confidences, I was shocked when I read in the newspapers on Monday, March 27, that three small creditors had forced MCorp to seek protection under Chapter 11 of the U.S. Bankruptcy Code.[2]

In a sense, MCorp's strategy had backfired. The company had sold assets to build a warehouse of cash to assure its survival. Instead, that cash had become a source of contention between the company and federal regulators. Management wanted to keep it in the parent company, whereas the regulators wanted the company to use it to recapitalize its subsidiary banks. In fall 1988, MCorp said that it might either have to file for bankruptcy protection or be forced into bankruptcy in order to shield the cash from the regulators, which ultimately led to the standstill agreement of November 1988.

But that much cash became an irresistible lure for creditors, who had continuously threatened to file on the company. Finally, three bondholders from S. N. Phelps & Company, a Greenwich, Connecticut, bond broker, filed for involuntary liquidation under Chapter 7 of the U.S. Bankruptcy Code on Friday, March 24. Stan Phelps, whom I had worked with, coincidentally, at Citibank in the early 1960s, filed in fear that MCorp would be forced by the regulators to use its cash to recapitalize its banks.

In response to Phelps's action, MCorp had no choice but to file its own petition to transfer the bankruptcy from involuntary liquidation under Chapter 7 to reorganization under Chapter 11.

On the surface, this seemed like it might be a blessing in disguise. Neither MCorp, TAB, nor NBC had made any progress negotiating with the FDIC, and we had frequently suggested that we might fare better under the protection of the court. However, the trick was getting there without incurring the ire of Seidman and severe reprisals against management. In the case of MCorp, this burden had been assumed by Phelps. Of course, no one knew what the reaction of the FDIC would be, since they had never been confronted with a bankruptcy. In commenting on the predicament to the *Wall Street Journal*, Bill Isaac said, "We've never been through anything like that before. It really does muddy the water."[3]

Analysts predicted that the FDIC would abandon its efforts to save the entire holding company on an "open bank" basis and concentrate on selling off the insolvent banks piecemeal as they were closed. This would scuttle the bid for the company by the takeover firm Kohlberg Kravis Roberts & Company, whose interest, according to Bishop, was genuine. Likewise, it would derail management's plan of reorganization, although privately Bishop didn't give their own plan a "snowball's chance in hell" of being approved–there had been just too much rancor between Bishop and the agency over the use of the $400 million in cash at the holding company.

I had called Bishop on Tuesday, March 28, to get an update on what was happening. At that time, there was no hint of what was to follow. However, probably as we spoke, events were unfolding that would sweep MCorp into a morass from which it probably wouldn't emerge for years.

As I was later told by Bishop and MCorp's president, John Cater, MBank New Braunfels, a solvent state bank, had demanded that the federal funds it had sold overnight on Monday to MBank Dallas be repaid. The process of repayment had actually begun, with all but approximately $17 million of about $60 million having been repaid, when they realized that if they repaid MBank New Braunfels, it would start a run by their other banks.

But it was too late. According to insiders within the FDIC, once they learned that MCorp's "internal plumbing" was on the verge of collapsing–as a result of paying off its intercompany federal funds (overnight borrowings)–the FDIC decided to move.

Preventing the dismantling or unraveling of the internal plumbing was critical to the FDIC in accomplishing their objective of seizing as many of the MCorp banks as possible: the FDIC believed, and correctly so, that the value of the franchise of the entire MCorp system of banks was greater than the value of any single bank. As in the case of First Republic, MBank Dallas was declared insolvent and unable to repay federal funds bought from solvent MCorp banks, thus rendering the seller banks insolvent.

Bishop had worked late that night and had left the office troubled, but with no forewarning of what was to follow. After spending several hours at home, he received a call with news that the FDIC was in the process of taking over all of MCorp's banks that were still connected to the lead Dallas bank through federal fund sales.

At 9:30 A.M. eastern time, Wednesday, March 29, details of the seizure came over the various wire services. Tuesday night, federal banking regulators had declared twenty of MCorp's twenty-five banks insolvent and had assumed their deposits. A "bridge bank" had been formed under ownership of the FDIC as the successor to the insolvent banks. MCorp was left with ownership in banks in Brownsville, Corpus Christi, El Paso, New Braunfels, and Waco; enough of the approximately $60 million sold by New Braunfels was repaid to assure its solvency. In addition, MCorp retained ownership in MTrust, its trust subsidiary.[4]

In commenting on the seizure, Seidman said that the FDIC would pursue potential claims against MCorp "for liabilities and obligations of MCorp to the twenty subsidiary banks that were closed." He elaborated that the claims involved "transactions between the banks and the holding company," and the claims were "substantial and material."[5]

Seidman's official explanation for the FDIC's action was that it was precipitated by a run on deposits at MBank Dallas–involving banks inside and outside the holding company–which led to a liquidity crisis. According to Comptroller Bob Clarke, federal regulators began monitoring the bank's situation throughout the day on Tuesday. "But it became clear as the day wore on that the bank was not going to meet the demands of its depositors," Clarke said.[6]

While liquidity and funding concerns may have been the official reason for the FDIC's action, MBank Dallas had additional borrowing capacity at the Federal Reserve Bank of Dallas and had met its funding requirements for the day. In retrospect, it is clear that the FDIC moved on MCorp because of fears that the repayment of funds to MBank New Braunfels would precipitate a run by the other subsidiary banks, and the repayment of funds to those banks would isolate them from potential seizure. The FDIC justified closing MCorp's solvent banks that had sold federal funds to MBank Dallas by refusing to honor all liabilities of MBank Dallas on a pro rata basis–intercompany accounts were specifically excluded. This basically meant that all liabilities were paid in full (all deposits, even those in excess of $100,000 were honored) except those of the solvent banks. The solvent banks were thus left with an asset on their books that exceeded their capital and that couldn't be collected, thereby rendering them insolvent. It was to the FDIC's advantage to seize as many of the solvent banks as possible in order to minimize their losses on the takeover.

The FDIC's swift and decisive action against MCorp was a real eye-opener to all those working on TAB and NBC. It clearly demonstrated the new bravado that existed in the FDIC: they had flexed their muscles and dared anyone to challenge them. They were willing to do whatever was necessary to accomplish their objective, and they would justify it later in court. However, many experts felt that they had overstepped their authority in seizing the solvent banks, and it was a certainty that their actions would be tested in court.

The message we got–loud and clear–was that the bankruptcy court offered no refuge from the FDIC. We had to play out the hand we had been dealt and hope that we got an "open bank" transaction.

"TAB's Capital Is Gone"

During March, TAB continued to be buffeted by bad news. On March 2, the *Fort Worth Star-Telegram* reported that a lawsuit had been filed against TAB the previous December by the Bank of New York, as trustee for holders of notes held by Merrill, Lynch, Pierce, Fenner and Smith Corporate Income Fund, for failure to pay $506,000 in interest due in November.[7] We hadn't previously disclosed the filing of the suit since damages weren't being sought, and public disclosure had been made when we missed the payment. By that time, our every action and decision was being influenced by liquidity and funding concerns. We feared that the lawsuit, on top of everything else, might push us over the edge.

Even though Bank of New York had filed against us, we had effectively stayed their suit by filing a counter suit alleging usury, among other things. This was clearly a delaying tactic on our part, but it worked–we had learned something from the millions of dollars in lender liability suits filed against us.

On Thursday, March 16, we received another shock when we were contacted by the press seeking confirmation that FDIC examiners were in both TAB and NBC. Our gravest concerns about the presence of the examiners had been realized.

The stories reporting the exam speculated that the examinations could be the precursor of a "closed bank" deal.[8] The March 17 edition of *American Banker* quoted sources as saying that Pohlad now wanted to buy the franchises on a "closed bank" basis, which would remove the necessity of negotiating with creditors and shareholders.[9] A "closed bank" purchase would also cut off litigation claims against both companies, thus removing a major obstacle in the negotiations between Pohlad and the FDIC.

Lender liability lawsuits filed against TAB alone totaled $650 million. Such lawsuits had become a favorite ploy used by attorneys, mostly on a contingent fee basis, in defending borrowers who were in default on loans and who were either being sued for repayment or in threat of losing their collateral through foreclosure. The tactic usually involved suing the lender based on an allegation of a misrepresentation or broken commitment or a violation of regulation or law. Although these allegations, in the vast majority of instances, were without merit, they bought time for the borrower and imposed an enormous legal expense on the lender, often forcing a settlement. They had become a scourge to the troubled Texas banks.

Although it was disquieting to read speculation about a closed bank in the newspapers, Pohlad's people assured us that they were still negotiating on an "open bank" basis. Even the stories about the examiners didn't panic our depositors: it seemed they were almost impervious to bad news by this time. So far, we had been able to handle all customer needs on a business-as-usual basis. But this was about to change.

At 11:30 on the morning of March 30, we were given a grim report of the charge-offs we were required to take to close the books for the first quarter of 1989 at TAB/Fort Worth. The amount, $131.1 million, would wipe out primary capital at TAB/Fort Worth. (Primary capital consisted of equity plus the loan loss reserve from which charge-offs are deducted.) This would effectively put us out of business at our largest and most important bank, because without primary capital we had no ability to make loans or to approve the smallest overdraft on an account. Tellers couldn't even cash a check unless they were certain there were funds available to pay it. There was no margin for error, as any loan or overdraft constituted a violation of law.

It was clear that the end for TAB was very near, but we had to stay open and operating–out of the hands of the FDIC–to keep our chances for an "open bank" solution alive. We had made it this far and were determined that we could jury-rig our operations and continue to serve our customers.

Coincidentally, TAB's board of directors met at 1:00 on the same day. The news of our plight cast an additional air of gloom over an already dejected board. At this point, we only had six outside board members left: Robert Hallam, Gary Pace, John Snyder, Earl Wilson, George Young, and Don Williamson. The other six had resigned to protect themselves from further potential liability from the FDIC or shareholders.

Subsequently, we notified all the appropriate regulators of our pending insolvency, fearing that this might be the catalyst that would cause them to move on us. To my astonishment, the OCC responded that we weren't insolvent until they so declared. Their primary worry was that we might inadvertently violate the law, and they admonished me accordingly.

John Stone seemed unruffled by this latest development and assured me the FDIC was still interested in an "open bank" deal. Either Stone was sincere or he was the best actor in the world; I feared it might be the latter.

By this time, we had become expert in grabbing victory out of the jaws of defeat. In this instance, the news of our capital deficiency provided a lever for us to turn up the heat on Pohlad, hopefully creating a greater sense of urgency.

Richard Calvert and I reached Tom Herbst at about 5:00 on March 30. "Tom, we're running out of gas," I said. "As of March 31, we'll be flat out of primary capital, and we won't be able to make any new loans or cover overdrafts. This thing is winding down. It's the ninth inning of the ball game, and you guys are at bat. A 'closed bank' deal would be bad for everyone," I added, almost desperately.

"It would rip the companies apart," Calvert said, equally as desperate. "The holding company staff would be separated from the bank staff, which would be working for the FDIC until the new owner took over. And the holding company would be at war with the FDIC. It wouldn't be a happy scenario."

"Carl is still committed to the 'open bank' concept; he won't abandon it," Herbst assured us, which came as a great relief.

I had called an officers' meeting at 4:00 that afternoon to explain the situation, and to give the officers instructions as to how we were going to handle our business. No sooner was that meeting over than I got calls from the *Wall Street Journal* and from the *Fort Worth Star-Telegram* telling me that they had each heard about our meeting and that there was a rumor we would be closed over the weekend by regulators. "Do you have regulators on the scene at any of your banks?" they asked.

I was aghast. How could they know about our meeting? Was the grapevine so efficient that reporters were hearing of internal events almost as they were happening? The thought was very disturbing.

Hundreds of man-hours of effort went into preparation for our first day of business at TAB/Fort Worth under the new procedures. On Monday, we operated as if it was business as usual. We took applications for installment loans, faxed them to TAB/Grand Prairie for approval, advised the customer, and then funded the loan from Grand Prairie, transferring the funds to TAB/Fort Worth without the customer knowing the difference. By the end of the day, we had also sold $23 million in overdrafts to TAB/Amarillo. Considering these procedures hadn't existed the previous

Thursday, these accomplishments were nothing short of astounding. By any measure, TAB was a great organization with extraordinary people who, in this instance, had performed the impossible. I was proud of every one of them.

To our knowledge, until that time, the regulators had not allowed any other large commercial bank in the country to continue operations after it had run out of capital and could no longer make loans, since a bank's legal loan limit is calculated as a percent of capital.

On April 28, TAB issued a press release announcing its first-quarter loss, exhausting its capital. The *Fort Worth Star-Telegram* coverage of the story was titled, "TAB's Capital Is Gone," but the newspaper hadn't picked up on the most important part of the story–that we were out of gas at TAB/Fort Worth.[10]

Playing It Straight

Our attorneys, our advisors, and the managements at TAB and NBC followed the FDIC's seizure of MCorp with the greatest interest, knowing that it could be a precursor of what might follow at our organizations. Each company had to prepare its defenses for a worst-case scenario. At TAB, we had been discussing contingency plans for months–the Continental-type transaction was just one such plan.

At our board meeting of March 30, we explored the two remaining available options. The first was to protect as many solvent banks as possible by changing the internal plumbing. All of TAB's solvent banks, of which there were twelve at this time (Levelland, Amarillo, Tyler, Duncanville, Fredericksburg, Midland, Denison, Richardson, Farmers Branch, Wichita Falls, Breckenridge, and Greater Southwest) were selling all of their excess funds through the federal funds market to TAB/Fort Worth. We believed that on any given day, TAB/Fort Worth had enough excess liquidity to repay up to three or four of the largest banks, thus protecting them from being seized by the FDIC in the same manner that the FDIC had seized MCorp's solvent banks.

It was patently evident from the FDIC's action with MCorp that any tinkering with internal plumbing would bring on an immediate and extremely harmful response. We were also certain that we couldn't get away with changing any of our internal plumbing without the OCC and the FDIC knowing about it instantly, as they were monitoring our federal funds position daily. We further believed that the FDIC would regard any change as a breach of faith, which would destroy any chance for an "open bank" deal. Given these assumptions, we unanimously concluded that we would play it straight and change nothing.

The second category of strategies was to create a greater sense of urgency on the part of the FDIC through moral suasion and political influence.

But now we had an additional motive to accelerate the process–the FDIC had thrown us another curve ball. In drafting of the Financial Institutions Reform, Recovery, and Enforcement Act of 1989 (FIRREA), the FDIC had included a provision requiring cross-guarantees between holding company subsidiaries. Under this provision, solvent banks would be liable for the losses of insolvent banks in a commonly controlled group.

If this provision remained part of the bill, and it passed before the TAB and NBC situation was resolved, we would lose an enormous amount of leverage to influence an "open bank" deal; presently there was no legally foolproof way for the FDIC to seize our solvent banks. Those assets they couldn't confiscate would be available for creditors and shareholders, two of the three constituencies the FDIC wanted to punish under their policy statement on "open bank" assistance.

Considering our precarious position, we decided to do whatever we could on the political front.

Accordingly, on Sunday, April 16, I went to Washington, D.C., with Richard Calvert and Mark Johnson to call on Senator Lloyd Bentsen (D) and on Representative Henry B. Gonzales (D), chairman of the House Banking Committee from San Antonio. Unfortunately, our efforts were in vain, as we were only able to see aides of Bentsen and Gonzales.

Before calling on Bentsen and Gonzales, however, we went to see John Stone to stress once again the urgency of the situation and to get a progress report. I opened the conversation by reminding Stone that TAB had no capital and that we were holding our operation together with "baling wire." Richard Calvert underscored the urgency of the situation by detailing the circumstances at NBC. I then said, "Frankly, John, we couldn't help but wonder if you were dragging your feet waiting for the legislation to pass." While Stone may have been incensed by this suggestion, he maintained his usual cool demeanor and replied, "We're not waiting for the legislation."

Stone's reply to Calvert's question of whether or not they were still committed to the merger wasn't as straight. "We have to do whatever is the lowest cost to the fund," he answered.

This was the first time anyone had equivocated with regard to the

FDIC's intentions concerning the proposed merger, a concept they had revived and used as an inducement to get TAB and NBC to "come in early." While we showed no disappointment, we were deeply disturbed that Stone was wavering. We weren't surprised, though. So far, the FDIC had sent out strong messages that they were prepared to renege on every commitment they had made.

While the chance of an "open bank" deal continued to lessen, as long as there was any chance at all, we had to conduct our business so as to optimize that chance.

A Missile From Levelland

Among all the CEOs of our subsidiary banks, Thad McDonnell, CEO of TAB/Levelland, stood out as a maverick. He was also the most talented manager of our community banks, consistently producing the highest returns on equity and on assets.

One of the anomalies of a bank holding company structure is that each subsidiary bank has a board of directors, whose fiduciary responsibility is to that particular bank rather than to the holding company. Another anomaly is that the supervision of bank holding companies and their subsidiary banks is divided among four entities: the Federal Reserve System is responsible for regulating holding companies; the OCC is responsible for the supervision of nationally chartered banks; and the FDIC and the Texas Department of Banking are responsible for regulating state-chartered banks in Texas.

As a consequence, state bank regulators criticized the directors of TAB's banks for keeping concentrations of credit–through the sale of federal funds–in the lead bank, TAB/Fort Worth, even though TAB/Fort Worth couldn't survive without those funds. This created a conflict for the directors between their fiduciary responsibility to the bank and their loyalty to the holding company. It likewise presented a dilemma to the TAB management: we were sympathetic to the plight of the directors, but we couldn't allow them to withdraw their bank's federal funds and possibly create a chain reaction that could bring down the entire company. The answer was to convert the boards to advisory status–where the directors had no power to vote–or to dissolve the boards completely.

We had dealt with each subsidiary bank on a case-by-case basis as the liability of the directors had become an issue. For example, we had dissolved the TAB/Dallas board and had converted the TAB/Houston board to advisory status; in each case the banks had exhausted their primary capital. The fact of the matter was that the regulators didn't want us to change the internal funding. It was precisely this situation–the concentration of funds by the solvent banks with the insolvent lead bank–that had enabled the regulators to seize most of MCorp's solvent banks.

At TAB/Levelland's board meeting of April 12, McDonnell explained that neither Ken Walker, deputy director of the FDIC in charge of the Dallas office, nor Ken Littlefield, commissioner of banking in Texas, would instruct TAB/Levelland to move the funds, nor would they guarantee or insure the funds in any way–it was strictly a board decision of TAB/Levelland. It was further revealed that the FDIC examiner Mike Williams told the TAB/Levelland management that he intended to criticize the concentration of funds with TAB/Fort Worth in his report on TAB/Levelland, but he was told not to do so by the Dallas office.

To appease the directors, who were determined to protect themselves, we agreed to allow them to withdraw the funds for one day–a day of extremely high liquidity at TAB/Fort Worth, when there would be no need to purchase federal funds from TAB/Levelland–during which the TAB/Levelland board would resign. April 20 was determined to be a day when we could accommodate the transaction without borrowing from the Federal Reserve Bank.

At 11:30 A.M. on Wednesday, April 19, Gary Cage and I were visiting with two representatives of Chase Manhattan Bank in TAB's offices, when Gary was called out of the meeting. At about 12:15, when Gary hadn't returned, I excused myself and went next door to my office where I found a scene of quiet chaos. Cage was sitting at my desk talking into the speakerphone, and a host of others were either sitting or milling around with grim expressions on their faces. Several were whispering among themselves while Gary spoke. The others appeared as though they were waiting for the coach to send in the next play from the sidelines. The tension level was so high that I immediately knew something was terribly wrong: we were in another crisis.

Bob Scott, TAB's treasurer, pulled me aside and filled me in on what was going on–a palace revolt was underway in Levelland. Shortly before 11:30 A.M., Susan Miller, TAB's senior operations officer, had received a call from a clerk at Texas Commerce Bank of Dallas, informing us that they had been notified that a messenger would soon present a draft for $63 million drawn by TAB/Levelland on TAB/Fort Worth, payable to TAB/Levelland's account at Texas Commerce. As Bob related the story,

I could feel a rush of adrenaline surge through my body as I prepared to meet this new challenge: the situation was grave, and the consequences could be catastrophic if we made the wrong move.

Thad and his directors had done the unthinkable: they had fired a missile directly at TAB/Fort Worth that could blow away whatever chance we had to salvage any value for our shareholders. If the draft were allowed to clear, it could precipitate a run on TAB/Fort Worth by our own banks, which could be joined by others, undoubtedly causing the regulators to take us over. We had to stop the draft before it was presented for payment.

I was already in the process of verifying the facts from Thad, when Bob Scott handed me what I needed. Standing at the edge of my desk, I spoke loudly and authoritatively into the speakerphone: "Thad, as chairman of the sole shareholder of TAB/Levelland, I'm calling a meeting of the shareholder, Texas American Bancshares, Inc., pursuant to Chapter IV, Article 9a, of the Texas Banking Code for the purpose of adopting the following resolution:

> As authorized by Section 2.9 of the Bylaws of Texas American Bank/ Levelland, Levelland, Texas (the "Bank"), BE IT RESOLVED by Texas American Bancshares, Inc., the sole shareholder of the Bank, that the current members of the Board of Directors of the Bank, being Thad McDonnell, Eddie Crawley, R. S. Reid, C. A. Parker, Jr., and Frank Watts, be and they are each hereby removed as Directors of the Bank effective this 19th day of April, 1989; and
>
> BE IT FURTHER RESOLVED that Joseph M. Grant, L. O. Brightbill III, Gary W. Cage, J. C. Brown, Bob G. Scott, and Richard Chapin are each hereby elected to succeed the removed Directors, each to serve until the next annual meeting of the shareholders of the Bank or until his death, resignation, or his successor is elected and shall qualify.[11]

You could have heard a pin drop on the other end of the phone. Thad was speechless. He hadn't thought we would be prepared to deal with them in this way. We had turned the tables on them and stolen the initiative. Before signing off from Thad, I told him that I would be in Levelland the next morning.

We then convened a meeting of the new board of directors of TAB/ Levelland in order to recall the draft, which we subsequently retrieved from Texas Commerce.[12]

As everyone realized the crisis had passed, a great sense first of relief and then of joy came over the room. Congratulations, handshakes, and hugs were exchanged over a job well done.

Once again, disaster had been averted, this time because a clerk at Texas Commerce had enough initiative and presence of mind to alert us to the incoming draft and because Bob Scott and others at TAB had done their homework. I had a profound feeling of pride and gratitude for this group of dedicated and talented people.

J. C. Brown, the executive vice president in charge of the TAB/Levelland relationship, and I fired Thad McDonnell the next day, although the official story in Levelland was that he retired.

FIFTEEN 15

THE FINAL CURTAIN

Upon arriving at the office on Thursday afternoon, April 20, I had an urgent call from the arbitrageur Jay Lustig of Drake Capital Securities in Santa Monica, California, who had invested heavily in our publicly traded 15.5 percent notes.

Only a month earlier, Lustig had threatened to put NBC into involuntary bankruptcy. I had talked with Lustig and his associate, Chuck Lewsadder, off and on for the last several months in an attempt to be very open, with the hope that the more information they had, the more patient they would be. So far, it had worked.

On this occasion, however, Lustig wasn't seeking information. His first words when I returned his call were, "We've decided we're going to file to put you into involuntary bankruptcy. We just don't see any advantage in waiting any longer."

I knew we had to stave him off or TAB was dead. We would suffer the same fate as MCorp, and our shareholders would be left with nothing. We couldn't allow it to end this way.

After pausing to catch my breath, I said as convincingly as I could, "Jay, I can understand your frustration. We are frustrated too. The FDIC is still talking 'open bank' solution. Besides, there is nothing that can be done to protect the solvent banks. If you file now, you destroy any chance of our getting an 'open bank' deal, and you haven't gained anything."

I then explained in detail how our "internal plumbing" worked. "Remember, all of our banks are 'plumbed' to our lead bank in Fort Worth through federal funds sales. The FDIC would refuse to repay any of these funds and would declare all of these banks insolvent, as they did in the cases of First Republic and MCorp. We wouldn't be able to save any of ours, whereas MCorp saved five. Every last one of our banks is selling all of its excess liquidity into Fort Worth."

"If you file, it would be a terrible mistake, for you, for us, for everyone," I added, hoping desperately to persuade him.

"Well, you've shot straight with us so far," Lustig responded. "I'm inclined to give you the benefit of the doubt, but we are growing very impatient."

I breathed a sigh of relief but realized that I had only bought us a little time–how little, I didn't know.

The next morning when I got the *Fort Worth Star-Telegram* from my front yard, I hadn't even gotten back to the front door when I stopped abruptly upon reading the headline, "Bank's Creditors Seek Help." I thought I had made some headway with Lustig, but it was apparent that he was an ever-present threat.

The article reported that creditors were seeking the counsel of the well-known bankruptcy law firm of Weil, Gotshal & Manges of New York, which had represented Texaco in its bankruptcy in 1987 and was representing bondholders of First RepublicBank and MCorp.

Lustig was quoted extensively:

> Bondholders have shown an enormous amount of patience so far. But now we're turning over every rock. We're just trying to find out, given what happened to First Republic and MCorp, what might happen here. . . . If I knew, for a fact, that the regulators were going to do a closed-bank assistance deal here [by implementing a bridge bank], we'd file for [Chapter 7] bankruptcy tomorrow. If we knew for a fact that it was going to be open bank, we wouldn't file at all.[1]

Additionally, Lustig said that the bondholders were becoming increasingly concerned about the long delay and any further delays that might make it possible for regulators to seize our solvent banks under pending legislation (FIRREA).

It was clear to me that this wasn't just an idle threat, but that Lustig was deadly serious. We had learned only a few days earlier that American National Insurance Company of Galveston had liquidated their entire $9 million position in our publicly traded bonds and that Lustig had bought no less than $5 million and possibly the entire $9 million, paying in all likelihood $.10 to $.15 on the dollar. So he had the incentive.

The heat was being turned up, and the survival of TAB was at stake. The specter of bankruptcy hung over the company like an oppressive cloud. Anxiety levels were high, and morale was plunging.

After talking to Lustig on Thursday, I immediately called Rodgin Cohen at Sullivan & Cromwell. Rodgin decided that we needed to move urgently on two fronts: he would call John Douglas, chief legal counsel for the FDIC, and explain that a crisis was developing; Michael Maney, of the same firm, would contact Martin Bienenstock of Weil, Gotshal to see if we could buy some additional time.

By conference call on Saturday, April 22, at 12:15 P.M. Fort Worth time, we got the results of these efforts from Cohen. The news from Maney's conversation with Bienenstock was good.

"Marty understands the 'internal plumbing' situation and the downside risk of filing now," Maney said. "I believe they will stand pat for awhile. But he said that they would file before the new legislation is passed that would leave the bondholders with nothing."

Cohen next reported on his conversation with Douglas. His report was both startling and disturbing:

> John understands the urgency of the situation and the need for a rapid resolution. I was really surprised over how forthcoming he was when he acknowledged that the FDIC could be terribly embarrassed over their handling of TAB and NBC. I don't want to read too much into that, but if they recognize that they would have a real public relations problem, an "open bank" solution would enable them to avoid the threat of possible disclosures that we might make in attempting to block a "closed bank" effort.
>
> John had just come from a meeting with Stone and Seidman prior to our conversation. He believes that a deal could be struck within three or four weeks, but the only deal they have on the table at this time for both companies is very difficult.

"Well, Rodge," I said, thinking dubiously of Lustig's threat. "I don't know if Lustig can be held off for three weeks."

In an effort to be ready to preempt Lustig, we instructed Sullivan & Cromwell to begin preparing a Chapter 11 bankruptcy filing, just so we would be prepared to take the offensive should we need to.

An integral part of this strategy would be to file a lawsuit against the regulators enjoining them from illegally grabbing our solvent banks. Our defense would be based on legal precedent, but our lever was that the FDIC didn't have "clean hands" in their handling of TAB and NBC.

Cohen further explained:

> We could justifiably point out that the FDIC asked us to "come in early," and they promised us more favorable treatment as a lure. They agreed to an "open bank" solution, and they invited us to find an investor. They have taken us through two bidding processes–and there is a strong possibility of a third–and this transaction has taken longer than any similar transaction on record, at a significantly greater cost to the FDIC fund.
>
> One of our strategies is to play upon our position as the wronged party. We would defend our lawsuit on the grounds that the FDIC doesn't have clean hands, and they shouldn't get relief since they behaved so badly.

Even as the "wronged party," the thought of fighting the FDIC in court was a frightening alternative. The chances of winning in a federal court, battling a federal agency, were very low indeed, and the legal costs would be astronomical.

Rebid: Round III

While we were trying to hold things together, the FDIC was busy attempting to line up additional bidders. We had learned that during the time Pohlad was supposed to have had an "exclusive," John Stone and Jim Thickson, assistant regional director for Chicago who was on special assignment helping Stone, were contacting potential bidders to form a "second tier" who could be activated at the appropriate time.

On Monday, May 1, the FDIC made it official: the bidding was being reopened, for the third excruciating time.

On this occasion, there was no drama. The phone call from Christie Sciacca, advising us that he had heard from Stone that the FDIC was "opening bidding to the standby bidders," was anticlimactic, since we had already gotten feedback from several of the prospects they had contacted.

"Christie," I said listlessly, "they've lived up to our every expectation. They've done it to us again. Hell, we might as well just give them the banks. Every time we turn around they are changing the rules. I think their aim is to wear us out to the point of submission–to where we will just hand over the keys."

"You may be right, but we have to keep on fighting–and cooperating–as long as there is any chance at all of an 'open bank' deal," Sciacca said, trying his hardest to be reassuring.

I knew Christie was right, but I was extremely discouraged.

Coincidentally, Pohlad had called me on Thursday, April 27, to inform me that they had taken a partner in order to provide the additional $100 million that the "good bank/bad bank" structure dictated. "I am convinced we are going to win," Pohlad said confidently. "No one knows these banks as we do, and no one is going to spend the time we have on due diligence. We have the advantage. Our new partner gives us financial clout and credibility. I can't tell you now, but you'll find out in a couple of days, and you'll be pleased.

"We're going to hang in there to the end," Pohlad added emphatically. "We're not going to abandon you. We're more enthusiastic than ever, and we'll be submitting a new bid within the next two weeks."

I had been exhausted and discouraged beyond belief. Pohlad was giving me a lifeline–hope–something positive to think about. My spirits rose as I listened to him. Pohlad had shown a will and determination that were genuinely admirable. There was no question that he was a winner, and he showed extraordinary sensitivity to the agony we were experiencing and the depth of our concerns about the banks and their employees. I sensed a mutual admiration and bonding that can only result from a commonality of purpose, as well as shared frustration and disappointment.

We badly wanted Pohlad to win, and we would fight as hard as we could to see that it happened. Unfortunately, there wasn't much we could do, since the FDIC had completely taken over the process. We were merely pawns on their chessboard.

Shortly after I received the official word of the rebidding, Tom Herbst called to arrange for the initial meeting with their partner. Assuming that Herbst already knew about the rebidding process, I mentioned it in passing.

"You can't be serious! I can't believe this!" The usually composed Tom Herbst was furious. He fumed, "They've abused us at every turn. They've misled us, and they've lied to us." He paused, regaining his composure somewhat, and added, "In any event, Jody, we're still committed to see it through to the end."

Herbst then disclosed that their partner was Norwest. Norwest was a venerable Minneapolis-based banking organization, with about $20 billion in assets, which had itself come through some very difficult times in the early 1980s.

This was good news on the one hand, but bad news on the other. Norwest was brought in by Pohlad because they could supply the additional $100 million needed to reach the required $300 million. On the negative side, it meant that the Pohlad organization, with which we had built such a great relationship, would take a secondary role even though the partnership was billed as fifty-fifty.

We also had heard from Bill Isaac that Security Pacific would definitely bid and that its president, Bob Smith, and several of his associates wanted to visit Fort Worth on Monday, May 8, on a whirlwind tour, staying for two to three hours after visiting San Antonio for a similar period that morning.

Upon their visit, Bob Smith was extremely impressed with Fort Worth and the franchise potential. With their California orientation, where there is a bank branch office on every street corner, he kept asking where all the banks were? There was no question in my mind: they were going to bid.

Buzz Brightbill and I were impressed with Smith, but neither of us was impressed with his four lieutenants. They were quiet, not bothering to ask questions or exchange niceties. During the entire time they were with us, their dour expressions never changed.

Two days later, the Security Pacific team arrived, some thirty strong, for due diligence. The general impression our people had of the Security Pacific team was that they had an icy demeanor, lacked sensitivity to our people and our circumstances, and looked upon us as second-class citizens.

The Norwest personnel, on the other hand, treated our people with great respect. Perhaps the difference was that the Norwest group had been in a similar situation and knew what it was like to suffer adversity.

On Thursday, May 11, Richard Calvert and I went to Washington once again to stress the urgency of getting the deal done. Stone was his usual chain-smoking, verbose self. We did learn that the FDIC had set a date of June 12 for the submission of bids.

In the meantime, prospective bidders were lining up: Pohlad/Norwest and Security Pacific would bid for both banks; Alan Fellheimer through his Pittsburgh-based Equimark Corporation would bid for NBC alone; and Ron Steinhart through Texop Bancshares would bid for TAB. There was still speculation in the press that Rainwater was in the fray, but we knew better.

More Deterioration

Most of the rest of May was spent aiding Norwest and Security Pacific with their due diligence. In the meantime, the progress of the TAB/NBC transaction was reported almost daily in the Fort Worth, Dallas, and San Antonio newspapers and in the *Wall Street Journal.* The fact that we hadn't had a massive defection of customers had been a real surprise, but I realized that the longer this went on and the more publicity we received, the more likely we would suffer losses. I was right.

The first major piece of business we lost was that of Texas Christian University (TCU), which moved its major operating account and a $41 million trust fund. Shortly thereafter, on Monday, June 5, we were notified by Dee Kelly, the Basses' attorney, that the Basses were moving $200 million in trust assets that we had under management.

These losses followed a newspaper report in the *Fort Worth Star-Telegram* that TAB had borrowed funds from the Federal Reserve Bank of Dallas in an amount averaging $33 million on each of two days during the first quarter of 1989, which amazingly was the only borrowing since May 1986.[2] This wasn't alarming unto itself, but the article also cited that deposits had declined 12 percent from the previous year, including a 22 percent drop in uninsured deposits. This was a clear signal that the confidence of our uninsured customers had been severely shaken.

Although the loss of the TCU and the Bass business came as a real blow because of the importance of the relationships, they represented only a small portion of what we lost in the first six months of 1989.

The Bids Are In

With the bids due on June 12, the level of activity accelerated among the bidders, as did our efforts to influence the bids. Our main focus was on structure, emphasizing an "open" versus "closed" approach and the merger of the companies.

As late as May 13, the *Fort Worth Star-Telegram* printed an article concluding that the two companies would be sold as a package in keeping with the original intent and our agreement with the FDIC.[3] This was good to read and was reassuring, although we were certain that the sources weren't unimpeachable. Yet we continued to receive signals that the FDIC preferred a "closed bank" solution.

On May 24, Bill Isaac reported that he had learned through his contact at Security Pacific that all discussions they had held with the FDIC up to that point had been on a "closed bank" basis, and only after the fact had they learned that the FDIC would consider an "open bank" bid. On June 13, the day after the bids had been submitted, Bill Isaac spoke to Stone, who indicated that the FDIC would like to finalize the deal within a month. Isaac received the distinct impression that Stone preferred an "open bank" structure. Apparently, two issues were important to Stone: to wrap it all up at once and to treat shareholders and creditors fairly.

With anticipation of the bids being filed on Monday, June 12, the media was filled with news of TAB and NBC and the bidders. On June 13, the *Wall Street Journal* reported that "Failing Banks of National Bancshares and Texas American Draw Few Bidders."[4] It reported accurately that Security Pacific and Norwest had bid for both companies and that Steinhart's Texop Bancshares, through its lead bank Deposit Guaranty, had bid for TAB, and that Alan Fellheimer's Equimark had bid for NBC.

While no one could predict the outcome, the odds-on betting among the TAB and NBC personnel, management, and advisors was that it was a toss-up between Norwest and Security Pacific. Norwest's advantage was that they were teamed with Pohlad, who knew us exceedingly well by this time, whereas Security Pacific had the advantage of being three times the size of Norwest, and thus could take somewhat more risk in their bid. Steinhart and Fellheimer were considered long shots. The countdown had begun, and our anxiety had increased accordingly.

Preparing for the Worst

With the tension mounting as each day passed, we continued to do everything we could to prepare for the worst and to expedite a decision.

On Wednesday, June 21, I went to Washington where Christie Sciacca and I visited the FDIC for a progress report. John Stone and Harrison Young of Prudential Bache were present. (Prudential Bache had been hired by the FDIC to advise them on the transaction.) Stone advised that he hoped to complete the bidding for MCorp before July 4, that they were not waiting for the legislation to pass, and that the legislation would not allow them to act even if it passed immediately due to the necessity for the FDIC to develop administrative procedures.

We had been concerned about Stone's preference between an "open bank" bid and a "closed bank" bid since we had learned of the confusion on this issue at Security Pacific. As a consequence, we decided to discuss the subject with Stone. He did not preclude an "open bank" deal, and we discussed the pros and cons of "open" versus "closed." I pointed out the cooperative attitude of TAB and NBC and that neither company wanted a declaration of war, which was what a "closed bank" deal would constitute.

Stone concluded the meeting by saying that "they [the OCC and FDIC] had looked at TAB very carefully and found no questionable transactions [that would lead to significant claims being filed by the FDIC]."

During the course of the meeting with the FDIC, Stone confirmed that MCorp would be handled before TAB. Consequently, we waited for an announcement on MCorp with great anticipation, assuming that an announcement on TAB would follow in three or four weeks.

Our waiting ended on Wednesday, June 28. At about 9:00 P.M., I received a call from Mike Dietrich, chairman of MBank Fort Worth, informing me that the FDIC had awarded MBank to Banc One Corporation of Columbus, Ohio. This was a surprise to everyone, and once again emphasized that the only thing one could count on from the FDIC was that they would do the unexpected. The heavy favorites for MCorp had been First City, NCNB, and Texas Commerce.

On July 14, Sciacca met with Jim Thickson and Harrison Young of Prudential Bache to try once again to stress the urgency of the situation and to urge them to expedite the transaction. The meeting was entirely unsatisfactory. After Christie had conveyed our concerns and had implored them to move with alacrity, Harrison responded, "Listen, Christie, you've been on this side of the table before and know what we can tell you and what we can't. Either we can sit here and look at each other or you can get up and leave. This may be abrupt, but that's where we are."

This was one of the most puzzling exchanges of the entire transaction. We didn't know what to make of it.

We considered, once again, with our legal counsel whether or not to make a preemptive strike by putting the company into bankruptcy voluntarily. After many hours of debate, we decided against this strategy because it would probably preclude any chance for an "open bank" deal.

All we could do now was wait.

SIXTEEN

JULY 20, 1989

At the start of the week of July 17, after one and a half years of negotiations with the FDIC, I knew we were close to the end, but I was impatient and restless. On Monday morning, I decided to call John Stone to see if I could learn anything.

Stone was, as usual, guarded and noncommittal in what he said. Finally, in response to my concerns about being forced into bankruptcy by Lustig and Lewsadder, Stone said, "We're concerned too and are working as hard as we can to try to wrap this up. In fact, we have two groups in today. I'm sure it's going to be within the next three weeks. Jody, that's all I can say; you just have to do the best you can to hold off Lustig and Lewsadder." In reflecting on Stone's comments, I assumed the "two groups" he was talking about were Norwest and Security Pacific.

After spending Tuesday and Wednesday working mostly on routine bank matters, I looked forward to Thursday, which was to begin with a Chamber of Commerce breakfast, followed by our usual weekly officers' meeting. These meetings were always a high point of the week for me, as I thoroughly enjoyed the interaction with the officers.

The Final Day

Thursday, July 20, began like any other Thursday, but it would prove to be one of the most memorable days in my life. The Chamber of Commerce meeting was at the City Club, located in the silver, glass-sheathed City Place Tower Two of Bass Brothers. Upon entering the club, I noticed that the cold decor, with its black, gray, and white tones, accentuated the mood of an economically devastated Fort Worth. Probably a suitable place for the chamber to meet, I mused, given the pall of desperation that embraced many of its members.

While I enjoyed seeing my friends at these meetings, I wasn't looking forward to answering the inevitable questions about the fate of TAB. I spotted Bayard Friedman across the room and immediately moved toward him. Friedman had been a great ally throughout the ordeal, but he had been unusually out-of-touch lately. I was anxious to bring him up to date.

"Good morning, Joseph. How are you?" Friedman frequently called me Joseph when greeting me, but this morning he was tight-lipped, and his blue eyes were unusually serious.

"Still waiting," I responded, knowing that no further explanation was needed. "But it should be soon now."

"It's today," Friedman said, his jaw set firmly.

"What?"

"It's today."

"How do you know?" I asked.

"Believe me, I know, but I can't tell you any more. Call me though, I want to talk to you when it's over."

I stared at him in disbelief, my stomach churning. The coldness of the room closed in and seemed to envelop me. What was going on here?

I'm not sure I really wanted the answer to that question. What appetite I had for breakfast quickly vanished, and I didn't hear much of the chamber proceedings. I was completely stunned; not by the reality that today was the day, but by the strange way in which I had learned what was happening. I instinctively knew how Bayard Friedman had this information. I wondered how long he had known, and suddenly I knew why I hadn't heard from him lately. I also understood why he had advised me about thirty days previously to begin looking for another career opportunity, to start looking after myself. At the time, I hadn't taken him too seriously.

I had to leave the chamber meeting early in order to be at the 8:30 TAB officers' meeting on time. It was just as well, because I really didn't want to talk to anyone. I needed the time to think about what I would say to the officers and to plan the rest of the day.

The ride up the elevator from the garage to the auditorium seemed to take forever. I now knew that this probably would be my last meeting. (I believed Friedman's information to be correct. Although I couldn't be 100 percent certain, I was 95 percent sure he was right.) I had already decided to conduct the meeting routinely. After all, there wasn't anything anybody could do. Why alarm them?

I walked to the center of the stage, faced the audience, and said, "Well here we are for one more meeting." No one in the audience knew how true those words were. The meeting was business as usual, after which I answered questions. To those questions concerning the status of the deal, I merely said, "I think we are very close."

As soon as the meeting ended, Whit Smith, who was in charge of recruiting at TAB, pulled me aside. "Jody, I got a call at home last night from Linda Brown at TAB/Dallas. She had just heard from a close acquaintance at the OCC that they are coming in today."

"Did she have any details?" I asked.

"No, but she claims that her source is in a position to be sure. I think she knows what she is talking about."

"I heard something similar earlier this morning," I said. "Today is probably the day. If you hear anything else, let me know." I struggled to keep my emotions in check and my voice clear, forcing a smile as I turned to leave.

Upon arriving at my office after the meeting, the calls confirming what I had already heard began coming in from all sources.

9:25 A.M. "Jody, this is Jack McSpadden. It's either today or tomorrow, and Steinhart appears to be in great shape."

As soon as Jack hung up I thought of what a fool I had been. My thoughts went back to McSpadden's call in April when he asked if we would object to Goldman Sachs representing Steinhart, as well as TAB. Jack assured us that it would be two different groups. One group, headed by McSpadden, working in the financial institutions area, would represent us. The other group, working under their M&A (mergers and acquisitions) department, would represent Steinhart. There would be a Chinese wall between the two groups; neither would know what the other was doing.

After considerable debate, we acquiesced to this request, primarily because we felt that McSpadden was trustworthy, and we didn't feel that Steinhart was a serious contender in any case. Now I wondered if Steinhart unknowingly had benefited from this unusual circumstance, and whether or not he would have had a chance without Goldman's support. The fact that McSpadden believed he knew something now indicated that the Chinese wall wasn't too effective. We had been naive at best. Had we known at the time that Goldman would be an investor, on behalf of its partners, with Steinhart, we never would have agreed to them being on both sides of the deal.

9:30 A.M. My assistant, Libby Dotson, buzzed to tell me that Martin Bowen, CEO of TAB/Houston, was on the phone.

"Hi, Martin, what's up?"

"Jody, we've just learned through a source at the OCC that today is the day. Supposedly it's a split deal, Security Pacific gets us and NBC goes to Norwest."

"Martin, we've been getting conflicting reports. The only one that's been consistent is that it will happen today. If it is a split deal, it makes sense that Norwest would go for NBC since that was Pohlad's first choice. Keep us posted if you hear anything else."

After the call I thought to myself, the OCC is leaking like a sieve. There's nothing we can do to head off the inevitable, but knowing that this is the day does give us a chance to consider any defensive moves we might want to make to preserve assets before the banks are closed.

9:50 A.M. No sooner had I hung up with Martin Bowen, than Jim Grant, CEO of TAB/Dallas, was on the phone.

"It looks like this is the day. We've heard from two sources. Wally Reed [head of consumer banking at TAB/Dallas] got a call from one of his friends at the FDIC. Also, we heard through Winstead McGuire, a prominent Dallas law firm, that we would be 'bridged' today, but that the FDIC hasn't made a decision as to the owner. It will be an MCorp-type deal where they will keep us open, pending a sale."

"Jim, that could be," I said. "We've been getting rumors all morning that it's today. I'm not so sure as to the ultimate disposition, though, or when."

My heart went out to Jim. I had hired him from InterFirst, and we had worked together for ten years. If it were Norwest/Pohlad or Security Pacific, Jim would survive. But if it were Steinhart, with his existing presence in the Dallas market, Jim's job would be in jeopardy. The whole process was so impersonal, it made me sick. And, yet, ironically banking was supposed to be a "personal" business.

10:10 A.M. It was curious, given all the rumors, that I hadn't heard from Richard Calvert and Mark Johnson. But, if they had been as busy as I had, they hadn't had a chance to call. I told Libby to get them on the phone and to say it was urgent.

Cued by the buzz from Libby indicating they were on the line, I leaned across my desk to activate the speakerphone. Gary Cage had joined me for the call.

"Hi, Richard, Mark. Gary is here with me. Is anything happening down there? Our phone has been ringing off the wall with reports that today is the day."

"Jody, we haven't heard anything," Richard responded with deep concern in his voice. "It's business as usual here, all is quiet. What's going on?"

After giving them a complete rundown on the morning's activities, we concluded that the action might be unilateral against TAB. This was bad news, as it was further confirmation that the merger was off, which saddened us all tremendously. We had grown exceedingly close over the past year and a half. Together we had experienced the emotional highs of near victory and the lows of continuous disappointment. We shared a common problem, and we understood the impact of the constant stress we were all under. We had fought long and hard for the merger, which we now saw slipping away from us. The reality of the moment was especially bitter.

Hanging up, an overwhelming sense of sorrow, disillusionment, and defeat washed over me, as I knew that our dreams of working together in one unified company would never be realized. I looked at Gary as he stood up, his face reflecting the disappointment we both felt. He glanced at me sympathetically and said, "I'll see you later."

10:45 A.M. With the expectation of imminent action by the OCC, I arranged for a conference call between TAB and all of our advisors.

After bringing everyone up to date with respect to the current status, we reviewed our state of readiness. Representatives of Carrington, Coleman, Sloman & Blumenthal, TAB's Dallas bankruptcy law firm, were poised to seek injunctions in federal courts with regard to our ten solvent national banks, and in state courts with regard to our two solvent state banks, in order to preclude the seizure and commingling of the assets of those banks with the insolvent banks. As of June 30, the solvent banks had total equity of $38.3 million and total primary capital of $63.9 million. We wouldn't activate the plan until the OCC or the State Banking Department of Texas, which had jurisdiction over state banks, made the first move. Simultaneously, we would file suit against the OCC and the FDIC for illegally declaring these banks insolvent and for illegally seizing them.

With these plans in place, the only remaining decision was whether or not to disconnect the plumbing between as many of our solvent banks and TAB/Fort Worth as possible. We would have to pay back the federal funds that we had bought from those banks, which would preclude federal regulators from declaring them insolvent. In the MCorp case, after declaring the lead bank insolvent, regulators had refused to repay 100 percent of the federal funds that bank had purchased from the solvent subsidiaries, thereby rendering the subsidiaries insolvent as well. Ironically, the pending bank-reform legislation, FIRREA, would provide for cross-guarantees of the liabilities of all subsidiaries of holding companies, thus making it impossible to isolate the solvent banks from the insolvent banks.

A principal requirement of receivers of national banks is that they treat the recognizable claims of all creditors on a pro rata basis; there could be no discrimination between creditors–all had to be treated equally. This had already been adjudicated in the case of First Empire Bank–New York versus the FDIC. The agency, which had refused to treat all claims ratably, argued that the law (12 U.S.C. Section 194) did not apply to it and that it was not required to comply with that section when assisting in the takeover of a closed bank. The Ninth Circuit ruled against the FDIC, asserting that, as a receiver of a national bank, it must make a ratable distribution of assets. Consequently, we felt our chances in court would be relatively good. On this issue, Rodgin Cohen's counsel would determine our approach.

Cohen advised:

> In court, they would characterize our repayment as a preference payment in anticipation of liquidation, claiming that we had favored one class of creditor over another. Their counsel would contend that this was in violation of the preference provision of the National Bank Act. It's the same principle as a preference payment to a creditor by a borrower, to the detriment of other creditors, in anticipation of bankruptcy.
>
> Court decisions are made 25 percent based on law and 75 percent based on who is the good guy and who is the bad guy. We want to look like the injured party. Based on First Empire, I like our odds in court. By paying off TAB/Levelland and TAB/Greater Southwest, TAB's remaining solvent state-chartered banks, we would hurt our chances. Besides, we still can't be sure it's a "closed bank" deal. Repaying the fed funds now would jeopardize an "open bank" solution. Additionally, I don't see any risk vis-à-vis the creditors. They won't bring a lawsuit on a voidable preference.

On Rodgin's advice, we stood pat on our interbank plumbing.

12:00 NOON As our conference call concluded, Libby handed me a note taken at 11:55 A.M. "Jim Cockrell [CEO of TAB/Temple] just called with the following message: A representative from the FDIC just arrived and is waiting to meet a representative from the OCC between 12:00 and 1:00. The representative from the FDIC has not said anything about why he is there."

The calls were now flooding in; regulators were arriving at all of our banks. Their presence was positive confirmation of the rumors. There was no doubt, we were being taken over. It's a "closed bank" deal. The only reason regulators would be at the banks would be to declare them insolvent: we were being closed and bridged. This was a horrible development. I felt like I had been shot with a stun gun by confirmation of the bad news I had been expecting all day.

1:30 P.M. John Foucault, the senior OCC examiner assigned to TAB, and his immediate superior, George Smith, came to see me. All they could tell me was that the OCC would take action today. I would learn the details after the close of business at 5:00 P.M.

As I sat alone in my office, thinking of the consequences, my head throbbed and my muscles ached, as if I had just finished a marathon. But my pain was emotional, not physical. What I had worked so long and hard for would never be, and the thought of separation from the bank and its people was numbing. Time passed quickly as I sat among the mementos and relics of my short career as CEO of TAB. My eyes focused on the gold medallion on my desk commemorating TAB's listing on the New York Stock Exchange on June 23, 1982. The stock had opened at $30 per share. Tomorrow it would be worthless.

2:00 P.M. I called Bayard Friedman to see if I could talk him into telling me who the winner was, although I was sure I already knew based on his previous comments. There was only one situation that would enable Bayard to be informed of the winner.

After Bayard acknowledged who it was, he said, "I really went to bat for you, but there was no way the FDIC was going to bend from their policy. If they made an exception in your case, they would have to do the same in others. You and Bond and the directors have to go."

I heard the words, and I knew he was right. I thanked him and hung up. I stared unseeingly out my window remembering that, since the FDIC's current policy statement had been promulgated under Seidman, there hadn't been any exceptions. Yet had it been an "open bank" deal under the concessions the FDIC had offered eighteen months earlier, the directors would have remained, and there was a very high probability Bond and I would have kept our jobs as well. I knew Pohlad would have fought hard to see that it happened that way.

I had called Pohlad earlier to let him know what was happening. He had already been told by the FDIC that he had lost, but of course, was precluded from calling us. He was as sick at heart as I was over the outcome. After the gargantuan effort, the emotional commitment, the time, and the money, to lose had to be a totally discouraging and depressing experience for Pohlad and his team. I was grateful, however, that we had become friends through this strange and unbelievable series of events. It was a friendship that I knew would endure.

Realizing that the bank would soon be part of my past, I tried to focus on the future, the job at hand. I had an obligation to the TAB shareholders and creditors. Someone had to steer TAB through certain bankruptcy and possible liquidation, and that someone had to be me–there was no one else. Bond couldn't do it because he was now fighting his own bigger battle. His prostate cancer, first detected in the early 1980s, had reappeared.

2:30 P.M. I spent the next hour calling directors and other insiders, such as attorneys Ed Keltner and Rice Tilley.

I had put Sheila on notice early in the day. Whenever I had a break, I would give her a call to keep her advised. The real reason, though, was to hear her voice and reassuring words.

3:30 P.M. Richard Calvert and Mark Johnson called. "We've just gotten a call from John Stone. He will be in our offices at 5:30 this afternoon. He wouldn't say more, but we know it won't be what we wanted. It looks like the merger is out of the question."

"I know, and I'm sick about it," I said. "I would really have enjoyed working with you, trying to turn these banks around. Best of luck in your meeting with Stone. Keep us informed, and we'll do the same." I could imagine how apprehensive they were feeling.

Although this was difficult for all of us, there was an air of good humor in this conversation. No matter how bad things seemed to be, dealings between TAB and NBC had always been good natured. People on both sides had maintained a sense of humor and a general spirit of optimism. This afternoon was no exception.

4:25 P.M. As I walked out of my office to conduct the officers' meeting, which I had called for 4:30, I thought about the apprehensions and fears of our people. They wanted the Norwest/Pohlad team to win; they were going to be terribly disappointed and worried about their jobs. Any change brings fear, but this was worse because everyone was in the dark as to who the new owner would be. Even though I couldn't tell them who the winner was, I knew that I needed to be reassuring. This had to be an upbeat meeting; I couldn't let them see my own anguish over this turn of events.

There was a standing-room-only crowd of three hundred people, the largest I had ever seen at an officers' meeting. Rumors had been reverberating through the organization all day, and it appeared that the entire officer corps, plus many others, were there. People had dropped whatever they were doing, no matter how urgent it was. The anxiety level had to be high enough to blow the roof off the auditorium. It was a somber crowd, so quiet that I was sure I could hear three hundred hearts beating. From center stage, I could see every questioning face, hoping for good news, but probably expecting something else based on the rumors that had been circulating.

I took a deep breath and began.

> This is the day that we all were beginning to think would never arrive. Let me tell you what is going to happen the rest of the day. Representatives from the OCC will arrive at my office at 5:00, and I will surrender the charter of the bank. I expect it to be a "closed bank" deal. I can't tell you who the new owner is, because I'm not sure. However, those long shots that I told you didn't have a chance–well, I may have spoken too soon. You will be told more as soon as possible, but, unfortunately, you probably won't be hearing from me again.
>
> [Trying to make this as light as I could, I continued.] I do know that you're going to have a new CEO. I will remain with the holding company. Someone has to stay there and guide the company through probable liquidation; it will be a big job. Don't worry about me, I'm going to be fine. I'll be here in the building, and I hope to see all of you frequently. You'll be fine too. You are a terrific group of people. You accomplished the impossible: you kept this franchise together for the new owner, and it's only due to your diligence and hard work. It is a great franchise, not because of the bricks and mortar or the communities it serves, but because of you, the people who make it all happen.

> You are winners, and you will make this organization a winner once more. Finally, thanks, once again, for all that you have done. I have been privileged to have been associated with you. God bless each and every one of you.

After the meeting, there was a continuous stream of people coming up to say thanks, to wish me luck, or in some cases to just shake my hand or give me a pat on the back. I was gratified by their caring gestures. But I wasn't surprised. People at TAB had always been supportive. I was reminded of fall 1988 when Tom Sassman, one of our senior vice presidents, had died suddenly of a stroke at the relatively young age of forty-three. I had been overwhelmed by the outpouring of sympathy and support for his family at the time. I was equally overwhelmed now, holding back the tears that I knew weren't far away.

5:00 P.M. By the time I returned to my office, it was already 5:00. Libby informed me that representatives of the OCC and the FDIC were in the building and were on their way to the executive offices.

They arrived on the sixteenth floor en masse and marched into the executive conference room next to my office. My first thought was that the scene reminded me of a scene from a movie, in which conquering soldiers march in to overwhelm their foe. I wondered to myself why the OCC and the FDIC needed so many people for such a simple job. While I didn't count them, it seemed like there must have been twelve to fifteen. Did they expect resistance? We had been more than cooperative. Did they expect anything less now? All that was missing were photographers and the press to record this event for posterity.

Although I held my head high and conducted myself with dignity, this was a demeaning experience. I felt humiliated, like I had committed a crime and was being officially charged. Even in this small arena, mostly with people I didn't know in the room, I was embarrassed and self-conscious. In addition to the federal regulators, Buzz Brightbill, Gary Cage, Bob Herchert, and Bob Scott were present. Scott, TAB's treasurer, had the bank charter ready to surrender.

I listened to the litany, as the OCC representative read the order revoking TAB/Fort Worth's charter. I felt like I was having a nightmare, as if this wasn't really happening. At the same time, a kaleidoscope of thoughts raced through my mind. I thought of Major Van Zandt, the founder of the bank, and of all his successors. I felt completely demoralized, as though

I had failed, and yet, I knew I had done the best that I or anyone else could have done with a sinking ship that was beyond salvage.

I numbly surrendered bank charter number 3131 issued to the Fort Worth National Bank on March 4, 1884, signed by Comptroller of the Currency John Jay Knox. It was the worst moment of my life.

As the charter passed from my hands, a chapter of history closed on Texas banking: a proud and venerable institution that had withstood the test of time, surviving two world wars and the Great Depression, had died an inglorious death. The reality of the moment left me saddened and feeling perilously sick to my stomach. I took several deep breaths to quell my nausea.

After the short ceremony, I adjourned to my office with one of the FDIC representatives who had asked if he could visit with me. I wanted to be alone with my sadness and despair; however, I had no choice but to agree to see him.

Patrick P. McCarthy's card read, "FDIC–Addison Consolidated Office." He was a minor functionary, not even out of the FDIC's Dallas regional office, but out of a satellite of the Dallas office. This was not exactly a class act on the part of the FDIC. Seidman and Stone obviously didn't give a damn about the vanquished, no matter the degree of culpability or, indeed, the level of cooperation.

McCarthy began by apologizing: "I feel awkward being here. I don't know how this fell to me, since I haven't been previously involved, and we've never met."

I forced a smile, suddenly relieved that I was at least talking to a person who seemed human.

"It's okay," I said, trying to make him feel more at ease. "You've got a job to do. I understand that, and you don't need to apologize for it."

"Yes, sir. You will receive a call from John Stone explaining everything to you, and shortly the new owner will be here to see you. I do have to explain to you, however, that neither you nor Mr. Bond or the current directors of the bank or the holding company can serve as officers or directors of the new bank. This is in keeping with our policy." McCarthy fidgeted in his chair uncomfortably as he covered this last point.

"I am familiar with the policy," I acknowledged, as we moved toward the door. I looked him squarely in the eye, "Can you tell me who the new owner is?"

At the same time McCarthy told me who it was, I saw the new owner come around the corner from the elevator lobby toward my office. As Ron Steinhart approached me, my thoughts raced back to Tuesday, June

27, when he and I had met for lunch at the Melrose Hotel in Dallas. At the time, I didn't think he had a chance of emerging the winner, and I as much as told him so when I said, "I hope you haven't spent much money on this." Now I felt somewhat embarrassed, but I was pleased for Ron.

"Congratulations, Ron. You've won a hell of a franchise with a terrific group of employees!" I exclaimed sincerely. "Come on in."

Ron, along with Terry Kelley who had been Ron's partner in acquiring the ten or so failed banks that formed their company's base, followed me into my office and sat at the conference table.

Although Ron had to be bursting with pride and excitement, his demeanor was understated given the circumstances. I had always liked Ron, as he had never taken himself too seriously. He wasn't the least bit pretentious; in fact, he was the opposite of flashy, in his four-door Ford Taurus sedan. Even his wardrobe, like his car, was subdued.

Even though we knew each other well, I was sure that Ron felt tentative walking into the office of the CEO he was replacing. I was also sure he was sympathetic to my plight.

After exchanging the normal pleasantries, I said, "Ron, my hat's off to you; I really didn't think you had a chance. How did you do it?"

"They never could come to terms with Pohlad. And I suppose that neither the Security Pacific nor the Norwest bids were competitive. We began to feel as though we had a real chance about three weeks ago," he replied, as he nervously tapped his Cross pen on the table.

"What about NBC, what happens to them?" I asked worriedly.

"It's an 'open bank' deal, and it goes to Fellheimer. He apparently put an attractive deal on the table."

That's a hell-of-a note to end on, I thought to myself. There isn't a whit of difference between the two organizations, yet they get an "open bank" deal and we don't. It was the luck of the draw, the way the bids had fallen. Still, my heart went out to Richard Calvert and Mark Johnson. Fellheimer was supposed to be a wild man. TAB was better off, by far, with Steinhart.

"TAB is the winner in this deal," I said with a smile. "They are lucky to have you."

"Ron, whatever I can do to be helpful, I hope you'll call on me," I offered, as Libby interrupted to tell me that John Stone was on the phone.

Steinhart and Kelly stood up.

"We have to go anyhow. We have an officers' meeting to introduce the new management," Ron explained. I watched as he and Terry walked to the door and let themselves out, then I drew a deep breath and picked up the phone.

5:30 P.M. As I sat down behind my desk, I heard Stone say, "Jody, this is John Stone. I'm in San Antonio, but I wanted to call and explain what happened. We tried, but we couldn't do an 'open bank' deal. The merger won't work; we just didn't get an acceptable bid for both banks together."

"John, this is a terrible disappointment. We put everything we had, a year and a half of effort, into getting an 'open bank' deal. I can't help but feel like we have been had."

"We greatly appreciate your cooperation, as well as that of your whole team. We couldn't have asked for more. We considered you as part of the solution, not part of the problem. And I hope you understand our position with regard to you, Bond, and the directors. We have our rules, and we have to abide by them."

Stone's words seemed empty. I was bitter, and I didn't trust him or anyone else in the FDIC, which had demonstrated repeatedly that it would shift positions, repudiate previous commitments, and use whatever means available to accomplish its objective. To the agency, the end justified the means. Anything was legitimate. It really didn't matter who got run over or hurt in the process. The individuals involved would justify their actions based on FDIC policies, which were designed to remove the burden of responsibility. Neither the FDIC nor its operatives seemed to have a conscience.

In their handling of TAB's case, the FDIC's quest for the best deal, the accompanying delays and ineptness, had cost the taxpayers hundreds of millions of dollars.

Even though I felt anything but gracious, I forced myself to be polite to Stone. I knew I would have future dealings with him as I attempted to liquidate TAB's assets, and that I might need to call on him to explain my role at TAB to some prospective employer. I had learned long ago never to burn my bridges behind me, so, after a short conversation, I thanked him for his call.

5:45 P.M. No sooner had I hung up with Stone, than Bob Clarke, the comptroller of the currency, called.

"Jody, I'm sorry that it worked out this way. Your cooperation was outstanding. We just couldn't make it work, and believe me, we gave it every effort."

I did believe that Clarke had given it his every effort. He was a man of integrity, and I trusted him.

"Bob, I know you did everything that you could," I responded earnestly.

Clarke continued as if he had not yet gotten to the real purpose of his call. "You're familiar with our policies with regard to the treatment of executive officers and directors of failed banks. As much as we wanted to, we couldn't make an exception in your case. I'm sorry."

"Bob, I understand, and I know you wouldn't have called if you weren't genuinely concerned."

"Jody, you're not precluded from serving in the future in some other bank. I would be happy to talk to anyone on your behalf, or give you a letter of recommendation," he offered.

"I appreciate that very much, and I may very well need to take you up on it. Bob, your call is a bright spot in what otherwise is a dismal situation. Thanks!"

6:00 P.M. With confirmation of a closed bank from Stone, it was time to launch our defense. The war I had tried to avoid with the FDIC was about to begin. There would be no winners in this conflict; both TAB and the FDIC would be trying to cut their losses short. The FDIC's goal would be to protect the insurance fund, while I would be working for TAB's creditors, as I was sure there would be nothing left for the shareholders. I had already witnessed firsthand that the FDIC had no scruples. They would fight as dirty and as hard as they needed to in order to win. I would have to fight equally as hard for the creditors. It was clear to me that I was the only one who personally had anything at risk: any future I might have in banking.

As the sole officer still on TAB's payroll, I authorized our attorneys to activate our plans.

First, we dissolved the boards of directors of all of our banks so we could act without their approval and so they would have no liability with regard to any of the actions we were about to take.

Then, attorneys from Carrington, Coleman went into federal court in Fort Worth and in state courts in Hockley County (the domicile of TAB/Levelland) and in Tarrant County (the domicile of TAB/Greater Southwest) in an attempt to block the FDIC from seizing our solvent banks and commingling their assets with those of the other banks. We had to preserve the separateness of the solvent banks so they could be returned to TAB in the event we prevailed in the lawsuit.

6:30 P.M. Steinhart had told me during our brief visit that initially the bank would be called "Texas American Bridge Bank," and that he would be chairman and CEO and Terry Kelley would be president and chief operating officer. In addition, Steinhart would offer Buzz Brightbill, Gary

Cage, and Bob Herchert positions with his company, and I had already urged all of them to accept. One-by-one they now came in to tell me of their decision. Brightbill would be vice chairman of the bank (by virtue of the FDIC's action, all of TAB's former subsidiary banks became branches of the lead bank in Fort Worth); Cage would become chief financial officer of both the bank and Steinhart's holding company; and Herchert would assume a position in administration in the bank, presumably similar to the one he had with TAB.

I expressed my appreciation and wished each one well as he left my office. I tried to keep a stiff upper lip, but this was an emotional experience for me. These men had become like brothers to me. We had gone through so much together. I could hardly believe it was all over.

I now not only felt alone, I *was* alone, except for Libby, who stayed with me until 10:00 that night while I conferred with TAB's attorneys and talked to the press.

Libby had been my assistant for the last ten years, and there was always the presumption that she would stay with me regardless of what happened to TAB. As in the case of the other employees, though, I had transferred her employment to the bank. I now would have to ask Steinhart to let her work for me until TAB's affairs were settled and then return to the bank. I wanted to be sure that Libby ultimately had a job.

Although I was very sad, I felt a flicker of relief that it was finally over. All the TAB people could get on with their lives, the bank would once again be able to serve its customers, and funds should begin to flow back into Fort Worth and TAB's other markets to help finance the recovery.

After leaving the office, I joined Sheila and a few friends for a late meal. I greeted Sheila with a kiss and a hug; she had been my sanctuary during TAB's decline. Now we faced an unknown future together. I would have a job and income, as long as TAB was in bankruptcy, probably for six to nine months, after which I would be cut off. TAB had followed a long-standing policy of not having contracts with its employees, thus there was no "golden parachute," no severance payment, and no continuation of income. Because of my insider position as CEO, I had never sold any of the forty thousand shares of TAB stock I owned. Once valued at about $2 million, the shares were now worthless. Additionally, the real estate interests I owned in Texas and in New York City were of questionable value given the depressed real estate markets. All I had left was the debt incurred to purchase part of the stock and that associated with the real estate. The thought of what I faced following TAB's bankruptcy–no job, huge debts, and no financial reserves–was a scary prospect.

I spent most of Friday, July 21–my first day as a banker with no bank to manage–in conference with attorneys and responding to phone calls from shareholders, creditors, and the press.

As I walked into my home that night, the phone was ringing. It was Marvin Sloman and Peter Tierney from Carrington, Coleman, and Bruce Clark from Sullivan & Cromwell. A temporary restraining order (TRO) had been issued by Tarrant County District Judge Sidney Farrar, Jr., in response to the injunction we had sought. It prevented the FDIC from taking over TAB/Greater Southwest in Tarrant County until a hearing was held on July 31. Our attempts to block the seizure of the other eleven banks had been rejected.

In commenting on the TRO to the *Star-Telegram*, Judge Farrar said, "It was not an attempt to block the transfer; it was an effort to hold the status quo of the state-chartered bank and its assets, separate and apart, until they could determine the question of whether the bank was insolvent or not."[1]

After I had been brought up to date, Peter Tierney said, "The FDIC is playing hardball. They are threatening to close Greater Southwest and pay off the depositors unless we release the TRO."

Marvin Sloman added, "We can keep the injunction in place, but we don't think they are bluffing. The fear is that they will liquidate the bank, and, even though we will have won the battle, we will have lost the war. We will own a bank, but it will be closed and be worth nothing."

"In addition," I said, resigned to the inevitable, "the FDIC might decide not to honor deposits over $100,000 just to make it as onerous as possible. None of us want to have on our conscience the loss that those depositors would sustain. They have been faithful to TAB by keeping their money with us. As innocent bystanders, they would be the real victims."

"Jody, this is Bruce Clark. We recommend that we lift the TRO, but in return, we require the FDIC to agree not to commingle the assets of the twelve banks we believe are solvent."

"Bruce, do you think there is a chance they will agree to that?" I asked.

"We think there is a good chance," Bruce responded.

"They don't really want to close that bank," Marvin Sloman added.

"Okay, let's go for it. And, if they don't agree, I want to lift the TRO in any event; we're not going to let the depositors of the bank suffer."

Those instructions to TAB's attorneys constituted my last decision related to any of TAB's banks. The TRO was lifted, and the FDIC agreed not to commingle assets until the courts reached a decision concerning the solvency of the twelve banks in question.

TAB in Bankruptcy

Reorganization under Chapter 11 of the U.S. Bankruptcy Code was chosen by the company, rather than liquidation under Chapter 7, so management and directors could stay in control until a future course of action could be determined. Privately, I had concluded that liquidation was the only likely outcome.

In its filing, TAB listed total assets of $55,029,000 and liabilities of $108,866,000. The most valuable asset was Texas American Services, Inc. (TASI), TAB's data processing and bank operations subsidiary, which Touche Ross had valued at $40 million to $50 million.

TASI's only customer, and only source of revenue, was the bank consisting of the old TAB banks. Conversely, the bank was totally dependent on TASI for its operations and bookkeeping. The FDIC had an agreement with Steinhart to provide the funds to purchase TASI, which meant they would have to approve the terms of the purchase. John Stone had already gone on record with Christie Sciacca that the FDIC believed TASI to be worth only $5 million to $10 million, and anything above that amount they would consider hostage money. I could envision that we were headed for a standoff with Steinhart and the FDIC over the disposition of the company.

It wasn't until the first meeting of the creditors' committee on October 11, 1989, that I came to fully appreciate the problems I would have with the committee over the sale of TASI. In assessing the value of TASI, I said, "I believe $20 million is a slam-dunk, $25 million is possible, and $30 million would be an absolute home run."

In response, Martin "Marty" Bienenstock of the New York law firm Weil, Gotshal & Manges, legal counsel for the creditors' committee, went into a tirade. Yelling loudly and almost out of control, he shouted, "We want to hold up the FDIC–we want an obscene price for TASI. We don't want $30 million–we want $80 million and not a penny less. The FDIC screwed us and we want to screw them. If they don't pay the price, we'll turn off the electricity."

I knew where Bienenstock was coming from; $80 million was the price that was needed to enable TAB to fully extinguish its liabilities, that is, for the creditors to realize 100 percent of the amount owed them. But $80 million was impossible. Marty didn't know the FDIC as I did.

Finally, after two months of negotiations, considerable fencing with the creditors' committee, and behind-the-scenes negotiations between Rodgin Cohen and the FDIC, a deal was struck. The FDIC agreed to a price of $30 million. Additionally, the FDIC agreed to drop any claims against TAB and its subsidiaries, and TAB agreed to drop any claims against the FDIC and to seek a maximum of $5 million in its lawsuit against the FDIC for seizing its solvent banks.

A unique aspect of the settlement was the FDIC's release of all officers and directors of TAB and its subsidiaries of any claim (except in the case of criminal violations, debts owed and evidenced by promissory notes, and those claims that would lead to recovery under TAB's officers' and directors' liability insurance). To my knowledge, this is the only case in which the FDIC or any other regulatory agency has given such a release to the officers and directors of a failed institution.

On June 26, 1990, TAB's bankruptcy ended with the distribution of its cash assets to the creditors and its noncash assets to a liquidating trust for their benefit. They were expected to ultimately receive about $.50 on the dollar.

While I was saddened to preside over the final liquidation of the company, I was pleased with the resulting return to the creditors. More than that, though, I had accomplished my most important objective during bankruptcy: protecting the jobs of approximately six hundred TASI employees.

Although the TAB saga was finished, at the time I had no way of knowing the importance the sale of TASI and the accompanying waivers would have on events that would occur over two years later.

SEVENTEEN 17

POSTMORTEM

Five years have passed since the closing and seizure of TAB's banks. Texas is returning to normal after its long struggle, although the definition of normal is different than it used to be.

The real estate crash that began in Texas spread over the rest of the country, like a plague, from region to region, leaving the carcasses of failed or restructured banks, savings banks, and S&Ls in its wake. No area of the country fully escaped, although no other state suffered as Texas did. No other state lost 506 banks due to failure between 1983 and 1992, which was 36 percent of all failures in the nation during that period. No other state lost 225 S&Ls, or 82 percent, of the total S&Ls in existence as of December 31, 1987. Nor did any other state lose nine of its ten largest banks either due to failure or to acquisition by an out-of-state financial institution.

An unusual confluence of events and circumstances, unprecedented in the history of Texas or of any other state or region in the country, propelled Texas into economic free-fall. The protracted recession in the oil industry beginning in 1981, and the virtual collapse in oil prices in the first quarter of 1986, left the oil-dependent Texas economy in shambles. The financial redlining of Texas in 1986 by the rest of the country, and indeed by the rest of the world, exacerbated the situation, leaving Texas's bloated financial institutions starved for liquidity. The Tax Reform Act of 1986, passed in August, was the final blow for many of the Texas banks and S&Ls. Already weak and vulnerable from five years of economic battering, they could not endure the ensuing 30 to 40 percent devaluation of real estate values. The carnage was devastating. Not even the Great Depression produced such a disastrous effect in Texas, as the major Texas banks that succumbed in the 1980s had managed to survive through the depression.

Texas was, indeed, unique. No other state was as dependent on oil, and none suffered from such a severe recession. As a consequence, what happened in Texas did not occur elsewhere. The full impact of the Tax Reform Act of 1986 was felt first in Texas, and it was several years before its reverberations rolled up the East Coast and then down into Florida; it was not until 1992 that the full impact was felt in California. By then, federal examiners had adopted much more lenient standards than those used to judge the Texas banks.

Although the Texas banking crash was caused largely by economic forces, the remedy was planned and executed by the FDIC under the direction of its chairman, L. William Seidman. As a result, the financial landscape of Texas was permanently and indelibly changed. The FDIC's policies and decisions left the state without a viable major banking organization that was locally based and managed. Additionally, the failure of the FDIC to move swiftly to address all the needs of the state crippled the state's recovery and left its businesses and individuals without adequate banking services.

TAB and NBC were among the most notable casualties. I'm still trying to put together the pieces of the TAB/NBC saga, but I realize that the full story may never be revealed because of the cloak of secrecy under which the FDIC operates. However, five years of research, including interviews with those involved and information not previously available, has led to some conclusions. With the clarity of twenty-twenty hindsight, it is now easy to see that the cards were stacked against TAB in its effort to get an "open bank" transaction.

Aftermath

WHAT HAPPENED?

In the first place, the interminable delays by the FDIC pushed TAB's banks into insolvency, making it politically difficult for the FDIC to justify an "open bank" transaction.

The FDIC's avowed motive in wanting an "open bank" solution was to avoid the costly consequences to the insurance fund of a bank failure. They believed that by addressing a situation early and avoiding a failure, perhaps hundreds of millions, if not billions, of dollars could be saved. History has shown this assessment to be correct, as evidenced by the extremely successful 1984 early "open bank" bailout of Chicago's Continental Bank. Conversely, it is now widely recognized that the practice of keeping banks open long after they are known to be insolvent increases the ultimate cost to the insurance fund. This was vividly demonstrated during 1985–1989 when this practice, known as "forbearance," was followed widely by the FHLB board in its handling of the S&L crisis.

In TAB's case, time was most assuredly the company's worst enemy: the longer it took to apply a tourniquet to TAB's gaping wounds, the greater the deterioration, the greater the ultimate cost to the FDIC, and the less likely the chance of an "open bank" resolution.

Yet, as we were to discover, under the best of circumstances the process of steering a proposal through the bureaucratic maze of the FDIC was itself lengthy and difficult, which augured against a timely conclusion. And the circumstances were far from ideal during the time when TAB and NBC were involved with the FDIC. Internal politics and power struggles within the FDIC; the changes from Poling to Roelle and finally to Stone; the furor over the costly 1988 year-end bailouts of the S&Ls under the Southwest Plan; the preoccupation of the FDIC board with the larger problems of First Republic and MCorp; and Seidman's power grab for FDIC jurisdiction over the S&Ls, all created unnecessary and costly delays.

Additionally, the FDIC had no sense of urgency to bring closure to the negotiations as long as the companies had no funding problems. In the cases of First Republic and MCorp, a funding crisis had precipitated FDIC intervention. In the cases of TAB and NBC, in the absence of a similar crisis, the FDIC was content to let the companies twist in the wind. It is ironic that short-term funding crises prompted the FDIC to action, while chronic, debilitating franchise deterioration, which drastically deepened the FDIC's losses, elicited no response.

It is also true that, as more time elapsed and TAB slipped closer toward insolvency, the more difficulty the FDIC had in justifying an "open bank" deal. As long as there was shareholders' equity on the books, the FDIC could rationalize giving the shareholders an equity stake in the restructured organization. But, in the case of an insolvent institution, when could such an action be justified? Could it be justified based upon extraordinary cooperation of the bank's officers and directors? The deeper the red ink, the more difficult it would be to sustain this argument.

Second, there was a hardcore nucleus at the staff level within the FDIC that strongly favored "closed bank" resolutions. This sentiment gained momentum with the successful "bridging" of First Republic.

We were concerned when we learned several months into the process that some of the FDIC staff had developed a strong preference for "closed bank" solutions, which they regarded as generally the lowest-cost alternative. In mid-1988, the FDIC had rejected the "open bank" proposal of Al Casey for First Republic in favor of the "closed bank" purchase by NCNB (NationsBank). However, we had believed that there were special circumstances in the First Republic deal; namely, they had not "come in early," and they were suspected of having covered up their problems.

We were even more disturbed, however, by Christie Sciacca's report in January 1989 that there had been a power struggle within the FDIC between the proponents of the "come in early, 'open bank' assistance" approach and the "closed bank, we'll deal with you when you're dead" philosophy. In the cases of First Republic, MCorp, and TAB, the "when you're dead" proponents prevailed.

It is now quite apparent that the FDIC had been considering a "closed bank" transaction as early as fall 1988, eight months into our eighteen-month ordeal, if not earlier. Approximately a year after TAB's banks were seized, I learned from the transcripts of FDIC proceedings obtained by MCorp's attorneys through legal discovery that, in a meeting of the FDIC board of directors on October 25, 1988, Bill Roelle advised the board that "assuming a 70 percent valuation of the Fed funds sold . . . we would grab a great number . . . in terms . . . of failures . . . of the subsidiary banks in both TAB and MBank."[1]

In other words, if the FDIC devalued by 30 percent the federal funds sold by the lead banks of each organization to the subsidiary banks, it would cause most of the subsidiaries to fail (twelve MCorp banks and twelve TAB banks actually were rendered insolvent in this manner). From the transcripts, it is evident that the FDIC had calculated the amount required to cause the failures and was seriously considering such an option. By grabbing as many of the banks as possible, they would be able to command higher prices for the franchises from prospective bidders.

Third, the character of the transaction and the negotiations changed with the entry of John Stone.

John Stone had his own agenda, a preferred structure incorporating a "collecting bank" or "bad bank" concept, similar to the one he used in the Abboud/First City transaction, which changed the capital requirement for TAB/NBC from $200 million to $300 million, putting the merger proposal beyond the reach of private investors. Thus, if neither Security Pacific nor Norwest/Pohlad made an acceptable bid, there was no alternative except to abandon the merger. Additionally, abandoning the merger wasn't as difficult for Stone, since he hadn't been involved in the original negotiations and was not committed to the concept.

Had Stan Poling stayed with the process, our chances of getting an "open bank" deal probably would have been higher.

Fourth, the FDIC's strong belief that management and shareholders should be penalized–in accordance with the policy statement on "open bank" assistance–made it extremely difficult for the FDIC to grant exceptions. In the case of an insolvent bank, there was a strong motivation to affect a "closed bank" transaction.

The FDIC board of directors had problems from the outset with granting an exception to their "open bank" policy statement of December 8, 1986. Although they agreed to concessions–specifically allowing shareholders to retain an equity interest in the restructured bank–they did so reluctantly and probably never fully embraced the concept. Although they agreed to allow directors and officers to continue with the restructured institution, they were not specific with regard to the details. Bill Isaac believed that it would have been a tactical error for us to have pressed this politically sensitive issue until the financial terms of a deal were agreed upon. Since the continuance of directors and officers was a secondary issue, we were content to follow Isaac's advice.

With my present perspective, after having carefully examined the record of TAB's experience with the FDIC, we should have recognized that a "closed bank" transaction was a strong possibility. Stone articulated the governing criteria in our first conversation on February 8, 1989, when he reminded me that, in an "open bank" transaction, shareholders should get no more than if their bank were allowed to fail. When TAB and its major banks actually became insolvent on March 31, 1989, the die was probably cast.

Shortly thereafter, when the TAB and NBC directors were told during the meeting of March 3 with Seidman that the FDIC examination of our banks was necessary in order to evaluate the assets for a "closed bank" scenario, we should have gotten the message. But we had hoped that in return for coming in early, we would be treated fairly, as they had promised.

Finally, the FDIC's ability to seize all of TAB's banks due to their linkage through federal fund sales to TAB/Fort Worth provided a powerful and irresistible incentive to do a "closed bank" transaction.

The respective internal-plumbing circumstances encouraged an "open bank" solution with NBC, but discouraged the same with TAB. NBC was able to avoid a "closed bank" outcome because three of their subsidiary banks were disconnected, in that they had no federal funds sold from any of their three solvent banks to their insolvent banks. In the final analysis, it is likely that the ability to declare all of TAB's banks insolvent, thus keeping the entire franchise intact for sale, was compelling. There was no incentive for the FDIC to ask for "open bank" bids on a stand-alone basis for TAB from Norwest/Pohlad or from Security Pacific when they had Steinhart's "closed bank" bid on the table. As it was, the bids for TAB/NBC from Norwest/Pohlad and from Security Pacific were for both banks, and there was no way for the FDIC to allocate portions of each bid to the individual franchises.

From a fiduciary point of view, we were obliged to do everything possible to obtain an "open bank" solution. Now, I realize that we should have unhooked our internal plumbing to free up as many banks as possible. But, at the time, we were convinced that had we initiated such action the FDIC would have moved on us precipitously, creating a "bridge bank" in a "closed bank" transaction, as they had in the case of MCorp.

We now know that we should have taken that chance, given the ultimate outcome.

HOW DID STEINHART AND FELLHEIMER WIN?

One of the most puzzling aspects of the case is how Fellheimer and Steinhart won. By any standard, they were both long shots, with relatively small banking franchises behind them–in Steinhart's case, a fledgling combination of small failed banks–pitted against banking giants Norwest/Pohlad and Security Pacific. It was a shocking, unbelievable, and incomprehensible decision: no one could understand how this happened or the FDIC's rationale.

Given how well Pohlad knew the companies, and given the amount of due diligence Norwest and Pohlad did independently and collectively, they should have had the inside track. The informed assessment of those associated with the transaction, including principals and advisors, was that Pohlad just negotiated too hard. With the FDIC just as determined to strike the best deal possible for the insurance fund, they were just as intransigent. An indication of the tough negotiating climate and the impasse they reached was conveyed by Seidman in the March 3, 1989, meeting with the company's representatives, when he said, "I've been talking to Carl Pohlad, who just finished telling me how disappointed he was with me and the FDIC, and I told him how disappointed I was with him." By then, the two sides were hopelessly deadlocked.

What happened to Security Pacific's bid? Bill Isaac, who represented Security Pacific in a consulting capacity with regard to other transactions, was told by Security Pacific CEO Bob Smith that they just had not been aggressive enough in their bid. We should have anticipated this, since at the outset they had wanted to bid on a "closed bank" basis. Isaac talked them out of that approach by convincing them that the FDIC would be more favorably disposed to an "open bank" transaction.

At the time, I believed that Security Pacific would be the winner. They wanted to be in Texas, and TAB/NBC was essentially the only viable acquisition available. Additionally, as the nation's fifth-largest bank, with $77.9 billion in assets, Security Pacific had the capacity to be the most aggressive bidder. The dilution they might have taken on TAB/NBC, with aggregate assets of about $7 billion, wouldn't have been significant. In the final analysis, however, they were just too conservative.

Most likely, Fellheimer represented the fly in the ointment. Richard Calvert and Mark Johnson reported that Fellheimer put a "hell-of-a deal" on the table for NBC, which was verified by Christie Sciacca through his sources at the FDIC. In a meeting with me on August 23, 1989, Fellheimer disclosed that the FDIC had picked his bid to purchase NBC three weeks before the transaction occurred on July 20. This coincides with Steinhart's comment that he began to feel he had a chance to win about three weeks before TAB was bridged. In retrospect, it is now clear that the FDIC began to negotiate in earnest with Steinhart when they decided they wanted to choose Fellheimer for NBC and realized that Steinhart was the only alternative for TAB, since he had submitted the only bid.

Even though he had the only bid on the table, Steinhart still had to pass muster with the FDIC. This was achieved with the assistance of Robert S. Strauss. Strauss, former ambassador to Russia, former special trade representative during President Jimmy Carter's administration, and past national chairman of the Democratic Party, is acknowledged to be one of the most effective lobbyists in either party. His influence crosses partisan lines, as evidenced by his appointment to Moscow by President Bush. Steinhart and Strauss were extremely close: when Strauss went into government service, he turned over his business affairs to Steinhart. Strauss, his son, and his law firm were all investors in Steinhart's company when it won the bid for TAB. Informed sources believe that it was Strauss who won the day for Steinhart.

It has been suggested that Strauss may even have gone all the way to the White House. However, even if he didn't intervene personally, just having his name associated with the bid would have swayed the decision makers. In the opinion of many, Strauss, at the time, was the most powerful man in Washington, next to the president.

THE FDIC VERSUS TAB AND MCORP

In court action following the lawsuit filed by TAB against federal regulators, U.S. District Judge Robert "Barefoot" Sanders for the Northern District of Texas ruled on June 25, 1990, that the FDIC illegally provoked the failure of twelve solvent TAB banks in trying to limit its cost.[2] In ruling in TAB's favor, Judge Sanders found that the FDIC illegally paid off all outside creditors of TAB/Fort Worth one hundred cents on the dollar, while it repaid otherwise solvent TAB subsidiary banks only a portion of what they were owed. As a result, a loss was sustained on the books of those banks, wiping out their capital and rendering them insolvent.

Judge Sanders's ruling supported a preliminary opinion rendered on September 7, 1989, by U.S. District Judge Robert Porter in the MCorp case. Judge Porter ruled that the FDIC had violated federal banking laws when it seized MBank Dallas and subsequently refused to return $17 million to MBank New Braunfels, which MBank New Braunfels had loaned to the Dallas bank in the form of overnight federal funds.[3]

In his ruling, Judge Sanders was particularly critical of the FDIC's apparent disregard for fairness and of its abuse of power. He stated:

> The closure and sale of solvent banks through arbitrary devaluation of their assets in another bank cannot be fair. . . . The facts of this case indicate an . . . egregious use of the FDIC's extensive (but not unlimited) powers by manipulating the recovery of affiliated banks on the obligations owed to them in order to make those banks insolvent as well.[4]

The National Bank Act of 1864 requires the OCC and the FDIC, as receiver, to distribute an insolvent bank's assets on a pro rata basis to all unsecured creditors. Although the FDIC had previously challenged the law in 1978 in First Empire and had lost, they repeatedly ignored the law during the Texas banking crisis. In assessing the FDIC's actions, Judge Sanders wrote: "The appearance of impropriety, whether real or not, in the FDIC/Receiver and the FDIC/Corporate deciding who gets how much, is quite worrisome, especially in light of the fiduciary duty owed by a receiver to the creditors."[5]

In a ruling issued on February 27, 1992, the Fifth Circuit Court of Appeals in New Orleans reversed Judge Sanders's opinion.[6] The Fifth Circuit said that the district court failed to consider that TAB/Fort Worth could not have repaid the solvent banks without the $900 million that the FDIC injected into the bank. Had the solvent banks received a distribution only from the assets of the failed bank, they would have received no more than 67 percent of their claims. Thus, the court found that TAB's solvent banks did receive a ratable distribution.

The trustee of TAB in liquidation decided not to appeal the Fifth Circuit's decision in view of the cost to pursue such action versus the $5 million maximum award of damages to which TAB had agreed.

TAB's attorneys did not have an opportunity to present a rebuttal to the Fifth Circuit's contention that TAB couldn't have repaid its federal funds from its borrowing banks without the injection of the aforementioned $900 million from the FDIC. However, if the decision had been appealed to the Supreme Court, TAB's attorneys would have maintained, among other arguments, that the FDIC's injection of funds was to restore capital, not liquidity. At the time of its closing on July 20, 1989, TAB had sufficient liquidity to repay in full the federal funds borrowings from some of its solvent banks.

In fall 1993, MCorp, its senior creditors, and the FDIC entered into a settlement in which MCorp would pay the FDIC $30 million. In a separate agreement, concluded in August 1993, the carriers of MCorp's directors' and officers' liability insurance agreed to pay the FDIC $39.2 million. Additionally, the parties to both settlements released each other from all claims and counterclaims.[7] Consequently, the question of whether or not the FDIC illegally seized MCorp's banks will never be addressed or resolved in the courts.

In a subsequent development, however, a federal judge rendered a decision that makes future challenges of FDIC actions much more likely. In the case of Dr. Ben Branch (trustee of the Bank of New England Corporation) versus the United States, Court of Federal Claims Judge Christine Cook Nettesheim ruled that the FDIC cannot seize a healthy affiliate of a failed bank if the healthy bank operated independently.[8] This ruling effectively invalidates the provision under the 1989 Financial Institutions Reform, Recovery, and Enforcement Act (FIRREA) that enables the FDIC to collect damages from commonly controlled institutions under cross-guarantee provisions. In ruling that the provision violates the Fifth

Amendment to the U.S. Constitution, Judge Nettesheim acknowledged the need to protect the insurance fund, but said, "Nonetheless, Congress may not remedy the problems now confronting the federal banking system by placing the financial burden on the back of innocents."[9]

The case involved the 1991 failure of Bank of New England, which in 1985 had acquired Maine National Bank. Upon the failure of Bank of New England, the FDIC presented a bill for $1 billion under the cross-guarantee statute to Maine National Bank, which had operated independently and profitably throughout. With an equity of $65 million, Maine National couldn't pay and was taken over by the FDIC.

If Judge Nettesheim's ruling is upheld, future cases will test the 1978 First Empire precedent and the Fifth Circuit Court of Appeals ruling of February 27, 1992, overturning Judge Barefoot Sanders's opinion that the FDIC's seizure of TAB's solvent banks did not violate the principle of ratable distribution, as established by the National Bank Act and upheld in First Empire.

EIGHTEEN

REFLECTIONS

Five years after the seizure of TAB, as I reflected on the experiences of TAB and NBC and the rest of the major Texas holding companies, I achieved a much greater understanding of the situation that brought about their downfall.

The forces that precipitated the financial collapse of Texas's major banks could not have been predicted, or probably avoided. What happened was inconceivable. The state, and its bankers, were blindsided and caught totally unprepared. As a result, no one took precautions to prevent it or made preparations to weather it. In reality, though, there was little that could have been done given the depth of the real estate devaluation. In fact, there are few banks in the country that could have survived the 40 percent devaluation in their real estate loan portfolio, which the Texas banks experienced.

MANY LEGITIMATE QUESTIONS EXIST CONCERNING THE TEXAS BANKING CRASH

Why didn't we see it coming?

In the first place, the problems with the Texas economy had emanated from the decline in oil and gas prices beginning in 1981 and were mostly isolated to that industry and to the communities that it heavily influenced: Houston, Midland, Odessa, and the smaller cities in the "oil patch." This seemed far removed from Dallas and Fort Worth, where TAB's banks and assets were concentrated. The general attitude in Dallas and Fort Worth was that we were essentially immune to the problem. It took the crash in oil prices in the first quarter of 1986, and the passage in August of the Tax Reform Act of 1986, to bring the crisis to North Texas.

Second, no one anticipated the crash in oil prices in 1986, which took the price per barrel from over $30 to under $10 in about ninety days, or the profound impact it would have on the entire economy. Nor did anyone foresee the passage of the Tax Reform Act of 1986, which sealed the fate of the Texas real estate economy.

And even if we had anticipated these events, I don't believe there would have been a general recognition of the extent to which the real estate markets would be impacted. Certainly, as events later revealed, lenders in the rest of the country largely ignored the potential impact of the Tax Reform Act. They continued to make real estate loans long after Texas had quit, even with the Texas disaster being played out before their eyes. The disastrous consequence of the reform act was to discourage investment at a time when the Texas markets were starved for funds. The depreciation in real estate values vastly accelerated after its passage.

Third, the flight of funds from the state and the redlining of Texas by the rest of the world, following the 1986 oil price crash, came as a shock. Funds were so plentiful that it was unthinkable that they could disappear, literally within a matter of days. Sources of funds within Texas also evaporated, partially out of shock over the withdrawal of funds from external sources and partially due to the attitude of the regulators. In 1986 and 1987, the banking and the thrift regulators had made it very clear that they would severely criticize any institution in the Southwest that made additional commitments to real estate. Lenders, understandably, had a knee-jerk reaction to this heavy-handed approach.

Finally, the general attitude that Texas and its economy were largely invincible prevailed until 1986. This was a product of Texas heritage, the oil and gas boom, and the inflation of the 1970s and the early 1980s. No one believed that a depression of such magnitude was possible.

Why didn't the abuses and the aggressive, if not irresponsible, lending by the S&Ls provide a clue to what might follow?

Historically, the S&L industry had not been a significant competitor in the eyes of Texas bankers. The advantages they enjoyed were well recognized: they could branch, and banks could not; they could pay higher rates on savings than banks; and, as savings institutions, they had a more stable source of funds than banks to make home mortgages. As a result, Texas banks didn't compete aggressively in these segments of the market.

Additionally, there were no S&Ls of significant size in Texas to pose a threat to the larger banks. The largest S&L was First Gibraltar with assets of about $6 billion compared to First RepublicBankCorporation, the largest banking organization, with $36 billion in assets. Consequently, the S&Ls were largely ignored.

The abuses and aggressive lending of the S&Ls weren't widely known until after 1985. There were isolated cases of abuse but they were believed to be extraordinary, and not an indicator of the extent of a widespread problem or of a bankrupt industry. That there were a total of only twelve S&L failures during 1982–1985 in Texas corroborates this notion. It is true that in 1986 and 1987, when the Federal Home Loan Bank board's practice of forbearance vastly understated thrift failures (there were two in 1986 and four in 1987), the extent of the S&L problem was becoming evident. By then, however, it was too late, as the damage to the Texas commercial banks had already occurred. The magnitude of the S&L problem and its impact on Texas real estate just wasn't contemplated.

In this environment, we believed TAB was taking acceptable risks in its approach to real estate lending. Not until years later would we be aware of the many circumstances that came together to produce the biggest real estate debacle in the history of Texas and the U.S.

So who was to blame?

Whereas, in the S&L crisis, there was plenty of blame to go around, such was not the case in the Texas banking crisis. With the exception of only a few minor incidents, there was no fraud, no insider dealing, no personal gain on the part of the bankers involved. To the contrary, the banking crisis was a personal tragedy to the insiders. In many instances, their personal finances and net worths were decimated and their careers ruined or, at best, put on hold.

Was management culpable? There is no doubt that bankers in Texas were blinded by the prosperity and the overly optimistic outlook for the future. However, the loans they made were extended in good faith in response to the perceived needs of the borrowers and of the communities they served. The concentration in real estate loans at 35 percent to 45 percent at the Texas banks seems high when looked at in isolation. However, when compared to December 31, 1991, concentrations in banks in the growth states of California and Florida–in California, 59 percent at Wells Fargo, 43 percent at Bank of America, and 39 percent at First Interstate, and, in Florida, 56 percent at Barnett Banks and 48 percent at SunTrust–the Texas percentages seem more reasonable.[1]

Once the loans were on the books in the Texas banks, management did the best job they could under the most difficult circumstances, as they helplessly watched the relentless and precipitous depreciation of their loan portfolios. As far as I am aware, without exception, they worked tirelessly in an attempt to save the institutions they had helped build.

Certainly, these individuals had significant incentive, since not only were they dependent on their banks for their income, but many had substantially all of their net worth tied up in stock in their banks. Many of the senior managers had sold their community banks for stock in the holding companies that later were among the most troubled. The stakes were, indeed, extremely high for most of the Texas bankers.

These bankers, accused by some of being negligent, were the same individuals who were the envy of the banking world in the early 1980s, when the Texas banks defined the meaning of high performance. They were held in the highest esteem by their peers, as evidenced by the election of Charles Pistor, vice chairman of First Republic, as chairman in 1988 of the American Bankers Association (ABA), the highest post in the industry. Many other executives held high leadership positions in the ABA and in the prestigious Association of Reserve City Bankers (now known as Bankers' Roundtable), of which both Ben Love of Texas Commerce and Robert H. Stewart III of InterFirst had served as president.

Did the skill and good judgment possessed by these executives evaporate overnight?

It is extremely unlikely that nine of the ten largest banks in Texas were all mismanaged. The fact that they either failed or were restructured through merger is conclusive evidence that the cause of the banking crisis in Texas was economic, not the result of bad management. Mismanagement is a random event: these failures and restructurings were not random, as all nine banks were involved.

What happened to the ninth-largest banking company, Cullen/Frost Bankers of San Antonio? Were they smarter than everyone else? Not necessarily. Cullen/Frost had been a relatively large oil lender and had suffered from severe loan problems beginning in 1983, when they sustained an annual loss of $23 million. Also in 1983, the company entered into a merger agreement with First City Bancorporation of Houston. As a consequence, during 1983–1985, Cullen/Frost was preoccupied cleaning up oil lending problems and dressing the bank up for the pending merger. Thus, while the other major Texas banks were actively booking real estate loans during 1983–1985, Cullen/Frost was on the sidelines. As it developed, it was an extremely opportune time not to be making real estate loans. Subsequently, the merger was called off because of First City's troubles, but the timing of these events probably saved Cullen/Frost.

Who, then, was at fault? In response to a report released by the House Banking Committee criticizing federal regulators for their handling of the MCorp failure, the Office of the Comptroller of the Currency said the "fundamental cause of the bank's failure" was "the drop in oil prices and the crash in the Texas real estate market. When the bottom dropped out of Texas real estate in 1985, [MCorp's] fate was sealed."[2] What was true of MCorp was also true of TAB and of the rest of the Texas banks that either failed or were restructured.

It is generally acknowledged that the real estate depression was attributed to the deregulation of the S&L industry and to the passage of the Tax Reform Act of 1986, both of which must be laid at the doorstep of Congress. Additionally, many analysts and politicians believe that federal and state regulators must share the blame for the commercial banking crisis. The OCC in particular is accused of having been too lax in examinations in the 1970s and early 1980s, which encouraged loose and aggressive banking practices, and of being too harsh in their approach thereafter, which created tight liquidity and credit conditions and pushed some banks into insolvency. Both practices contributed to the large number of bank failures in the 1980s.

Some banking pundits place the blame more directly on Congress, but Congress of an earlier generation–the Congress that passed federal deposit insurance in 1933. The theory is that deposit insurance encourages loose banking practices by not placing the full burden of accountability on bankers for their actions. The insurance cushions the fall by reimbursing depositors, who otherwise would demand responsibility and accountability. Although the logic of this theory is appealing, it ignores the virtue of deposit insurance, which fosters confidence and stability in the banking system.

It is further argued that successive increases in the amount of the coverage to the $100,000 level enabled financial institutions to raise huge sums of money to fund their growth and to fuel the escalation in real estate prices. This is a valid argument, but it was also the $100,000 coverage that allowed TAB, NBC, and other troubled Texas banks to launch and operate "spread" CD programs, which provided liquidity while they worked with the FDIC to resolve their problems.

Another factor that contributed to the severity of the commercial banking crisis in Texas was the state's unit banking structure. The concept of unit banking had been a time-honored tradition in Texas, dating back to the Texas Constitution of 1876. Although, in an effort to ameliorate the banking crisis, branching became permissible in 1987, it was too late to allow the major banks to diversify their portfolios. Under unit banking, they forfeited the consumer banking business to the more convenient suburban banks and the home mortgage business to the S&Ls, which had unlimited branching powers. Instead, the banks filled their portfolios with business, oil and gas, and real estate loans. The lack of diversification in the major bank portfolios set them up for failure.

Finally, the losses to the FSLIC and the FDIC insurance funds were exacerbated, the demise of some of the thrifts and banks was accelerated, and the weakening of others was worsened by the FHLB's practice of forbearance and by the FDIC's 100 percent guarantee of deposits over $100,000 at some banks. The insolvent thrifts, well known to the depositing public, had to pay an average premium for their deposits of nearly 1 percent over the national average, thereby deepening their losses. To counter the competition of the insolvent thrifts and the unlimited FDIC guarantee of deposits at some banks, healthy institutions were forced to pay higher rates than otherwise would have been necessary, at a cost of millions of dollars. The resultant higher available rates, which became pervasive in Texas, became known as the "Texas Premium." This is another example of well-intentioned government practices that deepened the crisis and penalized solvent institutions.

MANY QUESTIONS ALSO EXIST CONCERNING THE TAB CASE IN PARTICULAR

Would TAB have failed had it not gone voluntarily to the FDIC for assistance?

That question is, of course, problematical. Shortly after the banks were seized, I would have said, given the regulatory environment and the collapse of the Texas real estate markets, TAB's failure was inevitable. However, from today's perspective, I'm not so certain.

On March 23, 1992, just thirty-two short months after the bailout and after TAB became Team Bank, Ron Steinhart announced that Team Bank would be sold to Banc One Corporation in an exchange of stock valued at $782 million. The price tag, a hefty 22 times Team Bank's 1991 earnings and 2.4 times its book value, provided the investors with a $522 million profit, or a return on investment of over 200 percent.[3]

The sale of Team Bank validates the intrinsic value of the TAB franchise, which I believe was well recognized by the investment community and the existing TAB shareholders. Consequently, had we been able to stop the bleeding and stabilize the company, I believe that we could have raised additional capital through a rights offering to shareholders. Additionally, there is a possibility that, had we taken a different course, we could have persuaded the bondholders to exchange their debt for equity, with the concession that the original shareholders would have been significantly diluted.

Could TAB have been stabilized? Had we not been in the hands of the FDIC, I don't believe that the OCC's examination in the second quarter of 1988, which produced additions to the loan loss reserve of $195 million, would have been nearly so severe. Nor would we have suffered the mark-to-market due diligence of August 1988, which took another $216 million of value out of the company.

The true value of TAB's assets will never be known. In the "fire sale" environment that we were in, and with the mark-to-market due diligence and the FDIC's philosophy of dumping real estate, value realization at rock-bottom prices became self-fulfilling. Under a different approach, I believe, the devaluation of assets would have been far less.

Admittedly, saving TAB would have required impeccable timing, major concessions from creditors, the courage of David facing Goliath on the part of the existing shareholders, and the luck of the Irish. But it still might have been possible.

However, in my estimation, it would have taken six to eight years to resurrect the company, during which TAB would have been an ineffective competitor, giving up ground to its peers. We would have lost so much momentum that it is questionable we would have had a viable company in the final analysis.

Although we didn't realize it at the time, the course we took of putting TAB in the hands of the FDIC determined TAB's destiny. We had taken a calculated risk by going to the FDIC in hopes of obtaining "open bank" assistance with concessions, thereby salvaging some value for our shareholders. Instead, we were subjected to federal examination after federal examination, and to repeated due diligence, during which TAB's assets were hammered to liquidation values. Additionally, the long delay by the FDIC in resolving the TAB situation caused extensive deterioration in its franchise and in its value.

In retrospect, we had no better alternative in 1988 when the decision was made to seek an FDIC-assisted merger between TAB and NBC. However, if we had known then what we know today, clearly we would have been better advised to stay on our independent course and fight for survival.

How much did the FDIC's blunders contribute to the cost of the bailout?

In a meeting in the Washington offices of the FDIC on August 19, 1992, between representatives of TAB and representatives of the FDIC, Bill Isaac stated that, in his opinion, delays and mismanagement by the FDIC in the TAB case increased the company's losses by "at least $500 million." Whether or not Isaac's estimate is close to being correct, once in the hands of the FDIC, hundreds of millions of dollars were stripped from the value of TAB's assets.

Was the "closed bank" transaction the least costly alternative?

In light of subsequent events, there is no question that "open bank" assistance, with the FDIC retaining some ownership, would have been by far the least costly alternative.

The FDIC had left themselves with no option other than Steinhart's, which points out another blunder: they should have instructed the bidders to submit open or closed bids, or both, for the individual organizations, as well as for the combination.

By not doing so, the FDIC incurred a tremendous opportunity cost. They deprived themselves, and thus the taxpayers, of participating in the $522 million gain from the sale of Team Bank to Banc One Corporation.

Further, had the FDIC done a Continental-type transaction, where the agency retained most of the ownership–and, accordingly, most of the profit potential–it could have recovered much of the $1.04 billion estimated cost of the TAB bailout through the ultimate sale of its interest.

Even the most amateur analysts were aware of the intrinsic value of the TAB and NBC franchises separately, and further knew that the combination multiplied that value. Recognition of that franchise potential is why the FDIC was intrigued with the idea of assisting the merger in the first place.

The FDIC left billions of dollars on the table in the form of lost opportunities for itself and of tax concessions for the benefit of private investors. Is this what the FDIC intended? The agency should be exceedingly embarrassed over the Steinhart sale. The FDIC's lost opportunities raises critical questions about FDIC policy and the effectiveness of the agency.

THERE IS ONE FINAL QUESTION REGARDING THE CASE OF TEXAS IN GENERAL

Were the regulators unduly harsh on Texas?

Texans would answer this question with an unqualified and resounding "yes." In hindsight, even the FDIC acknowledged that it was overzealous in its treatment of Texas. William Taylor, Seidman's successor as chairman of the FDIC, confirmed the accusation in an April 5, 1992, interview with the *Dallas Morning News.* Taylor said, "The person who says things got a little aggressive in Texas probably isn't all wrong."[4]

In a broader context, there is evidence that regulators "exercised their power with an unprecedented lack of restraint" during the last years of TAB's existence. In a study done by David Bizer, deputy chief economist of the Securities and Exchange Commission, comparing regulator examinations against bank balance sheets for the four years beginning in mid-1988, Bizer concluded: "Examiner ratings went down in a way that cannot be explained by changes in balance sheets, regional economic conditions, or the fall in real estate prices."[5]

The evidence supports the charge that federal regulators took a much harder line in dealing with Texas than they did in dealing with the banking crisis in other parts of the country.

As the banking crash was winding down in Texas in 1989 and 1990, it was spreading to other parts of the U.S. The first area to be hit was New England. Almost simultaneously, the disease spread to another growth state, Florida, and to the Washington, D.C.–Maryland–Northern Virginia area. Finally, after about a two-year lag, California and Arizona were hit.

The building boom of the 1980s, fueled by a recovering economy and declining interest rates, embraced the entire country. The crash that followed began in Texas because the props under the Texas economy were blown away by the oil recession that started in 1982, accelerated in 1986, and evolved into a full-blown real estate debacle after the passage of the Tax Reform Act in August 1986.

But Texas was not an anomaly: it was a precursor of what was to happen elsewhere. By late 1989, concerns were being voiced about the Northeast. Among the ten states that showed the largest increases in delinquencies in bank real estate loans from the end of 1988, eight were in the Northeast, with New York, New Jersey, and Connecticut all on the list. A slowing of growth in defense spending, a recession in high technology companies in the Boston area, and the aftermath of the stock market crash of October 1987 paved the way for the decline. However, it was the glut of commercial real estate that created the problems for the banks. As in Texas, the Tax Reform Act of 1986 had diminished investors' demand for real estate throughout the country.

Banks with the greatest problems included Bank of New England Corporation in Boston, Shawmut Corporation of Boston and Hartford, and Bank of Boston Corporation; Citicorp, Chemical New York Corporation, and Chase Manhattan Corporation in New York City; and the five largest banks in New Hampshire. In the Washington, D.C., area, the list included Maryland National Corporation of Baltimore, Riggs National Corporation of Washington, and Sovran Financial Corporation and Signet Banking Corporation in Virginia.

The same mistakes that were made by bankers in Texas were made by their counterparts in the Northeast. According to Robert Litan, a banking expert with the Brookings Institute in Washington, D.C., "It's sort of the history of Finance: no one learns from the last disaster, especially when they didn't have any part in it."[6] Chairman Seidman of the FDIC agreed: "I suppose they thought it could happen to dumb Texans, but not happen to wise, conservative Yankees."[7]

The failure of Bank of New England Corporation on January 6, 1991, with the seizure of its banking subsidiaries–Bank of New England of Boston with $13.2 billion in assets, Connecticut Bank & Trust of Hartford with assets of $7.7 billion, and Maine National Bank with assets of $1.1 billion–was a watershed event. Attributed to "aggressive lending into the region's then robust real estate market," it was the largest failure outside of Texas and the third-largest failure ever. According to Lawrence Fish, chairman and CEO of Bank of New England Corporation, "No institution in New England is as concentrated in real estate as the Bank of New England."[8]

As in the case of First Republic and MCorp, the FDIC set up a bridge bank for each of the three banks, which they would run pending their sale. The move was described as essential to halt the erosion of confidence in the banking system and protect all depositors from loss, even those in excess of the $100,000 insurance limit.

The failure of Bank of New England served as a wake-up call to the Northeast. They had observed what had happened in Texas and had resolved not to allow a similar outcome. According to Wayne Ayers, chief economist of Bank of Boston, in an interview with the *Dallas Morning News*, "We want to avoid what happened in Texas. . . . We saw how Texas lost control of its major financial resources." The answer, in Ayers's opinion: "Do what Texas did not do–mount a political campaign to save an indigenous financial system."[9]

And they did!

David LaGesse of the *Dallas Morning News*, in his article "Leeway Sought for Banks: New England Uses Its Political Clout," reported that, in the aftermath of the Bank of New England failure, New England mounted an all-out lobbying effort, which involved "a dozen senators, six governors, and a couple dozen representatives."[10]

The result of these efforts paid off. According to Wayne Ayers, "I think there's a clear change of philosophy on the part of regulators."[11]

Indeed, a clamor for leniency from the Northeast political lobby was heard loud and clear in Washington. In response, the comptroller's office abandoned the "black box" exams, so called because of a computer model used to select candidates for specially targeted exams. Banks that were selected were those that seemed particularly vulnerable to a decline in real estate. Some bankers likened these exams to the Spanish Inquisition.[12]

Federal bank examiners were also instructed not to automatically criticize a bank's renewal of a commercial real estate loan. This move was intended to take pressure off banks that had made "mini-perms," short-term loans of five to seven years without takeout commitments from permanent lenders. Such loans, which were made extensively by the major Texas banks, were granted with the expectation that, upon maturity of the "mini-perm," the real estate project would be completed and fully leased, and that obtaining a long-term permanent loan would be routine. However, given the state of the real estate markets beginning in 1986, no loans were available. Bank examiners forced the Texas banks to put matured "mini-perms" on nonaccrual and to establish large loan loss reserves. This did not happen in the East.[13]

Additionally, the OCC encouraged examiners to allow banks more time to work with troubled borrowers, to evaluate loans based on the expected *future* cash flow from real estate rather than on current liquidation value, and to stress to bankers that reductions in the concentration of real estate loans could be gradual.[14]

In assessing the new attitude of Washington, the bank analyst Frank Anderson observed, "It's *forbearance.* The people in Washington just can't get the word out–they choke on it, and for good reason. . . . [It's] also discrimination–a change from how they did things in Texas."[15] According to Bert Ely, a highly respected bank and thrift consultant in Alexandria, Virginia, "In a word, it's forbearance, and it's because of an extraordinary political effort in New England."[16]

Federal regulators utilized another type of assistance not generally recognized as forbearance. In a conversation with Bill Isaac on August

20, 1992, he stated that the main reason the Federal Reserve system had significantly relaxed monetary policy beginning in the spring of 1989, resulting in a substantial decline in interest rates, was due to their fear that Citicorp and other major money center and regional banks would otherwise fail. Indeed, lower interest rates dramatically reduced the cost of funds of major banks, thus improving profit margins. Lower rates also vastly increased the valuation of bank bond portfolios, which in many instances subsequently were either partially or totally liquidated with large gains, thereby augmenting capital and creating an additional buffer against failure. Of course, this action came too late to help the Texas banks.

As early as October 1988, John Cater, president of MCorp, charged that Washington was insensitive to the Texas problem and that the Texas political leadership should have acted sooner to "preserve the banking franchises in Texas." In an interview with the *Fort Worth Star-Telegram*, Cater said:

> [T]here may be a lack of sensitivity in Washington relative to the problems in Texas that is almost unique.
>
> When they had the problems in the Midwest, in the Rust Belt, a lot of special legislation was enacted [involving] import duties and trade quotas.
>
> The same was true in the Northwest when they had problems in the timber and paper products industry, and in the Northeast with textiles and shoes.
>
> When it happened in Texas–either the politicians are afraid to touch it, or we are so unpopular. Maybe they think we're getting what we deserve. Maybe it's been a pipe dream all along that somebody in Washington would view the problems we have as something worthy of attention.[17]

Because of the greater leniency shown after the crash in Texas and after the Bank of New England failure, the number of major casualties in the rest of the country was far less than expected. No major commercial banks in New York City failed, although many of the savings banks and S&Ls were restructured. Washington lost its oldest bank when the National Bank of Washington failed in August 1990 (before forbearance had taken hold). But Riggs National, Maryland National, and the most troubled banks in Virginia were spared. And even though the California real estate economy was described as "much worse" than Texas, no major California commercial bank failed.[18] Security Pacific was forced to sell to Bank of

America because of heavy loan losses. According to filings with the Securities and Exchange Commission, Security Pacific decided it faced a bleak future as an independent.

The only top-one-hundred bank outside of Texas to fail after Bank of New England, the nation's twenty-second largest, was Southeast Bank in Miami, Florida, forty-third largest in the country, which failed in August 1991.

In retrospect, it seems clear that the regulators were unjustifiably harsh in their treatment of Texas, as confirmed by the FDIC chairman Bill Taylor in his April 5, 1992, interview with the *Dallas Morning News.*

However, Texans were also their own worst enemy. The political leadership lacked understanding of the situation and was totally ineffective. Governor Bill Clements told Bayard Friedman that the banks were broke, they deserved to be broke, and he wasn't going to do a damned thing to help them. Thus, the governor of the state, who was highly respected and in a position to assume a pivotal role of leadership, abandoned his state's major banks–the same banks that bankrolled his company, Sedco of Dallas, and made him a multimillionaire. By the time he realized his mistake, subsequent to the seizure of First Republic, his efforts were too late.

Some of the politicians who were willing to help compromised themselves early through efforts to help troubled S&Ls, most of which were run by crooks. By the time the banks' problems surfaced, these individuals were either afraid to help or had lost credibility due to their prior efforts. In the case of Speaker of the House Jim Wright, Democrat from Fort Worth, he had lost his job as Speaker and had relinquished his seat in the U.S. House of Representatives.

NINETEEN 19

THE FDIC'S TEXAS RECORD

The FDIC's record in dealing with the Texas banking crisis can be viewed from several perspectives. On the one hand, they successfully handled an extremely large number of bank failures in Texas: 506 banks during 1983–1992, which is 25 percent of all bank failures since the FDIC was established in 1933. This was accomplished with little loss to the depositors of these banks.

On the other hand, the "open bank" rescues of BancTexas, NBC, and First City were poorly structured and all came unraveled, much to the detriment of their customers and their communities.

"Closed Bank" Resolutions

In its 1992 annual report, the FDIC proclaimed that "banking went off the critical list" after bank failures in the previous decade had soared to "levels not seen since the Great Depression." During that period, "the FDIC was able to cushion the collapse of about one-tenth of our banking system, contain the damage from it, and proceed to cleaning up the wreckage–all means to the end of maintaining public confidence in our financial system."[1]

Indeed, the FDIC's work in Texas was prodigious. The 506 bank failures they handled in Texas during 1983–1992 represented 36.5 percent of all failures in the U.S. For the most critical period of the crisis, 1987–1990, the agency resolved 417 bank failures in Texas, or 52 percent of the nation's total. This doesn't begin to explain the magnitude of the task, however. These banks had total deposits of $48.6 billion, which was 70 percent of the deposits of all banks to fail in those years. This excludes the banks and deposits of First City, NBC, and BancTexas, all of which were handled on an "open bank" basis.

During the two worst years in Texas, 1988 and 1989, the magnitude of the task was even more astounding (see Table 1 on page 27). For 1988, when First Republic failed–the largest failure in FDIC history–Texas accounted for 57 percent of bank failures, with total deposits of $22.8 billion, which was a whopping 92 percent of the deposits of all banks to fail in that year. In the following year, which included the statistics of MCorp and TAB, Texas accounted for 65 percent of failures, containing $18.5 billion in deposits, which was 77 percent of the total.

The huge concentration of failures in Texas underscores the depth to which the economy plunged. In no other period since the Great Depression has a state, or the nation, experienced such problems. In explaining the magnitude of the challenge faced by the FDIC during this period, it should be pointed out that the agency carried an extremely large burden in liquidating billions of dollars in foreclosed assets of failed banks. Additionally, the normal business of examining and supervising several thousand insured banks in Texas continued, and a significant number of these were "problem banks," which created an added burden.

The benefit to Texas in the form of capital injected from the FDIC and from out-of-state banks, which purchased Texas's fallen giants, was most significant. Furthermore, the maintenance of confidence and the almost uninterrupted provision of banking services to the communities served eased the burden on the state and its citizens.

"Open Bank" Resolutions

As admirable as the FDIC's record in resolving failed banks was, its record in structuring "open bank" transactions was dismal. Not one of the large "open bank" transactions was successful. Either they were poorly timed with not enough assistance, as in the cases of BancTexas and First City, or they made mistakes in the banks or individuals they chose as "white knights" to recapitalize and assume ownership of the failed institutions. In the case of NBC, the transaction was never completed because Equimark was undercapitalized and itself fell on financial hard times. In the case of First City, A. Robert Abboud, who had a questionable reputation as a manager coming into the deal, grossly mismanaged the bank.

NATIONAL BANCSHARES OF TEXAS

My misgivings about Alan Fellheimer were confirmed on Saturday, April 28, 1990, when it was announced that Equimark had "pulled out" of its proposed takeover of NBC.[2] Nine months after the FDIC's decision, the NBC/Equimark deal was off. It was a situation that was unbelievable. What had happened and why?

The official reason was that the creditors, led by Jay Lustig, wouldn't accept an offer to exchange their debt for a security that would give investors about $.30 on the dollar. Lustig later said that the creditors would have gone along had the FDIC agreed to sweeten the deal by $6 million, increasing the return to $.60 on the dollar.

According to Mark Johnson and Richard Calvert, the real reason the deal fell through was because of Equimark's deteriorating financial condition, which had made it impossible for Equimark to raise the $116 million needed to complete the acquisition. The $6 million gap between the creditors and the FDIC provided a convenient excuse for the FDIC to scuttle the deal, without having to admit that the investor they chose couldn't complete the transaction. Thus, the FDIC saved face.

An article in the April 30 *Wall Street Journal* disclosed that Equimark lost $15.4 million in the first quarter of 1990 and that, because of its weak common stock price, the company had to abort the planned offering, which was to fund the NBC acquisition.[3] As a result, the company would have had to resort to such extreme measures as selling its credit card business to raise the required $116 million.

Equimark's second-quarter loss grew to $30 million, nearly twice that of the first quarter. During the second quarter, on May 29, Judith Fellheimer, Alan's wife and chairman of Equimark's lead bank, was fired. Alan Fellheimer explained that the withdrawal from the NBC transaction had necessitated layoffs, and that criticism of the husband/wife team since the layoffs had caused the firing. But, even after the firing, the accusations of nepotism and self-enrichment continued.[4]

Alan Fellheimer had been controversial before being chosen to acquire NBC. It is true, he had turned Equimark around from an $18.5 million loss in 1985 to a $4.2 million profit in 1986, and was known as a turnaround artist. But his methods were unconventional, including hiring a former Israeli tank commander to collect delinquent third-world loans. Fellheimer was an aggressive lender but lacking in experience, which caught up with him when the real estate and consumer markets began to turn sour in the

Northeast. He went on an ambitious acquisition campaign. In addition to attempting to purchase NBC, he bought Liberty Savings Bank in Philadelphia, a small bank in Idaho, a minority interest in a money-losing thrift in Wyoming, and finance companies in Tampa, Florida. He installed Judith Fellheimer's twenty-three-year-old son as head of all eight branches of the Idaho bank, which lost $203,000 in 1989.

Additionally, Fellheimer was flamboyant, as evidenced by the transporting of his Rolls Royce to San Antonio for his personal use. The FDIC later disclosed that they were reviewing how Equimark spent $10 million during the nine months the company was managing NBC.[5] The inquiry resulted in the filing of a claim for recovery against Equimark, which was subsequently settled for an undisclosed amount.[6]

The only time I was ever with Fellheimer was at a meeting on August 23, 1989, in Fort Worth. He had come with Richard Calvert and Mark Johnson on a courtesy visit. During the one hour we were together, he lived up to his reputation. With dark thinning hair, a rough complexion, and a stocky build, he looked street hardened, and I rapidly concluded that he was also street smart. A lawyer who had become a specialist in turnarounds, Fellheimer was a "gut-fighter" who would go for the jugular and show no mercy; for example, it didn't take him long to understand the leverage TAB had with the FDIC by owning TASI, or to recommend that we use it to our advantage. He couldn't sit in one place for over five minutes. He was in perpetual motion, blowing and blustering around the conference room during our meeting. He was a wheeler-dealer of gigantic proportions and a man with no small ego. Fellheimer is definitely not cut out of the same cloth as the average conservative banker.

On September 6, 1990, Alan Fellheimer said he would resign as chairman and CEO of Equimark.[7] On November 15, 1990, Maryland National Bank announced that it had filed suit against Alan and Judith Fellheimer, alleging that they had defaulted on an $11.3 million loan used to purchase an 8.4 percent stake in Equimark.[8]

Incredibly, this was the man that the FDIC picked to lead the recapitalization of NBC, when they could have chosen either Norwest/Pohlad or Security Pacific, two of the premier banks in the country at the time. Either choice would have brought a strong player into the Texas market: a player who would offer another banking alternative to the other new entrants in Texas; who had the resources to introduce new products into the market; who had the capital base to help finance the recovery of the battered economy; and perhaps, as importantly, a player who unquestionably could have closed the transaction.

On Friday, June 1, 1990, the FDIC seized the major banking assets of NBC and sold them in a "closed bank" transaction to NCNB (the name was subsequently changed to NationsBank Corporation).[9] NBC, left with three small banks in Laredo, Eagle Pass, and Rockdale, entered bankruptcy a few days later.

Thus, the long, intense struggle of TAB and NBC to save their banking franchises for their shareholders and their communities was finally over.

BANCTEXAS

BancTexas was the first of the Texas banks to receive "open bank" assistance from the FDIC when, in July 1987, it received an injection of $150 million in federal assistance and $50 million in new equity capital from the Cleveland-based Hallwood Group, Inc. Unfortunately, the fate of BancTexas was sealed from the outset. With the Texas economy continuing to slide, a scant eighteen months later BancTexas had lost half of its capital.[10] On January 26, 1990, BancTexas was sold in a "closed bank" transaction to Hibernia Corporation, the largest banking organization in Louisiana, at $6.2 billion.[11]

In addition to the BancTexas acquisition, Hallwood entered into an "open bank" transaction with the FDIC to acquire Alliance Bancorporation of Anchorage, Alaska, with similarly disastrous results. As in the case of BancTexas, less than a year after receiving $295 million in assistance from the FDIC and $65 million in capital from Hallwood, Alliance had exhausted $102.2 million in equity to post a capital deficit of $27.3 million.[12]

According to an article in the February 2, 1989, edition of *American Banker*, the FDIC made a series of mistakes in structuring the Hallwood transactions.[13] First, it broke one of its own policies that stated "assistance transactions should restore the recipient institutions to economic viability." Second, the FDIC had unfounded optimism concerning the economies of Texas and Alaska. Ironically, this was the same mistake Texas bankers made in assessing the economy of their state. Finally, the deals were done with a fixed amount of assistance, which left the banks with no margin for error. In subsequent transactions, the recipient banks had a "put agreement" with the FDIC to place a given amount of additional bad loans within a specific time frame. (The FDIC refused to be interviewed for the *American Banker* article.)

HIBERNIA-TEXAS

The FDIC made a disastrous mistake in choosing Hibernia Corporation to purchase the principal assets of BancTexas, in addition to enough other insolvent Texas banks to build a $1.1 billion Hibernia-Texas franchise. Based in New Orleans, Hibernia had been operating in an economy that had suffered from some of the same problems as Texas, an economy largely dependent on oil and oil-related industries. The difference between Louisiana and Texas was that Louisiana hadn't experienced the expansion in its economy or the boom in real estate during 1983–1985 that Texas had. Thus, the Louisiana economy didn't experience as hard a fall as Texas following the crash in oil prices in the first quarter of 1986 and the Tax Reform Act in August 1986. Indeed, it took several years for the aftermath of these events to be reflected in Louisiana's bank loan portfolios, including that of Hibernia.

However, less than a year and a half after purchasing BancTexas in January 1990, Hibernia was in deep trouble. Bludgeoned by high concentrations of loans on highly leveraged transactions (HLTs) and on real estate, Hibernia's nonperforming loans escalated, and it reported a loss of $82.2 million in the first half of 1991 and a loss of $164.7 million for the year.[14] To make matters worse, the Texas operation was capitalized largely with borrowed money under a $100 million revolving loan from Chase.[15] Regulators barred the company from paying dividends, and the board of directors fired the top four officers, following orders from the OCC, after the four had pocketed $8.94 million in compensation, an amount equal to 42.7 percent of cumulative earnings over forty-two months.[16] On December 19, 1991, Hibernia announced that Chase would take a 46 percent stake in the company in return for reducing their note from $95 million to $35 million.[17]

In the second quarter of 1992, Hibernia sold its Texas bank to Comerica of Detroit in order to reduce its assets and to comply with regulatory equity to asset ratio guidelines.

FIRST CITY BANCORPORATION

The First City transaction, awarded to the former Chicago banker Bob Abboud, contained the "put agreement" allowing Abboud to "put" newly discovered bad loans back to the FDIC subsequent to closing, but the transaction repeated the other mistakes previously noted. A major difference between this transaction and the Hallwood structure was that the

FDIC did not leave the nonperforming loans on the books of the bank; instead, it established a new bank, "The Collecting Bank," to house the bad loans. Such a vehicle had first been used in Chemical's acquisition of Texas Commerce. Unfortunately, there was still a linkage between restructured First City and the Collecting Bank, in that the latter issued notes to First City for the purchase of the bad assets in an amount equal to 80 percent to 100 percent of the book value of the assets.

The assistance package, which was completed on April 20, 1988, provided approximately $1 billion in assistance from the FDIC, an amount Bill Isaac, who was representing a competing bid, felt was deficient by $200 million to $300 million. "There's no question the deal was too thin," said Isaac. "I thought there was about a 25 percent chance [that Abboud's] deal would not work. Those odds are too high."[18]

According to a March 1992 article in *Institutional Investor*, John Stone, in his zeal to negotiate a good deal for the insurance fund, may have driven too hard a bargain. After telling Abboud that the competing bids for the bank were essentially even, Stone then demanded "a series of concessions–such as giving the agency a $100 million claim on the collecting bank's recoveries–that drove up the Abboud group's costs." As a source close to the deal affirmed, "if that [increasing the costs] happened once, it happened ten times."[19]

The package the FDIC received included the purchase of preferred stock and warrants to purchase common shares, so, had it worked, the FDIC had upside potential. The infusion of private capital was $500 million.[20]

The worst mistake the FDIC made in structuring the First City transaction was in picking Abboud, who had previously been fired as CEO of First National Bank of Chicago in 1980 and as president of Occidental Petroleum in 1984.[21] In addition to his track record, Abboud had a reputation of being difficult to get along with and of possessing a gargantuan ego. But with his vow to build a "Texas bank" to serve the needs of the state (Abboud told me that this was a "crusade") and with the existing outlook for an improving Texas economy, the success of the transaction seemed assured.

Unfortunately, the Texas economy didn't improve fast enough. Even though Houston, First City's major market, was improving, there was little loan demand to fuel the growth of the bank. To make matters worse, the Austin and the Dallas/Fort Worth economies were still declining, and the assets of First City's banks in these cities continued to deteriorate accordingly.

To compensate for the lack of growth from Texas sources, Abboud violated his own vow and turned to external sources for loans. This strategy proved disastrous. Six of the most prominent borrowers, including Drexel Burnham, Federated Department Stores, Circle K, Garfinckel's, Calumet Farms, and Midway Airlines–which collectively owed close to $100 million–slipped into bankruptcy. In the words of Frank Anderson, an analyst at Stephens, Inc., "They must have booked every bad HLT [highly leveraged transaction] loan that came down the pike."[22]

Abboud's quest for earning assets wasn't confined to the domestic market. Riding the company's $15 million private jet, he went on a ten thousand mile lending spree abroad, utilizing many of the contacts that he had made at First Chicago and Occidental. The loan that eventually proved to be the bank's single largest problem originated as a letter of credit (LOC), guaranteeing a Citibank loan of $140 million to the late Spanish industrialist, Ignacio Coca. When the loan fell into default, Citibank called upon First City to honor its commitment by funding the LOC. First City, in turn, attempted to foreclose on $200 million in real estate and other collateral, only to find this to be exceedingly difficult under Spanish law. First City's most embarrassing loan, however, was a $49 million loan made in early 1990 to the Iraqi government of Saddam Hussein, albeit with a U.S. guarantee.[23]

While Abboud and his hired guns were chasing deals outside of Texas, the local economy continued to slip, causing recoveries on loans in the bad bank to languish. By the third quarter of 1990, there was no question: the Collecting Bank was in trouble because of poor recoveries on real estate loans. Accordingly, First City took a $77 million write-off on the Collecting Bank's notes.

With aggregate losses of $229.5 million for 1990 and the first quarter of 1991, Abboud was ousted on March 27, 1991.[24] In an old-fashioned coup d'état, Abboud's lieutenants had risen up against their abrasive leader while he was in New York trying to restructure the Coca loan, a feat that he ironically thought would save the bank.[25]

Abboud's takeover of First City came to an inglorious end after three years. Handed a golden opportunity by a cooperative FDIC, Abboud misled and mismanaged First City to the point of needing another bailout. He was his own worst enemy: arrogance and poor judgment were the cause of his downfall. Abboud's stewardship of First City was further sullied by the indictment and subsequent conviction of his handpicked chief aid, Frank C. Cihak, president of First City Bancorporation, for money laundering, self-dealing, and accepting kickbacks.

In the wake of Abboud's firing, the veteran First City and Corpus Christi banker C. Ivan Wilson was given the reins, whereupon he immediately started working on a recapitalization plan. Seeking buyers for thirteen of First City's banks and a $150 million cash infusion, Wilson and his chief financial officer Robert Brown began scouring the Texas business community for commitments. With time running out due to pressure from the FDIC, Wilson was doing his best to bring the recapitalization to completion. On October 29, 1992, having lined up tentative commitments for the purchase of the banks, Brown was desperately trying to firm up pledges for the equity injection. One such commitment for $10 million was provided via fax by Electronic Data Systems of Dallas (EDS), which I had joined in December 1990 as chief financial officer.

In a completely unanticipated move on October 30, 1992, the FDIC seized First City's twenty banks in its second bailout of the company in four years. According to FDIC officials, the agency would put up $500 million to protect depositors and would sell the banks to the highest bidders.

I was totally shocked by the FDIC's takeover of First City, having been told less than twenty-four hours earlier that the recapitalization was close to being finalized.

Three months after their seizure, on January 27, 1993, the FDIC sold First City's banks to Houston rival Texas Commerce (owned by Chemical Banking Corporation of New York) and to others for an unexpected premium of $434 million.[26] "This bid is absolutely astonishing!" exclaimed Harrison Young, director, Division of Resolutions. "We had no idea we would get bids this strong. There have been some changes in the people's perception of the economy. But quite frankly, we were very surprised."[27]

In addition to the untimely seizure of First City's banks, this surprise development, when management was on the brink of completing their recapitalization plan, raised the ire of shareholders, creditors, and management, who claimed foul play and a breach of faith by the FDIC.

On September 24, 1993, First City filed suit against the FDIC, the OCC, and the Texas Banking Commissioner, claiming the closure of the bank was "arbitrary and capricious" and was done "with intentional or reckless disregard for the facts and circumstances then well known to these regulatory agencies."[28] The suit sought up to $2 billion in punitive damages and about $1 billion in ordinary damages. Among other things, it claimed that the surplus resulting from the difference between the costs of the liquidation and the premium from the sale of assets, which the FDIC estimated at $60 million and First City estimated at between

$450 million and $500 million, be returned to the company. Additionally, it asked that the uninsured depositors, who were forced to accept an 80 percent payment on balances over the $100,000 insurance limit, be reimbursed in full.

On October 8, 1993, First City agreed to abandon the lawsuit and enter settlement talks with the FDIC.[29] On June 24, 1994, the parties to the lawsuit announced a settlement agreement, pending approval of the bankruptcy court.[30]

Subsequently, First City announced in December 1994 that it would file a joint reorganization plan with J-Hawk Corporation of Waco, Texas, an acquirer of portfolios of distressed assets, under which J-Hawk would merge into First City for about 50 percent of the new entity's common stock.[31] The merger received the approval of the court in May 1995. At the same time, the terms of the previously announced settlement with the FDIC were approved. Under the settlement, it was estimated that the FDIC would return to First City $125 million in cash and $55 million in loans and real estate. The FDIC would also return $75 million from a reserve against a pool of distressed loans held by Texas Commerce and Frost National Bank of San Antonio, which would be purchased by First City at face value. Additionally, the FDIC would provide funds to allow restitution to those depositors in the First City banks–Austin, Dallas, Houston, and San Antonio–whose deposits were not fully insured and who were required to take approximately $.80 on the dollar on the amounts over the $100,000 insured limit. All other creditors would be paid in full. Senior preferred shareholders would be paid over two years, and Junior preferred shareholders would receive between $100 million and $150 million, depending on the liquidation value of the returned assets, as well as 35 percent of the new company's common stock. Common shareholders would get 15 percent of the new company's stock, with the remaining 50 percent going to J-Hawk shareholders. Steve Goodwin of Carrington, Coleman, Sloman & Blumenthal, legal counsel for First City, estimated the total value of the settlement to be about $350 million.[32]

Thus ended the long and painful saga of First City, which began about twelve years earlier with the decline in the oil business and the accompanying recession in Houston.

This action also brought to a close the golden era of banking in Texas, when the large Texas banks had been the envy of the country. With the closing and sale of First City, nine of the ten largest Texas banks had ceased to exist as Texas-based-and-managed entities due to merger or sale.

The preceding faux pas by the FDIC cost the insurance fund, and thus the taxpayers, hundreds of millions of dollars. The FDIC found that selecting investors to recapitalize insolvent banks is fraught with the same pitfalls that bankers face in making loans. They made mistakes in the investors they selected; they misjudged the amount of funds required to adequately recapitalize the banks; they grossly underestimated the losses on problem loans; and they failed to anticipate the depth of the real estate depression.

The FDIC's record under Chairman L. William Seidman was no better than that of the bankers and directors of insolvent banks that were sued for imprudence, negligence, and violation of their fiduciary responsibilities.

TWENTY

SEIDMAN'S TEXAS LEGACY

To some, L. William Seidman's tenure as chairman of the FDIC was a success. To others, it was blemished with astonishing failures. Overall, he was controversial; in 1990 the White House was trying to dump him because of his "self-confidence, independence, and tart tongue."[1] Regardless of how Seidman is perceived, there is no doubt that during his tenure major Texas banks in the hands of the FDIC fared horribly.

Fewer Banking Alternatives

At the beginning of 1987, Texans controlled the ten largest banking organizations in the state, with over $116 billion in assets, including the eighteenth, twentieth, twenty-fifth, and twenty-sixth largest banks in the country. A total of seven Texas banks ranked among the nation's top one-hundred largest banks. Just three years later, only one remained in local hands: Cullen/Frost Bankers, Inc., of San Antonio, the 108th-largest banking organization in the country, with about $3 billion in assets.

With the consolidation of banking in Texas, which began in 1986, the eight largest banking organizations were reduced to four: NationsBank absorbed NBC and First Republic (which had previously absorbed InterFirst); Banc One Corporation acquired MCorp and Team Bank (formerly TAB); Chemical bought Texas Commerce, which subsequently purchased the major assets of First City; and First Interstate acquired Allied. As a consequence, three banking alternatives were eliminated (four if InterFirst is included).

A critical test used to determine violations of antitrust provisions in considering bank mergers is based on the number of banking alternatives available to bank customers. Any decrease implies a greater concentration of banking resources and is considered to have negative implications for bank customers.

Out-of-State Control

The fact that control of the state's major banking resources has passed into out-of-state hands has been traumatic for Texans. The engine that drove the commercialization and industrialization of the state, and provided the early entrepreneurs with the seed money to build some of today's leading businesses, is gone.

An example of that engine's importance is provided by Tom Vandergriff, former mayor of Arlington, Texas. He described how the bankers' willing attitude helped to get the professional baseball team, the Washington Senators, to move to Arlington in 1971. The move hinged on the owner's ability to pay creditors $8 million. Vandergriff turned to a group of Dallas, Fort Worth, and Arlington bankers, who said, "You get the franchise–we'll provide the money." The team opened the 1972 season in Arlington under its new name, the Texas Rangers. "Without the bankers' full-speed-ahead spirit and action, we simply could not have done what we did in those days," Vandergriff said.[2]

Vandergriff and others fear that the demise of local control means the chairmen of Texas's largest bank holding companies will no longer be able to flex the financial muscle that in the past played a key role in the state's economic development. The institutions that were major power bases for the state's leaders have, in reality, been reduced to branch offices of the out-of-state owners. The power in those organizations normally resides in the headquarter cities. Even Banc One announced in May 1995 that it was abandoning its once hallowed decentralization–known as its "uncommon partnership"–which preserved the autonomy of its subsidiary banks. In the future, the authority that presidents once had to run their banks as they saw fit would be replaced by that of one executive in Columbus, Ohio; bank presidents would henceforth become market managers, an unfortunate decision for bank customers.

As a consequence of the centralization of authority, not only are the power bases gone, but so are the institutional incubators that in the past spawned so many of Texas's leaders. It is unlikely that the Texas banking system of the future will produce such leaders as R. L. Thornton, former chairman of MCorp's predecessor, Mercantile National Bank; Fred Florence, former chairman of Republic National Bank; Jesse Jones or Ben

Love of Texas Commerce; Judge James A. Elkins, or his son James A. Elkins, Jr., both former chairmen of First City; or K. M. Van Zandt, Lewis Bond, or Bayard Friedman of the Fort Worth National Bank (TAB's predecessor). Both Thornton and Friedman were mayors of their respective cities; Jones was head of the Reconstruction Finance Corporation under President Franklin D. Roosevelt; and the rest were giants in their cities and in Texas. What is true of the larger institutions and cities is also true, only on a smaller scale, of hundreds of smaller communities throughout Texas, which lost their leaders and their institutional power bases.

In its January 21, 1993, edition, *American Banker* listed its candidates for the nation's top forty bankers under forty years of age: not a single commercial banker from Texas was named, whereas ten years ago a similar listing would have included more than a proportional Texas representation.

Of equal concern, as a result of actions taken by the FDIC throughout the state, an entire generation of Texas leaders was virtually eradicated. Many of these leaders were purged from their banks: consequently, they had to leave the banking business and start anew in different fields. Many had to leave the state to find work. Others were damaged so severely, financially and professionally, that they were stripped of their dignity, power, and, thus, their effectiveness.

Likewise, the boardrooms were left empty, and the directors who once occupied those boardrooms were disenfranchised. Directors of the banks that failed–including the directors of the banks of First Republic, MCorp, First City, and TAB–were subjected to a reign of terror as the FDIC sought, in some cases unmercifully, to recover damages for negligence. In the process, the incentive for any responsible business person in Texas to serve as director of an FDIC-insured bank was all but destroyed.

The boardrooms of the major banks were seats of power where business and civic leaders, who were also bank directors, made many of the critical decisions affecting their communities. The case cited by Tom Vandergriff concerning the move of the Washington Senators to Texas is but one of many examples. With out-of-state ownership and statewide branching, local boards have either become legally unnecessary, or they have been de-emphasized. In some instances, they are filled largely with insiders, just to meet the legal requirement of five directors per national bank. The displacement of the boardroom as a power seat leaves an institutional void that cannot be easily filled.

Indeed, based on early evidence, Texans have regarded the presence of out-of-state banks more negatively than positively. NationsBank of Texas (formerly NCNB), the earliest entry as a result of an FDIC bailout, displayed an arrogance and lack of sensitivity that provoked open hostility by its detractors. NCNB became widely known to stand for "No Cash for No Body."[3]

According to the former Texas commissioner of banking James Sexton, in an October 1991 interview with the *Dallas Morning News*, "NCNB remains an unwelcome alien to many Texans." Chris Williston, executive director of the Independent Bankers Association of Texas, agreed: "Bridges are burned now that can't be repaired."[4]

Continued hostility toward the out-of-state invaders is cited as a principal reason why Texas opted out of the Riegle-Neal Interstate Banking and Branching Act of 1994, which allows banks to branch across state lines. In commenting on the signing of the opt-out bill on May 11, 1995, by Texas Governor George W. Bush, Chris Williston said,

> Certainly, there was a lot of emotion and a lot of history at work here. The economic aspects of a large share of the banking market being owned by out-of-state institutions is more pronounced here than anywhere else in the country. There's a hell of a lot of animosity here from bank customers over what's happened to the banking industry.
>
> With this law, they will be well served in that they will still have a local player that is responsive to their needs.[5]

On the other hand, economists and regulators argue that the presence of out-of-state banks means expanded banking services, particularly for consumers, and greater financial resources. There seems little question that the Texas major banks, which hadn't emphasized consumer banking in the then-existing, unit banking environment, will benefit from the consumer-banking expertise of their new owners. Also, the capital resources and lending limits of Banc One, Chemical, NationsBank, and First Interstate are much greater than those of the banks they bought.

Although NationsBank seems to have been the lightning rod for those who resent the presence of out-of-state banks, the real issue is the banks' commitment to the state and to the communities they serve.

While only time will tell, there are some certainties: there is no doubt that funds will leave the state in the form of dividends and management fees to the parent holding companies. Stricter credit standards will be imposed, and some investment and credit decisions will be made in distant corporate offices. (Based on the lending record of the 1980s in Texas, it could be argued that a more centralized control over the lending process is needed.) Loans for today's entrepreneurs will be harder to obtain, since they are by definition more relationship based. And support for civic and charitable purposes will probably diminish materially, as these budgets are set by corporate headquarters in faraway places. Indeed, based on recent reports, this appears to have happened, at least in regard to NationsBank and Banc One, Texas.

A branching study reported by the House Banking Committee in 1992 and conducted by the Federal Reserve Bank of Atlanta found that, in the case of mergers involving multistate banking organizations, the controlling organization was likely to drain funds from the state of the acquired institution. In the case of fifteen large holding companies, nine acted to drain funds from at least 40 percent of the satellite states in which the holding companies operate. In assessing the studies, James B. Watt, president of the Conference of State Bank Supervisors, said that the studies "at least ought to raise a question of whether bigger is better."[6]

With regard to civic and charitable contributions, NationsBank has been a major supporter of the arts. The commitment of Texas Commerce and its officers to corporate leadership hasn't noticeably changed since the acquisition by Chemical. By negotiating from a position of strength, Ben Love was able to preserve his bank's independence in setting their local agenda.

Consolidation

The massive consolidation of banks in Texas has had unwanted economic side effects in the short term: increased vacancy rates in commercial real estate and increased unemployment. For example, five years after the collapse of its banks, Dallas has the highest vacancy rate of commercial real estate in its downtown of any major city in the U.S., at about 40 percent. This is *partially* a legacy of the consolidation that occurred in major banks in the 1980s. Prior to the consolidation, InterFirst and Republic both occupied two towers in downtown Dallas; each complex was well over one million square feet. Today, after the merger and acquisition by NationsBank Corporation, they have downsized into one tower, where they occupy less than one million square feet. In Houston, with the demise of First City, the space it once occupied stands empty–in excess of one million square feet–as a ghostly reminder of its past glory. The consolidations have contributed greatly to the economic decline of downtown Dallas and downtown Houston. Other communities where branches were closed have also been significantly affected.

With regard to unemployment, thousands of bankers have been displaced from their jobs. In the Republic/InterFirst merger alone, consolidation plans called for the elimination of three thousand jobs. And this was before the purchase by NationsBank and the further consolidation of staff functions.

The consolidation and rationalization of personnel not only takes place at the outset of a merger–it is an ongoing process. For example, the goal to achieve higher total returns to shareholders can result in a company seeking increases from its subsidiary operations to offset lower returns elsewhere. In May 1995, Chemical announced that in order to improve its return on equity, it would seek to eliminate $50 million in annual costs, including 1,100 jobs, from its Texas Commerce subsidiary. The impact of unemployment alone has had a significant effect in some communities, not to mention the personal suffering of individuals and families, who often are forced to leave the industry and even move out-of-state.

In weighing the advantages of out-of-state ownership of Texas banks against the disadvantages, Texas is definitely the loser.

"Gross Abuse"

In its zeal to execute transactions that were of least cost to the insurance fund, the FDIC was accused of "gross abuse" in some instances. For example, in May 1994, U.S. District Judge Joe Kendall awarded a Fort Worth building owner $115 million in damages, ruling that the FDIC, in conjunction with NationsBank, unlawfully broke a long-term lease on a downtown office building once occupied by First Republic. In a stinging fifty-five-page opinion, the judge accused the FDIC of "high-handed and cavalier conduct." According to an account of the decision in the May 20, 1994, edition of *American Banker*, "NationsBank, with help from the FDIC, first bullied the building's landlord, Burnett Plaza Associates, and eventually illegally broke the lease."[7] Eight months after the sale of First Republic to NationsBank, the FDIC broke the lease.

In his opinion, the judge said, "The FDIC's eight-month delay is outrageous. The FDIC may not use the repudiation power, or conspire with, allow, and as here encourage others to intimidate landlords." NationsBank "intentionally and with reckless disregard to Burnett's rights acted jointly with the FDIC to abuse the otherwise legitimate disaffirmance power."[8]

In commenting on the ramifications of the ruling, William Lawley of Dallas's Wilcox Realty, observed, "There are literally hundreds of leases that were involved. The FDIC went through town with an ax, and it ruined a lot of owners and buildings."[9] There is, however, a four-year statute of limitations, which would limit the FDIC's potential liability since many of the broken leases occurred in the mid-1980s. The FDIC has stated its intention to appeal the decision.

Another court decision will certainly affect pending action in Texas. The Supreme Court ruled in mid-June 1994 that a law firm that represented an insolvent thrift in transactions with investors should not be held liable for amounts later paid by the S&L to investors, who claimed they were deceived concerning the thrifts' condition. The Court declared that "there is no federal policy that the [insurance] fund should always win."[10]

The attitude of the FDIC in Texas seemed to be that the FDIC should always win and that their actions were justified because they were in the best interest of the insurance fund. In the process, the FDIC created distrust and ill will on the part of Texans.

Lost Integrity

Under Seidman, the FDIC lost credibility as a result of their actions in Texas. Carl Pohlad, for example, believed that the FDIC broke promises to him and his representatives on numerous occasions. One incident occurred when they struck a deal with Stan Poling, only to have the FDIC board of directors later renege. Based on this incident, Poling asked to be removed from the TAB/NBC case, as he felt his credibility had been undermined.

Al Casey, chairman of First Republic, also believed he had been misled by the FDIC, according to his deposition taken in relation to the FDIC's suit against the directors of First Republic's lead bank in Dallas. Casey believed that "management's plan" of recapitalization for First Republic was acceptable to the FDIC, and he demanded an explanation from FDIC officials as to "why they had accepted the NCNB proposal, rejected . . . [management's] proposal and done so with no hint to . . . [management]." In response to questioning from counsel, Casey admitted that he felt "a sense at that time of betrayal toward the FDIC."[11]

In the same deposition, Casey accused Seidman of reneging on assurances Seidman made to the directors of First Republic. In answering questions about the FDIC's suit against the First Republic directors, Casey recalled a conversation he had with Seidman: Casey said to Seidman, ". . . how can they [the FDIC] file a suit against these people when the FDIC, as personified by you and your general counsel [the FDIC's general counsel, who was present at the time] present said you weren't going to sue them?" Seidman replied, "Al, I have been told that I must recluse myself. I cannot discuss it." According to Casey, they then "dropped the matter. 'I can't discuss it any further,' that's what [Seidman] said."[12]

Alleged breaches of faith by Seidman and the FDIC left many Texans totally disenchanted with the agency, a legacy that will endure.

Protecting the Fund

One legacy left by Seidman is not isolated to Texas, although the policies followed in Texas had a huge impact on the insurance fund. According to the FDIC's 1992 annual report, one of the principal purposes of banking regulation, and thus of the FDIC, "is to protect the insurance fund."[13] One would have to give the FDIC a terrible report card in this respect, as the fund slid deeply into the red from 1988 through 1991, and actually ended 1991 with a negative balance of $11.1 billion. In the private sector, a corporation with a negative net worth would be put in bankruptcy, its management would be fired, and its directors would be sued by shareholders for negligence.

During Seidman's tenure as chairman, the FDIC's experience in handling problem banks raises serious policy issues. The "open bank," early resolution approach, which the FDIC was very reluctant to use, is significantly less expensive than allowing a bank to go through the agonizing death throes of failure. The TAB/NBC experiment never had a chance to test this premise, although empirical evidence, academic studies, and congressional investigations attest to the efficacy of early resolutions.

According to FDIC annual reports, the estimated costs (losses) in resolving the major Texas banks increased as time went on: in 1989, the estimated cost to the FDIC of First Republic was $2.9 billion, whereas in 1991 the estimate had risen to $3.6 billion; in 1989, the estimate for resolving MCorp was $2.7 billion, versus $2.9 billion in 1991; and in 1989, the estimate for TAB was $900 million, whereas in 1991 it had risen to $1.039 billion.[14]

Additionally, the provision in the FDIC's policy statement of December 8, 1986–adopted and implemented during Seidman's reign–which discourages the FDIC from taking an equity interest in an assisted bank, cost the insurance fund billions of dollars. The FDIC's effective sale of their interests in Continental Illinois National Bank in Chicago and in Crossland Savings Bank of Brooklyn, New York, which will be discussed later in this chapter, clearly demonstrates the advantages of taking equity interests.

The policies and practices of the FDIC also left too many casualties in the form of failed banks. As previously indicated, the 506 banks that failed in Texas during 1983–1992 represent 25 percent of all banks to fail in the U.S. since the establishment of the FDIC in 1933.

A Different Approach

With a different approach, the sale of Texas's major banks to outsiders could have been avoided, and the cost to the taxpayer could have been greatly reduced. There were notable precedents. One was the Reconstruction Finance Corporation (RFC), which was created in January 1932 to deal with the banking crisis during the Great Depression. In the absence of federal deposit insurance, which became effective with the establishment of the FDIC on January 1, 1934, there was a crisis of confidence in the nation's banking system. In the months following the stock market crash of October 24, 1929, financial panic ensued as depositors lined up to withdraw funds from their banks. From June 30, 1929, to June 30, 1931, 4,202, or 16.7 percent, of the nation's banks failed. It was in response to this crisis that the RFC was established, admittedly under conditions far more compelling to the nation than those occasioned by the crash of the Texas economy in the 1980s.

However, according to an article by Sandra L. Planisek in *American Banker*, there are remarkable similarities between the 1989 Texas situation and the Great Depression in terms of the capital shortfalls and the institutions created to deal with them (the RFC and the RTC). The original economic anomalies were different, but both crises afflicted institutions that were "heavily invested in real estate." Planisek concludes that by taking equity positions in troubled institutions–in addition to making loans–the RFC was able to make "more types of deals."[15]

Over its life, the RFC invested $1 billion in the equity of six thousand banks and lent $2.6 billion to ten thousand banks. The agency successfully liquidated all of its equity, either by reselling it to the issuing bank or by selling it in the secondary market. It lost no money in the process. Of the $10.5 billion used in supporting banks and agriculture throughout the Great Depression, all was repaid to the U.S. Treasury, plus a profit of $500 million.[16] A phenomenal accomplishment!

Another precedent was set in 1982 during Bill Isaac's tenure as FDIC chairman. The FDIC injected capital in the form of interest-bearing notes into mutual savings banks in the East to prevent the entire industry from failing. According to Isaac, this worked, and he believes something similar would have worked for the Texas banks, as well.

Also under Bill Isaac, the FDIC's 1984 bailout of Continental Illinois Corporation, the parent of Continental Illinois National Bank & Trust Company in Chicago, provides a model for a successful restructuring involving "open bank" assistance. In that case, the FDIC purchased 80 percent of the bank's stock and purchased $5.2 billion in bad loans. Seven years later, on June 13, 1991, the FDIC sold its last 14.2 million shares. Whereas the original estimate of the cost of the bailout was $4.5 billion, the final figure was just under $1 billion.[17]

There is no doubt that the policies followed during the Texas crisis were driven by Seidman and represented, for the most part, his personal philosophy. After Seidman succeeded Isaac as FDIC chairman, a fundamental change in philosophy occurred inside the FDIC, which all but precluded a Continental-type bailout. The change was marked by the adoption of the "open bank" assistance policy on December 8, 1986, which required private sources of capital and discouraged the investment of equity by the FDIC in an "open bank" deal. The Continental model failed to meet either of these tests: it was restructured with FDIC capital and had no private capital.

The "open bank" assistance policy also dictates that the "cost to the FDIC of the proposal must clearly be less than other available alternatives."[18] The word "clearly" focuses the comparison of alternative proposals on that which can be clearly and accurately measured. This favors a proposal that preserves the current cash balance of the FDIC vis-à-vis a proposal that has a greater long-term return to the fund. Considerations such as which investor is the most viable financially, which can bring the most in terms of enhanced banking services, and which would be best for all the communities served become secondary. Yet it is these very considerations that ultimately determine the success of a transaction.

In an April 5, 1992, interview with the *Dallas Morning News*, Seidman's philosophy became patently clear. In responding to questions about the Southwest Plan, which contained elements of government ownership, Seidman said, "Even if it's a little more costly, my preference was for the government not to be running the bank."[19] On the issue of dumping real estate, he said that allowing the government to warehouse real estate distorted the local market; the government shouldn't be betting on a turnaround.

The reality is that Seidman's stance against taking equity positions cost the taxpayers billions of dollars. In some cases, the sale of the banks to Wall Street–backed interests rather than to the public resulted in massive transfers of wealth from the hands of small shareholders to a few wealthy investors and investment bankers. Additionally, the practice of dumping rather than withholding real estate distorted markets even more by creating a huge supply overload, which drove prices artificially low.

In summary, had it not been for Seidman, better decisions probably would have been made for the major Texas banks and for the nation.

A New Agenda

As the banking crisis spread to other parts of the country, the attitudes and approaches of politicians and regulators to addressing the problems changed.

For example, there were suggestions that some of the inequities of the 1986 Tax Reform Act should be reversed. On November 10, 1991, in an unprecedented acknowledgment of the role that the reform act had played in creating the country's banking crisis, the former FDIC chairman L. William Seidman told Congress that commercial real estate was in a depression and that efforts to correct abuses had gone overboard. He explained, "Retroactive changes in tax laws almost ensured that we'd have these real estate problems." To help remedy the situation, he endorsed restoring passive-loss rules for real estate investments and lowering the capital gains tax rate.[20]

Equally encouraging was the attitude of the FDIC chairman William Taylor. Under Taylor, the FDIC agreed in February 1992 to ease the burden on borrowers whose loans were classified as nonperforming at the defunct Bank of New England by guaranteeing $1.2 billion in existing and new loans.[21]

Furthermore, on January 24, 1992, in an action not taken since the rescue of Continental Illinois Bank, the FDIC under Taylor seized the $7 billion Crossland Savings Bank of Brooklyn, New York, which it would then run as conservator under authority granted to the agency by FIRREA. The FDIC explained that, in failing to receive an acceptable bid for the bank, the cheapest alternative was to manage the institution itself.[22]

Critics of the move contended that it was unfair for a government-run bank to compete with private institutions and that liquidation would be less costly than running the bank until the market rebounded. Others contended that the government shouldn't be in the business of running institutions, charging that, when it did, it often ran them "into the ground."

The Continental Illinois experience counters all of these assertions. Ken Guenther, executive vice president of the Independent Bankers Association, supported the action: "I do think that what he [Taylor] is trying to put in place is a lower-cost alternative. If it works, it helps."[23]

In a related development, federal regulators announced on February 17, 1992, that they were preparing a "new strategy" to deal with failing banks and S&Ls. As an alternative to liquidation, regulators were proposing to invest in weak institutions in hope of nursing them back to health. It was believed that this approach would be less costly than waiting for the banks to drift into insolvency, and it was also believed that it would provide needed credit in the affected communities and in the nation. As proposed, the plan would be equivalent to the existing "open bank" concept in that the current shareholders would retain a stake in the restructured bank, albeit significantly diluted by the government's holdings.[24]

Chairman Taylor's goal was to reduce the cost to the insurance fund and the taxpayers and to reduce the disruption to local markets. In commenting on the approach, he said, "We're not going to liquidate in a disorderly fashion [which could be interpreted as an implied criticism of his predecessor]–we're going to liquidate in an orderly fashion."[25]

In the *Dallas Morning News*, Seidman criticized Taylor's approach. "Yeah, I left him a powerful institution and now he's misusing it," Seidman said. "A bank hospital at the FDIC is a concept I would not have embraced."[26]

Clearly, with the departure of Seidman and the entry of Taylor, there was a new agenda among government regulators. Tragically, Taylor died suddenly on August 20, 1992, following surgery for cancer of the colon. In commenting on his death, the *New York Times* stated that one of Taylor's "highest and most controversial priorities was trying to resolve the problems of failing banks without liquidating them" by utilizing "bank hospitals" in which staffs of bankers would take over the management of weak banks on behalf of the FDIC and "nurse" them back to health before they were sold.[27]

Continuing Taylor's efforts to reduce the cost of bank failures to the insurance fund, the FDIC used a new "low-cost" formula in closing two banks in October 1992. In dealing with First Constitution Bank, New Haven, Connecticut, and Howard Savings Bank, Livingston, New Jersey, the FDIC closed both banks before they were technically insolvent to protect their franchise value. In addition, it provided incentives to the acquiring banks to work with borrowers who had troubled loans, and it agreed to absorb 80 percent of the losses on those loans for five years.[28]

Additionally, on December 8, 1992, the FDIC issued a new policy statement designed to encourage troubled banks and S&Ls to seek "open bank" assistance. The 1992 policy statement superseded a 1990 policy statement, which updated the 1986 statement to include minor changes required by FIRREA.[29] The 1992 statement was necessitated by a mandatory provision of the Federal Deposit Insurance Corporation Improvement Act of 1991, which encourages the early resolution of troubled institutions. It changes the requirement that the financial impact on shareholders and on subordinated debtholders approximate the effect if the bank had failed, by requiring only that they "make substantial concessions." It also permits the payment of contingent fees to investment bankers and lawyers, who help arrange "open bank" assistance rescues.[30]

The April 4, 1990, policy statement made a subtle change with respect to the FDIC taking equity interests to allow more flexibility. It provided that on a "case-by-case basis" the FDIC could consider taking an "equity or other financial interest" in an institution. While falling short of encouraging the taking of equity interests, the new language represented a departure from the 1986 statement, which stated a "preference" for not taking such interests. Even so, there continued to be great reluctance to take equity interests under Seidman and prior to the Crossland case.

Almost a year after Taylor's death, his approach in the Crossland case was validated with the successful conclusion of the experiment. On August 13, 1993, the FDIC announced that it was selling Crossland to a group of private investors for $332 million. In announcing the sale, Acting Chairman Andrew C. Hove declared that the Crossland approach "saved the Bank Insurance Fund approximately $400 million."[31]

The incentives to take equity interests are great. For example, by applying the percentage of savings from the estimated costs in the cases of Continental (77.8 percent) and Crossland Savings (29.4 percent) to First Republic, MCorp, and TAB, the FDIC could have saved between $2.2 billion and $5.8 billion from the 1991 estimated aggregate costs of $7.5 billion.

Hove's term expired in February 1993. It isn't clear whether or not the new chairman, Ricki Helfer, a Washington, D.C., lawyer who was confirmed by the Senate on October 4, 1994, will recommend adoption of the hospital plan.

Irrespective of what ultimately happens to the hospital plan, the FDIC's abysmal record in Texas demands a complete investigation and review of the agency's policies promulgated under the former chairman L. William Seidman. Also, it seems absurd for the FDIC to cling to the notion of not owning equity in once troubled banks if, by temporarily taking such positions, the cost to the insurance fund–and thus to the taxpayers–could be reduced by billions of dollars.

EPILOGUE
Three Years Later

With the acceptance of TAB's plan of liquidation and the dismissal of the bankruptcy on June 26, 1990, as far as I was concerned the final curtain had closed on the TAB drama.

I had joined Electronic Data Systems Corporation (EDS) in Dallas as chief financial officer, a job I was thoroughly enjoying after the turbulent last two years at TAB. Since being purchased by General Motors in 1984, EDS has grown into the world's largest information technology company, with over $12 billion in revenues and ninety thousand employees in over forty countries. As a member of the EDS board of directors and with the financial pulse of the company in my hands, I was in a great position to participate in the dynamic future of this exciting company.

To my great surprise, in February 1992, my equanimity at EDS was shattered by a ghost from the past.

At that time, I received a call from Gary Cage, who was CFO of Team Bancshares. As soon as I heard the tension in his voice, I felt a sinking sensation in my stomach.

"Jody," Cage said, "I thought you needed to know that we have just heard from a Tulsa law firm, Gable & Gotwals, which has been hired by the FDIC." He paused, took a deep breath, and then, struggling to check his emotion, added, "They have requested mountains of information on TAB. They've also contacted a number of former TAB people requesting interviews. They've taken space in the building and assigned three people here to carry on an investigation. They told our attorney that they're here to investigate whether or not to file a lawsuit against the former officers and directors of TAB's major banks."

As I heard Gary's explanation, I was totally astonished, particularly considering the "Reservation of Rights and Limited Release" the FDIC had given us when Team Bank bought TASI (TAB's data processing and bank operations company) from TAB on January 26, 1990. As I thought about the FDIC's actions, my astonishment passed quickly into seething anger.

"Gary," I said, "they're doing it again, breaking another promise, abrogating another commitment. I guess we shouldn't be surprised, though. They haven't kept a promise yet."

"You're right. This is unconscionable. In any event, I'll keep you informed as to what is going on."

In reflecting on our conversation, I was puzzled over the FDIC's actions. We had a written "Release" signed by John Stone and a "handshake" agreement that they would not pursue the personal assets of any of TAB's officers or directors. These agreements, along with TAB's history of cooperation, should have discouraged this step. That notwithstanding, I was concerned about the law firm that had been hired. Tulsa was struggling from the economic hangover of the 1980s and was more than likely void of bountiful opportunities for a law firm. Gable & Gotwals had only one incentive: to build a case against us, whether justified or not. A prospective three- to five-year lawsuit against us had to look like a gold mine to them. I cringed at the thought. I couldn't stand years of litigation, either financially or professionally.

I knew I had to move quickly if there was any hope of heading this off. With the help of Rice Tilley, who had been TAB/Fort Worth's legal counsel, we organized the directors of the Dallas, Fort Worth, and Houston banks into a "joint-defense group," and rehired the law firms that had represented TAB in the last months prior to its seizure and during its bankruptcy: Carrington, Coleman, Sloman & Blumenthal of Dallas and Sullivan & Cromwell of New York.

A meeting was scheduled for May 7, 1992, in Washington, D.C., between Steve Goodwin, Peter Tierney, and Rodgin Cohen representing the TAB group, and attorneys from Gable & Gotwals and from the FDIC.

Shortly after lunch, Peter Tierney and Steve Goodwin called from Washington. "Jody, the meeting began on a sour note," Peter said, sounding tired and discouraged. "Before we could say anything, John Rule of Gable & Gotwals announced that his law firm was going to recommend to the FDIC that they file a lawsuit against the officers and directors of TAB. From there it just went downhill. They demanded that we sign a tolling agreement extending the statute of limitations beyond its July 20, 1992, deadline, or they would sue prior to its expiration."

The impact of hearing this hit me like ten thousand volts. This was just inconceivable.

"Did you discuss the Release?" I asked. "Have they just completely ignored it?"

Steve Goodwin, who was always very precise and deliberate, responded: "The FDIC has taken the position that the provision added to the Release in the last hours before it was signed enables them to pursue the personal assets of the targeted individuals, in addition to the D&O [directors and officers] insurance. Just to refresh your memory, it reads: 'Nothing herein is intended to or shall prevent the FDIC from recovering the full amount of any such claim, as defined above from any officer.'" (In this context, the term "officer" included directors.)

Steve continued in an ironical tone. "They seem to have conveniently forgotten that they agreed to exclude personal assets from any recovery. The circumstances surrounding the addition of this language will obviously be a major issue in future discussions."

"I remember the circumstances as if it were yesterday," I said, recalling the last, tense, forty-eight hours before the deal was signed. "Tricia Connell [an attorney working with Rodgin Cohen from Sullivan & Cromwell] received an urgent call from the FDIC, which had brought in a so-called insurance expert from their internal legal staff to review a draft of the document. She was told that the release in its existing form would make it impossible for the FDIC to sue the officers and directors in order to make a claim, much less collect insurance proceeds in the event a claim was awarded."

"That's exactly right," Steve confirmed. "And the insurance companies would assert a policy defense: that all the individuals had been released and there is no one to sue."

Reflecting on the poor negotiating posture we were in at the time, I said "I wish we had dug our feet in and never allowed them to enter that language, but they promised they would limit any recovery to insurance proceeds, and we had no choice at the time: it was going to be that release or no release." "Well, they lied!" Steve said sardonically, ending the conversation.

In reflecting on what I had just learned, it appeared my worst fears had been realized. Once again events seemed out of our control, catapulting toward a climax by July 20. My anger had only grown as Steve Goodwin and Peter Tierney had described the meeting to me. While the Gable & Gotwals attorneys had prepared their case and were the spokesmen, the FDIC staff enthusiastically endorsed the recommendation, in total disregard of our agreement. But now that we knew where they were headed, all of our energies had to be focused on preparing our strategy and defense.

Ironically, whereas Ron Steinhart and I had been on opposite sides of the negotiating table in the sale of TASI (TAB's data processing subsidiary) to Team Bank, in this instance we were allies with a strong common interest: most of the potential targets were either officers or substantial customers of Team Bank.

Coincidentally, on May 7, the same day our counsel met with the FDIC's representatives, Ron Steinhart sat next to FDIC chairman William Taylor at a dinner in Washington, D.C. According to Steinhart, after he expressed his distress over the possibility of the FDIC suing some of his officers and best customers, the following exchange took place.

"Ron," Taylor responded, "I don't know anything about the TAB situation, but I don't believe that the FDIC should be suing officers and directors who didn't personally benefit from their actions."

"Mr. Chairman, we've been in the bank over two years, and I can tell you that we haven't uncovered any impropriety or misconduct," Steinhart assured Taylor. "These people did everything they could to save the bank and to cooperate with the FDIC."

"You're probably right. Frankly, our legal staff is overzealous in their pursuit of these lawsuits. They're out of control," Taylor said emphatically.

Upon learning of this conversation and in hope that he might intervene, I wrote to Taylor on July 28, detailing the background of the case and requesting a meeting, which was subsequently scheduled for August 20. Unfortunately, we never got to see Taylor because of his surgery on August 14 and subsequent death on August 21, at the early age of fifty-two.

As scheduled, however, on August 20, Rodgin Cohen, Bill Isaac (whose aid I had enlisted in the interim), and I met with the FDIC general counsel Al Byrne, John Stone, and Stan Poling. Déjà vu! I couldn't believe I was meeting one more time with the FDIC in their offices. I hated being there; I had only bitter memories of the place and the people. Our hosts were polite, but Poling and Stone looked sheepish and avoided making eye contact during the entire meeting.

Bill Isaac began the meeting by reviewing the history of the TAB/FDIC relationship. He reminded them that he had encouraged TAB and NBC to seek assistance from the FDIC, with assurances from Stan Poling that the companies and their officers and directors would receive favorable treatment for "coming in early." He recited in detail the extraordinary level of cooperation of TAB and its officials throughout the ordeal.

Finally, Isaac looked directly at Al Byrne and said, "Al, in my entire experience with the FDIC, including when I was chairman, the TAB/NBC episode is the darkest chapter I have witnessed." Then, turning to face Stone and Poling, as if to remind them of their culpability in the episode, he said, "The ineptness, mismanagement, and delays on the part of the FDIC cost TAB at least one-half billion dollars."

Although Isaac didn't say so, I am sure the FDIC understood that Isaac would be a witness for the defense should the case come to trial. Isaac had previously told me that he would testify in our behalf and he would charge no fee in order to add greater credibility to his testimony. Having a former chairman testifying against them had to be unnerving, particularly one who had played a pivotal role in TAB's negotiations with the agency.

Isaac then looked at Byrne, as the person of authority in the room, and concluded by saying, "Frankly, Al, I would be terribly embarrassed if the FDIC brought a suit against TAB." After Isaac finished, the room was absolutely quiet; no one said a word, no one moved. There was no question about the level of respect afforded a former chairman.

In accordance with our scripted agenda, Rodgin Cohen then discussed the public policy implications of the FDIC filing suit.

> I personally believe that in the future the FDIC is going to want to encourage early resolutions for problem banks. There is no question that it is the most cost-effective way to rescue a bank. If you file suit against these people, it will receive an inordinate amount of publicity. The facts surrounding this case will be terribly embarrassing; the FDIC's credibility will suffer a very significant setback, and as a consequence, it will be extremely difficult in the future to persuade the management of any problem bank to come in early.

Throughout these orations Byrne, Stone, and Poling listened quietly. In fact, Stone and Poling said very little during the entire meeting; they obviously had been well-coached in the event a lawsuit did ensue. But Poling's body language gave him away, as he nodded agreement with nearly every point that Isaac and Cohen made. I had always felt that Poling was a decent human being. After the meeting, Cohen, Isaac, and I agreed that if the FDIC decided to proceed, Poling's deposition would be helpful to our cause.

My role at the meeting was to explain further TAB's cooperation, after which I made an emotional plea to Byrne to reconsider their position and to honor the Release of January 26, 1990, and the underlying agreements. My concluding comment was:

> These are highly visible and respected individuals. They include a former mayor of Fort Worth, four past chairmen of the Fort Worth Chamber of Commerce, the current chairman of the Board of Trustees of Texas Christian University, three CEOs of companies listed on the New York Stock Exchange, and the CEO of a company listed on the American Exchange.
>
> Filing a suit against them will indelibly tarnish their images and reputations and will reflect unfavorably on their companies as well. Even complete exoneration in court can't erase the damage of being sued by the FDIC. Unfortunately, the general public doesn't differentiate between honest bank directors who are being sued for alleged negligence and those who are prosecuted and convicted for criminal activity. All are tarred with the same broad brush. Personally, I would be humiliated, and my company would be terribly embarrassed.

At this point Byrne interrupted: "We would make every effort to avoid filing a suit by seeing if we could reach some kind of settlement first."

"I know that," I responded, my emotions and anger rising as I spoke, "but it's hardly fair. We would come to the table armed with our checkbooks, while you would have a gun at our heads in the form of a threatened lawsuit, with the unlimited resources of the federal government behind you. I don't see how in good conscience you can even consider bringing a suit. Including all the heartache associated with TAB's failure and all the disappointments throughout our dealings with the FDIC, as bad as all of that was, this is the most disheartening thing that has happened."

I looked at Stone with accusing eyes and continued. "We came to the FDIC in good faith, expecting an 'open bank' transaction and to be treated fairly. What we got instead was a closed bank and the threat of a lawsuit. How could anything be worse than this?"

Stone started to respond, "Well, uh . . . ," but Byrne intervened.

"Well, perhaps the ADR process [alternative dispute resolution] will resolve the issue," he said.

Our reading of Byrne's attitude was that if he had his wish, it would be for the entire matter to go away. We were convinced that the FDIC didn't want the facts of this case to be aired in court, and the ADR process was a way out for the agency.

We very reluctantly had agreed to the ADR process and had signed a tolling agreement prior to July 20 when it became apparent that it was the only alternative. Under this arrangement, a neutral evaluator would be jointly selected to hear the dispute–confined in this instance only to the Release–and render a decision. While it would be nonbinding to both parties, Rodgin Cohen was convinced that if we won, the FDIC would not proceed with litigation. If, on the other hand, we lost, we would have the option of a preemptive strike: we would seek a "declaratory judgement" in federal court in Fort Worth, where we believed the judges would be more sympathetic to our case. We would ask the court to interpret the release in accordance with its original intent.

In a major concession to our side, the FDIC agreed to select a Texas judge as the neutral evaluator in the ADR process. Accordingly, we chose Frank G. Evans, a retired judge from Houston, who is associated with Judicial Arbitration and Mediation Services, Inc. Oral arguments would be held in Fort Worth on October 8, 1992, and Judge Evans would render his decision by October 23.

On the morning of the 8th, as I turned right on Main Street in Fort Worth, I thought how glad I was that the hearing was here. The meeting room in the Worthington Hotel, which was owned by the Bass family, had been arranged like a courtroom, and as I suspected, there was a full contingent of TAB supporters. The room itself, ultramodern like the rest of the hotel, was decorated in gray and white, giving it a cold feeling not unlike a courtroom. The TAB attorneys occupied the table and chairs on the right side of the room facing the front, with the TAB supporters sitting behind them. Looking to the left, I saw the three attorneys for the FDIC, with only empty chairs behind them.

The atmosphere of the TAB group was serious but optimistic. We knew the FDIC was not justified in suing against us, and we were confident that Judge Evans would agree. We were concerned, though, that even if we got a favorable opinion from Judge Evans, the zealots in the legal department of the FDIC would want to litigate.

Since the Release itself could be interpreted as being ambiguous and contradictory, the briefs, affidavits, and the hearing focused on the intent of the parties. Our side maintained that an agreement had been reached at a December 21, 1989, meeting between the parties in the FDIC offices, whereas their side alleged that no agreement had been reached. John Stone and the FDIC attorney Thomas A. Schulz, who was involved in the negotiations, said that the FDIC had determined at the outset that it would not give a release limited to recovery from insurance proceeds, and that Tom Schulz had called to notify TAB's attorneys prior to Stone signing the letter of intent dated December 29, 1989.

If that were true–and our attorneys had no recollection of such a call–it is curious that the December 29 letter of intent failed to document the FDIC's position. Instead, the letter of intent merely restated what had been agreed to at the meeting of December 21, all of which was included in the final release.

Affidavits supporting our position were provided by Steve Goodwin of Carrington, Coleman; Rodgin Cohen and Patricia Connell of Sullivan & Cromwell; and myself. In addition, corroborating affidavits by Ron Steinhart and his attorney John Kendrick, then with the Dallas law firm of Akin, Gump, Strauss, Hauer, and Feld, lent great credibility to our position, since they were "uninterested" third parties.

It appeared, based on conflicting affidavits, that Judge Evans had the unenviable task of determining which side had a better recollection of what was agreed to at the meeting of December 21.

Our attorneys, however, gave him some help when they pointed out that, in the affidavits submitted by Stone and Schulz, most of the language was word for word, exactly verbatim. Obviously, the affidavits weren't independently prepared; they instead were drafted by one of the FDIC's in-house attorneys and then presented to Stone and Schulz for their signatures.

As damaging as this was to the FDIC's credibility, the most important evidence was the so-called "rogue memorandum," which we strategically presented at the last possible minute in a "Reply Affidavit." This was a memorandum sent by the FDIC to Rodgin Cohen on December 26, 1989, just five days after the meeting of December 21. The memo set out, when memories were still fresh, the FDIC's interpretation of the commitment it had made. After confirming that they retained the right to assert claims for fraud, dishonesty, or self-dealing, the FDIC wrote:

> For other claims founded on transactions or conduct undertaken by persons acting as officers, directors, or employees of TAB, TASI, or TAB's banking subsidiaries, *the FDIC will not execute a judgment against the personal assets of such persons* [emphasis mine].
>
> The FDIC reserves the right to fully pursue any claim covered by directors' and officers' liability policy or any other form of insurance coverage, *but will limit execution of judgment to insurer* [emphasis mine].

In her argument before Judge Evans, Mary P. Davis, the FDIC's lead attorney, attempted to cast aspersion on the validity of the memorandum. She stated, "About this memorandum of December 26, we have searched our files and have interviewed anyone who could have any knowledge of it. We have no record of it and know nothing about it. It is a rogue memorandum."[1]

"Miss Davis, how then do you explain it?" Judge Evans asked tersely.

"We can't, your honor. We have a theory," she said laughing. "We believe it originated in the offices of Carrington, Coleman, was faxed to the FDIC, and somehow was faxed to Mr. Cohen."

Under normal courtroom procedures, our attorneys would have jumped to their feet in vigorous objection. As it was, they exchanged incredulous glances. The rest of us were literally left with our mouths hanging open in shock and outrage: to suggest that we had manufactured this very damaging evidence was despicable.

Judge Evans replied coolly, "Miss Davis, unless the FDIC can provide some evidence supporting your theory, I am going to accept Mr. Cohen's affidavit and the attached memorandum."

Davis looked at Judge Evans for a long moment. With reluctance, she said, "Unfortunately, we have no evidence to substantiate our theory."

The memo itself lent further credibility to its authenticity. It had an imprint, made by an outgoing fax machine, which read: "12.26.89 02:30. PM–FDIC LEGAL." Upon receipt, Rodgin Cohen had written "URGENT" across the top of the memo, with instructions to send copies to Steve Goodwin at Carrington, Coleman; Patricia Connell and Bruce Clark at Sullivan & Cromwell; and myself. Had the memorandum originated at Carrington, Coleman, as Mary Davis suggested, there would have been no reason for Rodgin Cohen to send a copy to Steve Goodwin, a Carrington, Coleman attorney.

After the hearing ended on what we considered to be a favorable note, we felt that our case was exceedingly strong. Even so, the two-week wait before we could expect an opinion was excruciating. The stakes were enormous.

Finally, Judge Evans's decision came to me in a phone call from Peter Tierney and Steve Goodwin on October 22, a day earlier than expected. "Jody, we have just received by fax Judge Evans's opinion. He sent it to us and to the FDIC simultaneously. We haven't heard from the FDIC."

As I listened to Peter, my pulse quickened and my muscles tightened. "How did Evans rule?" I asked, my anxiety level rising.

Steve Goodwin then interrupted: "There are nineteen pages of legal opinion here, but let me read you the conclusion: "The FDIC may seek recovery against TAB's Former Officers and Directors for the claims referred to and described in paragraph (a) (ii) of the Release, but the FDIC's recovery is *limited to the proceeds of available insurance coverage obtained for or purchased by TAB to cover its Officers and Directors* [emphasis mine]."

As I registered the meaning of these words, I felt a huge sense of relief. Now, if Rodgin was right, this whole thing would be over. Judge Evans had ruled, and we had won, but it was too early to celebrate. While this was a resounding victory, the FDIC still had to decide whether or not they were going to sue: they had until October 30. Predictably, they would once again keep us waiting until the last minute.

On October 28, Al Byrne called Rodgin Cohen to ask if Rodgin was sure that the "rogue memorandum" came out of the FDIC. Rodgin assured him that it had.

Finally, the following day, Byrne called Cohen with their decision: against the "vigorous objections" of some members of their legal staff, the FDIC had decided *not* to pursue litigation against the TAB group. This news was greeted with cheers and "high fives" by everyone on our side.

Besides relief, I felt a great sense of joy. This small victory over the FDIC was sweet consolation after the bitter defeat of three years earlier. I was especially pleased for our directors, who had the most to lose. This final chapter of the TAB saga had come to a favorable and just end.

After this episode, there was no question in my mind. Chairman Taylor had been right: the legal staff at the FDIC was "out of control." Even the former FDIC general counsel John L. Douglas, who was in office during the TAB saga, cautioned the FDIC in a June 30, 1992, article in *American Banker* not to "tarnish a good record by prosecuting the wrong people for the wrong reasons." He elaborated, "No one quibbles with the efforts to identify the real culprits. Fraud, criminal activity, self-dealing, and insider abuse are rightfully punished. But, we should be wary of the recent surge in 'bad loan' or 'risky business activity' cases being filed against directors."[2]

Perhaps some relief will come from a decision reached by U.S. District Judge Royce Lamberth on February 19, 1993, when he threw out most of the government's negligence and breach-of-duty charges against the former officers and directors of the failed National Bank of Washington (D.C.). In his ruling Judge Lamberth criticized the rationale for the lawsuit, said it was without merit, and required the FDIC to pay the defendants' legal expenses related to at least one of the charges.[3] Unfortunately, this decision came too late to influence the $23 million settlement that the former officers and directors of First Republic paid to the FDIC on January 29, 1993, in order to avoid litigation based on essentially the same charges of negligence and breach-of-duty as those alleged in the National Bank of Washington case.

An FDIC or RTC which is "out of control" is indeed a regrettable circumstance. The opportunity for unbridled abuse of power is great: the agencies have unlimited resources at their disposal and, in many cases, unlimited time due to the ability of lawyers to coerce defendants into tolling statutes of limitations. Also, under FIRREA, the statute of limitations was extended in 1989 from five to ten years for fraud. Moreover, law firms, such as Gable & Gotwals in the TAB case, have a tremendous incentive to litigate–an open checkbook from the agencies. In most instances, the law firms retained by the agencies are based in cities other than those in which the defendants reside. These firms swoop in, wreak havoc on the local citizens, and leave just as quickly as they arrived. They are, thus, not subject to any lasting public accountability for their actions in their hometowns where they would have to coexist with the defendants, where they could be criticized by other clients and potential clients, and where they make their living.

The efforts of the government to exact restitution from officers and directors of failed institutions undoubtedly have resulted in increased awareness of fiduciary responsibility. In the future, directors may be more diligent in questioning the purpose and soundness of loans and the viability of borrowers. However, it will certainly be more difficult to attract qualified directors due to the huge potential liability. The experience of the 1980s has clearly demonstrated that even loans that appear very solid and have been subjected to rigid standards and thorough due diligence can turn sour. And, with twenty-twenty hindsight, regulators have an easy time constructing a case of negligence.

Critics charge that the FDIC and the RTC are driven by politics in their pursuit of bank and S&L officers and directors; to these agencies, judgements and convictions become akin to notches on their guns. Additionally, government attorneys are accused of pressuring their targets into settling rather than incurring the often staggering costs of extended litigation. For example, I was told by one of the defendants in the First Republic case that the FDIC's attorneys threatened years of litigation in which the costs to the defendants would be far more than settling out of court. The same defendant said that his legal bills were running about $10,000 per month.

While the government's efforts to recover are monumental and relentless, their effectiveness is open to question. A large percentage has come from the Big Six accounting firms and from relatively few other accounting firms and law firms. While the amount the FDIC and RTC have spent on outside law firms and on their internal legal staffs is not readily available, it is estimated by some that the government spends far more than it will ever recover.

The government, or any agency thereof, has a responsibility to exercise its power with great discretion. It is apparent from the TAB case, as well as from many other cases, that this has not always been true. Additionally, appropriate oversight–and thus accountability–of the FDIC and the RTC has been conspicuously absent.

Breaking concrete for TAB's new operations center in downtown Fort Worth, Texas. Left to right, the author, Lewis H. Bond, and Bayard H. Friedman.

Lewis H. Bond and the author in front of TAB's headquarters building and The Eagle *by Alexander Calder, spring 1986.*

William M. Isaac, Chairman and CEO of The Secura Group, Washington, D.C.

Richard W. Calvert, Chairman and CEO of National Bancshares Corporation of Texas, San Antonio. Photo by Zavell's, Inc.

Mark M. Johnson, President, National Bancshares Corporation of Texas. Photo by Zavell's, Inc.

Richard E. Rainwater, investments, in his office in Fort Worth, Texas. Photo courtesy of the Dallas Morning News.

Carl R. Pohlad, Chairman and CEO, Bank Shares, Inc., in front of Marquette Bank in downtown Minneapolis, 1988. Photo courtesy of the Dallas Morning News.

The author, interview with the Dallas Morning News, *in TAB's sixteenth-floor executive offices, July 30, 1989. Photo courtesy of the* Dallas Morning News.

Press conference of July 20, 1988. Left to right, Gary W. Cage, Chief Financial Officer, TAB; Mark M. Johnson, President, NBC; Richard W. Calvert, Chairman and CEO, NBC; Carl R. Pohlad, Chairman and CEO, Bank Shares, Inc.; the author; and Jim Pohlad, Bank Shares, Inc. Photo courtesy of the Fort Worth Star-Telegram.

Left to right, Bayard H. Friedman, Fort Worth, and Ronald G. Steinhart, Chairman and CEO, Deposit Guaranty Bank of Dallas, at press conference of July 21, 1989. Photo courtesy of the Fort Worth Star-Telegram.

THE CAST
Where They Are Now

Texas American Bancshares

JOSEPH M. "JODY" GRANT, Chairman and Chief Executive Officer.
Resigned from TAB on March 29, 1990. Received a six-figure severance payment for the successful liquidation of TAB's assets (recommended by the creditors' committee in bankruptcy; approximately $.55 per $1.00 of investment was returned to the creditors). Joined American General Corporation (AG) as executive vice president on March 29, 1990. Two days earlier, Torchmark Corporation, Birmingham, Alabama, launched a hostile takeover of AG. Subsequently, AG was offered for sale. During this process, given the uncertainty and the turmoil, left AG and later joined Electronic Data Systems (EDS), Dallas, Texas, as chief financial officer.

L. O. "BUZZ" BRIGHTBILL III, President.
Vice chairman, Team Bank, Fort Worth, Texas, until the sale of Team Bancshares to Bank One Corporation on November 30, 1992. Currently Senior Vice President of Bank One, Texas in its Fort Worth office.

GARY W. CAGE, Executive Vice President and Chief Financial Officer.
Served as chief financial officer, Team Bancshares, Dallas, Texas, until shortly after the sale to Banc One Corporation on November 30, 1992. Currently chief financial officer of Emcare, Inc., a Dallas-based company that manages trauma units for hospitals.

GENE GRAY, Executive Vice President.
President, Bank of Commerce, Fort Worth, Texas.

ROBERT L. HERCHERT, Executive Vice President.
President and CEO of Freese and Nichols, Inc., a private civil engineering firm in Fort Worth, Texas.

LEWIS H. BOND, Chairman of the Executive Committee.
Deceased: died of cancer on December 29, 1990.

National Bancshares Corporation of Texas

RICHARD W. CALVERT, Chairman and Chief Executive Officer.
Retired in San Antonio, Texas.

MARK M. JOHNSON, President.
Served as president of National Bancshares Corporation of Texas during its bankruptcy. Currently president of Texas Bancshares, Inc., a San Antonio–based bank holding company, with assets of approximately $300 million, operating in South Texas.

Federal Deposit Insurance Corporation

L. WILLIAM SEIDMAN, Chairman.
Retired from the FDIC in 1991. Serves as a consultant to several public and private organizations and divides time between Washington, D.C., Florida, Phoenix, and Nantucket. Published his memoirs, *Full Faith and Credit: The Great S&L Debacle And Other Washington Sagas* (Times Books, Random House, 1993). Neither TAB nor NBC were mentioned in the book.

C. C. HOPE, Director.
Deceased: died on March 1, 1993.

ALFRED J. T. BYRNE, General Counsel.
Assumed position of general counsel in June 1990. Resigned on November 12, 1994, to join the Washington, D.C., law firm of Patton, Boggs & Blow.

STANLEY J. POLING, Director, Division of Accounting and Corporate Services.
Scheduled to retire in early 1996 from the position of Director of the Division of Bank Supervision, FDIC. Previously succeeded Harrison Young as director, Division of Resolutions.

WILLIAM H. ROELLE, Division Director, Failing Banks and Assistance Programs.
Presently on special assignment in Poland for the FDIC. Previously served as senior vice president and chief financial officer, Division of Institution Operations and Sales, RTC.

JOHN W. STONE, Associate Director, Division of Bank Supervision.
Retired on December 31, 1995, from the position of Acting Executive Director for Supervision, Resolutions, and Compliance, FDIC. Previously served as deputy to acting chairman Andrew C. Hove subsequent to being associate director, Division of Bank Supervision. Stone's career at the FDIC flourished after the banking crisis in spite of his culpability in the failure of the "open bank" resolutions in Texas and Alaska.

HARRISON YOUNG, Director, Division of Resolutions.
Joined the FDIC from Prudential Bache in 1991 in the above position. Announced his resignation on August 30, 1994, to join Morgan Stanley as a senior advisor in the company's Hong Kong office.

Office of the Comptroller of the Currency

ROBERT L. CLARKE, Comptroller of the Currency.
Failed to receive Senate Banking Committee confirmation for a second term for "contributing" to the wave of bank failures during his term. Subsequently rejoined the Houston law firm of Bracewell & Patterson, Houston, Texas.

Potential Investors

CARL R. POHLAD, Minneapolis Investor, Chairman and Chief Executive Officer of MEI Diversified, Inc., and of Bank Shares, Inc.
After failing to acquire TAB, purchased 80 percent of First State Bank, Denton, Texas, a $200 million community bank. A finders fee was paid to the author in this transaction. Sold Bank Shares, Inc., to Minneapolis-based First Bank System for $247.9 million. Pohlad's holding company, MEI Diversified, Inc., filed for Chapter 11 bankruptcy in March 1993 due to the unprofitable operations of its beauty-salon-operating subsidiary purchased in 1990. The company is aggressively pursuing litigation to recover damages from the sellers. *Forbes* magazine's 1994 Forbes Four Hundred estimated net worth: $710 million.

RICHARD E. RAINWATER, Fort Worth Investor.
Attempt to purchase TAB and NBC was his last venture in a regulated industry. Major investments have been in health care, oil, and real estate. Reported to have made several hundred million dollars in the leveraged buy out (LBO) of Hospital Corporation of America. Cofounder of Columbia Healthcare, which acquired Hospital Corporation after the LBO. In 1994, took public Crescent REIT (Real Estate Investment Trust) with Caroline Rose Hunt, daughter of H. L. Hunt. Now splits time between New York City, Santa Barbara, and Fort Worth. *Forbes* magazine's 1994 Forbes Four Hundred estimated net worth: $750 million.

GERALD J. FORD, Dallas Investor, Chairman of Ford Bank Group, Inc.
With Ron Perelman, Ford purchased First Gibraltar Bank, FSB, in a highly controversial transaction under the Southwest Plan. Perelman and Ford sold First Gibraltar to Bank of America in fall 1992 at a reported profit of $100 million, after realizing hundreds of millions of dollars in tax benefits. In October 1994, Ford and Perelman paid $1.1 billion to Ford Motor Company for San Francisco–based First Nationwide Bank. At about the same time, Ford sold his interest in Ford Bank Group to Norwest Bank in Minneapolis. Now splits time between Dallas and San Francisco, although Dallas remains his permanent residence.

ALAN N. FELLHEIMER, Equimark, Pittsburgh.
Reported to have returned to law practice after leaving Equimark.

RONALD G. STEINHART, Chairman, Deposit Guaranty Bank of Dallas.
Chairman and CEO, Team Bancshares, Dallas, Texas (successor to Deposit Guaranty). On November 30, 1992, sold Team Bank to Banc One Corporation, Columbus, Ohio, for a profit of over $500 million; Steinhart's share, $13 million. Steinhart is now chairman and CEO of Bank One, Texas.

NORWEST BANK, Minneapolis.
Now the seventeenth-largest bank holding company, with assets of $38.5 billion. Lloyd Johnson recently retired. He chose Dick Kovosovich as successor CEO.

SECURITY PACIFIC BANK, Los Angeles.
Because of losses on loans, Security Pacific was forced to sell out to Bank of America. Bob Smith negotiated the sale but was not included in management of the merged institutions. Reported to be currently in the consulting business.

The Secura Group

WILLIAM M. ISAAC, Chairman and CEO (former chairman of the Federal Deposit Insurance Corporation).
Remains as chairman and CEO of Secura, now considered the leading bank consulting firm. Led the nation in fees from bank M&A activity in 1991. In 1994, the Washington, D.C., law firm of Arnold & Porter sold its 25 percent interest in Secura to Arthur Anderson and Anderson Consulting.

CHRISTIE A. SCIACCA, Partner and Managing Director.
Remains with Secura as managing director.

Sullivan & Cromwell

H. RODGIN COHEN, Partner.
Remains with Sullivan & Cromwell. Considered the leading bank regulatory attorney in the country. Clients included First Bank System in its acquisition of Bank Shares, Inc. Represented the former officers and directors of TAB's subsidiary banks in their successful effort to avert a lawsuit by the FDIC to recover under the directors' and officers' liability insurance.

BRUCE CLARK, Partner.
Remains with Sullivan & Cromwell.

Carrington, Coleman, Sloman & Blumenthal

STEPHEN A. GOODWIN, Partner
MARVIN S. SLOMAN, Partner
PETER TIERNEY, Partner
All of the above remain with Carrington, Coleman, Sloman & Blumenthal in the same positions.

Advisors to Texas American Bancshares

BAYARD H. FRIEDMAN, Fort Worth Banker (former Chairman and Chief Executive Officer of Texas American Bank/Fort Worth).

Appointed senior chairman, Team Bank, Fort Worth, on July 21, 1989, the day after Steinhart was awarded the bank. Remained with Team Bank until its sale to Banc One on November 30, 1992, when he established an investment management business in Fort Worth.

SUPPORTING CAST

Texas American Bancshares Directors

H. L. "SONNY" BROWN, JR., Independent Oil Operator.
BEN J. FORTSON, Independent Oil Producer.
ROBERT HALLAM, Chairman, Ben E. Keith Company.
STUART HUNT, Partner in Headwaters Oil Company (nephew of H. L. Hunt).
CLARK A. JOHNSON, Chairman and Chief Executive Officer, Pier 1 Imports.
WILLIAM R. LUMMIS, Chairman, Chief Executive Officer, and President, Summa Corporation (nephew of Howard Hughes).
GARY H. PACE, Chairman, J. C. Pace & Company.
JOHN V. ROACH, Chairman, President, and Chief Executive Officer, Tandy Corporation.
JOHN C. SNYDER, Chairman and Chief Executive Officer, Snyder Oil Company.
EARL WILSON, General Partner, Ridglea Construction Company.
GEORGE M. YOUNG, Independent Producer of Oil and Gas.
DON WILLIAMSON, Consultant, Williamson-Dickie Manufacturing Company.

The former directors of TAB all continue in the same positions they previously held when they were directors of TAB, except for Lummis who retired to Houston and Wilson who died on November 21, 1992. Hallam, Johnson, Roach, Snyder, Wilson, and Williamson, who were also directors of TAB subsidiary banks, were identified as potential defendants by the FDIC in its aborted attempt to obtain a recovery from the bank's directors.

Texas American Advisors

JAMES L. SEXTON, Bracewell & Patterson (former Deputy Director of the FDIC and Commissioner of Banking in Texas).

Remains with Bracewell & Patterson in Austin, Texas.

JACK MCSPADDEN, Goldman Sachs & Company.
Left Goldman Sachs in 1992 to join C. S. First Boston in a similar position.

CHRIS FLOWERS, Partner, Goldman Sachs & Company.
Remains with Goldman Sachs.

RICE A. TILLEY, JR., Partner, Law, Snakard & Gambill.
Remains with Law, Snakard & Gambill. Also identified as a possible defendant by the FDIC in their unsuccessful effort to recover from the former directors of TAB/Fort Worth.

ED KELTNER, Attorney.
Retired. Serving as Of Counsel to the Fort Worth law firm of Shannon, Gracey.

DEE KELLY, Partner, Kelly, Hart & Hallman.
Remains with Kelly, Hart & Hallman. Represented Johnson, Roach, and other former TAB subsidiary directors in the threatened FDIC litigation.

National Bancshares Advisors

JAMES R. "JAMIE" SMITH, Partner, Cox & Smith, San Antonio, Texas.
Remains with Cox & Smith.

FREDERICK "RICK" WOLFF, Shearson, Lehman.
Remains with Lehman Brothers (Shearson was sold by American Express to Smith Barney).

Richard E. Rainwater Associates

PETER JOOST, Partner.
Remains as an associate of Rainwater. Moved his residence to California at the end of 1992.

MORT J. MEYERSON, Partner (former President of Electronic Data Systems).
Worked for Ross Perot in his campaign for president of the United States. Currently president and CEO of Perot Systems, Inc. Retains some interests in Rainwater investments.

Carl R. Pohlad Associates

DONALD E. BENSON, President of MEI Diversified, Inc.
THOMAS A. HERBST, Executive Vice President, Bank Shares, Inc.
ALBERT J. COLIANNI, Vice President, Bank Shares, Inc.
JIM POHLAD, son of Carl Pohlad.
IRWIN JACOBS, Minneapolis Investor.
All of the above are still associated with Pohlad.

First Republic Bancorporation of Dallas

ALBERT V. CASEY, Chairman and Chief Executive Officer (succeeded Fronterhouse on April 12, 1988; former Chairman of American Airlines and Postmaster General of the United States).

Chairman of the Resolution Trust Corporation (RTC), Washington, D.C., during the last two years of the Bush administration. Retired on March 31, 1993, to return to Dallas, Texas, where he teaches at Southern Methodist University.

GERALD FRONTERHOUSE, Chairman and Chief Executive Officer.

Retired.

CHARLES H. PISTOR, Vice Chairman of First Republic and President of the American Bankers Association.

Vice chairman for Development, Southern Methodist University, Dallas, Texas.

ROBERT H. STEWART III, Vice Chairman (former Chairman of InterFirst Bancorporation).

Joined Steinhart as vice chairman of Team Bancshares. Became vice chairman, Bank One, Texas, Inc., Dallas, upon its acquisition of Team Bancshares.

JOE MUSOLINO, President.

Chairman, NationsBank, Houston, Texas.

MCorp

GENE BISHOP, Chairman and Chief Executive Officer.

Retired as chairman and CEO, Life Partners, Inc., a life insurance holding company in Dallas, Texas. Reportedly made $6 million in an initial public offering of Life Partners in March 1993. Retired in 1994.

JOHN CATER, President.

President, Compass Bank–Houston, formerly Riveroaks Bank & Trust Company and now the lead bank of Compass Bancshares of Texas, the $2 billion Texas subsidiary of Compass Bancshares of Birmingham, Alabama.

Arbitrageurs

JAY LUSTIG, Drake Capital Securities, Santa Monica, California.

CHUCK LEWSADDER, Drake Capital Securities.

Lustig and Lewsadder were paid over $.50 on the dollar for their investment in TAB's 15 1/4 percent notes for which they paid between $.10 and $.20 cents on the dollar. Probably suffered a substantial loss in their investment in NBC's public debt.

STAN N. PHELPS, Stan N. Phelps Company, Greenwich, Connecticut.
Experienced similar gain as Lustig and Lewsadder on TAB investment. Continues to be a successful arbitrageur.

Texas American Bancshares Officers

DON COCKERHAM, President, TAB/Austin.
Released from federal prison in January 1992.

OLIVIA "LIBBY" DOTSON, Administrative Assistant.
Assistant vice president, Team Bank, Fort Worth, where she handled the author's family banking relationship until she resigned on January 22, 1993. Currently director of community affairs, All Saints Health Care, Inc., Fort Worth, Texas.

THAD MCDONNELL, Chairman, TAB/Levelland.
President, First National Bank, Grapevine, Texas.

NOTES

Chapter 1

1. "Lewis Bond–TAB Founding Father–Fondly Recalls 34-Year Career," *TABS* (published quarterly by Texas American Bancshares, Inc., Fort Worth, Texas), vol. 11, no. 2 (Second Quarter, 1986). Personal files of author.

2. "Texas American Rejects as Inadequate $50-a-Share Offer by Texas Commerce," *Wall Street Journal*, July 27, 1983.

3. "Merger Spree of Texas Banks," *New York Times*, August 3, 1983.

4. "Report of Examination," Comptroller of the Currency, Administrator of National Banks, Charter No. 3131-HC, examination for the period ended January 28, 1985. Personal files of author.

Chapter 2

1. *1988–1989 Texas Almanac* (Dallas: *Dallas Morning News*, 1987), 443–456.

2. *Profiles 1988–Midland, Texas* (Midland, Tex.: Midland Chamber of Commerce); Dave Clark, "Cities Seek to Diversify Despite 'Oil Boomtown' Atmosphere," *Texas Business* (June 1981), 62.

3. Letter to Lewis H. Bond, Chairman of the Board and Chief Executive Officer, Texas American Bancshares, Inc., from the Office of the Comptroller of the Currency, Administrator of National Banks, signed by Michael L. LaRusso, Director, Multinational and Regional Bank Supervision, February 6, 1987. Personal files of author.

4. *Texas Economic Indicators*, Bureau of Business Research, College and Graduate School of Business, University of Texas at Austin (February 1989), and the Greater Houston Chamber of Commerce.

5. "Chilling Specter at Continental," *New York Times*, May 20, 1984.

6. "Collapse of Abilene National Bank Is Tied to Loan Losses, Many in Energy Industry," *Wall Street Journal*, August 9, 1982.

7. "Bank in Midland, Texas, Has Assets Sold by FDIC," *Wall Street Journal*, October 17, 1983.

8. Texas Department of Banking, Austin, Texas.

9. "First Oklahoma Bank Unit Fails; FDIC Steps In," *Wall Street Journal*, July 15, 1986.

10. "BancOklahoma Seeks Rare Aid from the FDIC," *Wall Street Journal*, July 22, 1986.

11. "BancOklahoma Unit in Oklahoma City to Get $130 Million in FDIC Assistance," *Wall Street Journal*, August 18, 1986.

Chapter 3

1. "Who to Thank for the Thrift Crisis," *New York Times*, June 12, 1988.

2. "Texas S&L Toll: 80% Likely to Need Aid," *American Banker*, February 15, 1989.

3. "State Led '88 Thrift Losses," *Fort Worth Star-Telegram*, March 22, 1989.

4. "Meanwhile, Thrifts Lost $3.4 Billion," *American Banker*, June 14, 1989.

5. "The S&L Mess: How We Got Into It–And How to Get Out," *Business Week* (October 21, 1988), 130–136.

6. "Unrelated Series of Events Led to S&L Crisis," *American Banker*, May 3, 1989.

7. Governor's Task Force on the Savings and Loan Industry, *Report to the Honorable William P. Clements, Jr., Governor of the State of Texas*, January 25, 1988, p. 27. Personal files of author.

8. Much of the material on Sunbelt Savings was drawn from "The Party's Over," by Byron Harris, *Texas Monthly* (June 1987), 110–113, 168–174, 182, and from "Gunbelt S&L," by Howard Rudnitsky and John R. Hayes, *Forbes* (September 19, 1988), 120.

9. "The Party's Over," 169.

10. Ibid., 111.

11. Interview with E. Ridley Briggs, June 13, 1989, Fort Worth, Texas.

12. Allen Pusey and Lee Hancock, "Network Fueled $10 Billion S&L Loss," *Dallas Morning News*, December 4, 1988; Bill Lodge and Allen Pusey, "Beebe's Network Cast Long Shadow in Thrift Industry," *Dallas Morning News*, December 23, 1988.

13. Brian O'Reilly, "How Hutton Took a Texas-Sized Bath," *Fortune* (October 13, 1986), 95–96.

14. Ibid., 96.

15. Allen Pusey, "Problems, Players Surfaced in '70s Scandal–Key Figures Later Played Powerful Roles in Texas's Troubled Thrifts," *Dallas Morning News*, December 4, 1988.

16. "Network Fueled $10 Billion S&L Loss," *Dallas Morning News,* December 4, 1988.

17. "Dixon Is Convicted, McBirney Agrees to Plead Guilty in Separate S&L Case," *Wall Street Journal,* December 21, 1990.

18. "Ex-Thrift Owner Is Convicted," *Dallas Morning News,* April 1, 1992.

19. "Woods Gets 25 Years for S&L Fund Misuse," *Dallas Morning News,* July 17, 1992.

20. "Faulkner, 3 Others Guilty in I-30 Case," *Dallas Morning News,* November 7, 1991.

21. "Faulkner Given 20-Year Term in I-30 Scheme," *Dallas Morning News,* January 16, 1992.

22. "Houston Developer Sentenced to 10 Years," *Dallas Morning News,* October 14, 1994.

23. "Fraud Found at Half of Sickest S&Ls," *San Antonio Express News,* May 19, 1989.

24. "Oversight Agency Formally Established," *Dallas Morning News,* August 10, 1989.

25. Texas Savings and Community Bankers Association, Austin, Texas; Office of Thrift Supervision, Department of the Treasury, Washington, D.C.

26. Ibid.

27. "Ongoing Fiasco: Hundreds of S&Ls Fall Hopelessly Short of New Capital Rules," *Wall Street Journal,* December 7, 1989.

28. "*In Cold Pursuit*: RTC Chases Billions from Failed Thrifts, But Nets Small Change," *Wall Street Journal,* September 2, 1994.

29. "S&Ls: Where Did All Those Billions Go?" *Fortune,* (September 10, 1990), 82–88.

Chapter 4

1. Jerry Flemmons, *Amon: The Life of Amon Carter, Sr.* (Austin: Jenkins Publishing Company, 1978), 295–296.

2. Lewis H. Bond, *Century One: 1873–1973, A City . . . And the Bank That Bears Its Name, The Story of The Fort Worth National Bank,* Newcomen Publication Number 976 (Princeton, N.J.: Princeton University Press, November 1973), 5.

Chapter 5

1. Personal files of author.

2. "Six Banks in Trouble on Ratings," *Fort Worth Star-Telegram,* March 19, 1986.

3. "Report of Examination," Comptroller of the Currency, Administrator of National Banks, Charter No. 3131-HC, examination for the period ended March 31, 1986. Personal files of author.

4. Ibid.

5. "Report of Examination," Comptroller of the Currency, Administrator of National Banks, Charter No. 3131-HC, examination for the period ended January 28, 1985. Personal files of author.

6. "Bank Sees Its Largest Loss Ever," *Fort Worth Star-Telegram*, September 26, 1986.

Chapter 6

1. "Texas Commerce Agrees to Merge with NY Bank," *Dallas Morning News*, December 16, 1986.

2. Ibid.

3. "Chemical to Buy Houston Bank For $1.19 Billion," *Wall Street Journal*, December 16, 1986.

4. Ibid.

5. Ibid.

6. "S&P Issues Debt Watch on TCB, Chemical," *Dallas Times Herald*, December 17, 1986.

7. "Texas Commerce Plans Merger," *San Antonio Express-News*, December 16, 1986.

8. "Weakest TCB Assets in Real Estate," *Houston Post*, December 16, 1986.

9. "Texas Bank Accepts Bid by Chemical," *USA Today*, December 16, 1986.

10. Ibid.

11. "Texas Commerce Agrees to Merge with NY Bank."

12. "Chemical to Buy Houston Bank For $1.19 Billion."

13. "Chemical's Purchase of Texas Commerce Marks Reversal of Oil Region's Fortunes," *Wall Street Journal*, December 17, 1986.

14. Ibid.

15. "Bank on More Out-of-State Mergers," *USA Today*, December 16, 1986.

16. Ibid.

17. "RepublicBank, InterFirst to Merge," *Dallas Morning News*, December 17, 1986.

18. "RepublicBank Merger Is End of InterFirst," *Fort Worth Star-Telegram*, December 17, 1986.

19. "RepublicBank Will Be Largest in Texas," *Fort Worth Star-Telegram*, December 17, 1986.

20. "Merged Bank Will Become Texas's Largest," *Fort Worth Star-Telegram*, December 17, 1986.

21. "RepublicBank, InterFirst to Merge."

22. "RepublicBank Will Be Largest in Texas."

23. "Natural Resource," *Fort Worth Star-Telegram*, September 17, 1989.

24. "The Richest People in America," *Forbes* (October 23, 1989, special issue: The 1988 Forbes Four Hundred), 236.

25. "First Interstate to Acquire Allied Bancshares," *Dallas Morning News*, May 22, 1987.

26. Ibid.

27. Ibid.

28. "Revision of Terms Delays Allied Deal," *Dallas Morning News*, December 5, 1987.

29. "First City Bancorp To Get $970 Million U.S. Infusion In Pact That Gives Abboud Control of Management," *Wall Street Journal*, September 10, 1987.

Chapter 7

1. "First RepublicBank Mulls Asking FDIC For Aid to Avert Failure of Dallas Bank," *Wall Street Journal*, March 14, 1988.

2. "Texas Bank Fights a War of Independence," *Wall Street Journal*, December 10, 1987.

3. "The First Republic Rescue Chronology," *American Banker*, August 2, 1988.

4. "U.S. Steps Up Scrutiny of First RepublicBank," *Wall Street Journal*, February 19, 1988.

5. Ibid.

6. "Lender in Crisis–Big Texas Bank to Ride Out Troubles, Could Be Faltering," *Wall Street Journal*, February 22, 1988.

7. Ibid.

8. Ibid.

9. "First RepublicBank Rescue Chronology."

10. "First RepublicBank Says It Approached Regulators on Federally Assisted Bailout," *Wall Street Journal*, March 16, 1989.

11. "First Republic Banks Get $1 Billion Assist," *Dallas Morning News*, March 18, 1988.

12. "First RepublicBank Loss of $1.5 Billion Estimated for 1st Period; Chairman Quits," *Wall Street Journal*, April 13, 1988.

13. "First RepublicBank to Reduce Its Board," *Fort Worth Star-Telegram*, May 3, 1988.

14. "FDIC Denies Aid Planned For Bank Firm," *Fort Worth Star-Telegram*, April 7, 1988.

15. L. William Seidman, Chairman, Federal Deposit Insurance Corporation, "Remarks Before the Morin Center for Banking Law Studies," Boston, Massachusetts, April 19, 1988.

Chapter 8

1. "The Man Behind a $5 Billion Dynasty," *Business Week* (October 20, 1986), 96.

2. Ibid., 95.

3. "The Richest People in America," 273.

4. Ibid., 186.

5. Harvey MacKay, *Swim with the Sharks–Without Being Eaten Alive* (New York: William Morrow and Co., 1988).

6. "The Richest People in America," 158.

7. Ibid., 150.

Chapter 11

1. "Ex-Chief of Bank Indicted," *Austin American-Statesman*, September 21, 1988.

2. "Former Bank President Pleads Guilty to Fraud," *Austin American-Statesman*, May 31, 1989.

3. "Ex-Bank Executive Gets 3 Years for Fraud," *Dallas Morning News*, February 23, 1990.

4. "U.S. to Post $475 Million to Assist National-Texas American Merger," *Fort Worth Star-Telegram*, July 21, 1988.

5. "Minnesota Investor Is Former Owner of Central Air Lines," *Fort Worth Star-Telegram*, July 21, 1988.

6. "Citicorp May Edge Out NCNB in Bids to Join Bailout of First Republic-Bank," *Wall Street Journal*, July 7, 1988.

7. "NCNB Acquiring First Republic," *Dallas Morning News*, July 30, 1988.

8. "Muddling Through First Republic's Rescue," *American Banker*, August 8, 1988.

9. "Texas Bank Rescues Pit Wall Street Investors Against Regulators," *American Banker*, November 29, 1988.

Chapter 12

1. "FDIC Reopens Bidding for Texas Banks after Pohlad Asks It to Assume More Risk," *Wall Street Journal*, October 24, 1988.

2. "Bank Rescue Deal Falters," *New York Times*, October 22, 1988.

3. "Texas American Rescue Is Reopened–Minneapolis Banker's Deal with FDIC Fails," *Fort Worth Star-Telegram*, October 22, 1988.

4. MEI Diversified, Inc., and Bank Shares, Inc., press release, October 21, 1988, Minneapolis, Minnesota.

5. "Federal Agencies Scrutinize Another Texas Bank Firm," *Fort Worth Star-Telegram*, August 4, 1988; "MCorp Sees Belief Growing That It Needs FDIC Aid," *Wall Street Journal*, August 17, 1988.

6. "MCorp, Last Big Texas Bank Holdout, Seeks Help," *New York Times*, October 8, 1988.

7. "MCorp Bankruptcy Seen as Possible," *New York Times*, October 28, 1988.

8. "Emergency Fed Loans Rise Dramatically," *Dallas Morning News*, November 15, 1988.

9. "MCorp Admits Borrowing, Says Funding Stable," *Dallas Morning News*, November 16, 1988.

Chapter 13

1. "The Anatomy of an Arlington Bank Failure," *Fort Worth Star-Telegram*, September 11, 1988.

2. "Central Bank Pays $1,000 for Failed Capital National," *Fort Worth Star-Telegram*, September 20, 1988.

3. "Fidelity National Is Closed," *Fort Worth Star-Telegram*, October 7, 1988.

4. "Texas American Bancshares to Default on Notes Payments," *Wall Street Journal*, September 13, 1988.

5. "Ex-Chief of Bank Indicted," *Austin American-Statesman*, September 21, 1988; "Holding On to Local Dollars," *Fort Worth Star-Telegram*, October 31, 1988; "Texas American Rescue Is Reopened," *Fort Worth Star-Telegram*, October 22, 1988.

6. "Texas American Reports $216.5 Million Loss," *Fort Worth Star-Telegram*, October 29, 1988.

7. "Banking Panel Looks at Breaks Given to Thrifts," *Wall Street Journal*, January 11, 1989.

8. "Seidman Urges S&L Cash Infusion," *Dallas Morning News*, January 16, 1989.

9. "Seidman Wins One For the Banks," *New York Times*, February 12, 1989.

Chapter 14

1. "Texas Cases Cast Doubt on FDIC Skills," *American Banker*, February 8, 1989.

2. "MCorp Says 3 Minor Bondholders Force It to Seek Chapter 11 Status," *Wall Street Journal*, March 27, 1989.

3. Ibid.

4. Dow Jones, 9:32 A.M. EST, March 29, 1989.

5. "Deposit Run Blamed for MBank Seizures," *Dallas Morning News*, March 30, 1989.

6. Ibid.

7. "TAB Creditors File Suit," *Fort Worth Star-Telegram*, March 2, 1989.

8. "Examiners at 2 Texas Banks," *Dallas Morning News*, March 17, 1989; "Audits May Alter Merger," *Fort Worth Star-Telegram*, March 18, 1989.

9. "Fate of 2 Banks in Texas Hinges on U.S. Exams," *American Banker*, March 17, 1989.

10. "TAB's Capital Is Gone," *Fort Worth Star-Telegram*, April 29, 1989.

11. Resolution on the Sole Shareholder of Texas American Bank/Levelland, Texas, Adopted by Written Consent, April 19, 1989, Fort Worth, Texas. Personal files of author.

12. Texas American Bank/Levelland, Special Directors' Meeting, Fort Worth, Texas, April 19, 1989. Personal files of author.

Chapter 15

1. "Bank's Creditors Seek Help," *Fort Worth Star-Telegram,* April 21, 1989.

2. "TAB Borrowed Funds: Report," *Fort Worth Star-Telegram,* May 31, 1989.

3. "U.S. Still Wants 2 Texas Banks Sold as Package, Analysts Say," *Fort Worth Star-Telegram,* May 13, 1989.

4. "Failing Banks of National Bancshares and Texas American Draw Few Suitors," *Wall Street Journal,* June 13, 1989.

Chapter 16

1. "Grand Prairie Bank to Stay Shut," *Fort Worth Star-Telegram,* July 22, 1989.

Chapter 17

1. *Texas American Bancshares, Inc., et al., Plaintiffs-Appellees v. Robert Logan Clarke et al., Defendants-Appellants,* United States Court of Appeals, Fifth Circuit, No. 90-1674, Exhibit 1, Transcript of Meeting of the Board of Directors of the FDIC, October 25, 1988. Personal files of author.

2. *Texas American Bancshares, Inc., et al., Plaintiffs v. Robert Logan Clarke, Comptroller of the Currency, et al., Defendants,* Civil Action No. 3-89-1864-H, United States District Court for the Northern District of Texas, Dallas Division, filed June 25, 1990, p. 24. Personal files of author.

3. "Judge: FDIC Broke Law in MCorp Closing," *Dallas Times Herald,* September 8, 1989.

4. *Texas American Bancshares, Inc., et al., Plaintiffs v. Robert Logan Clarke, Comptroller of the Currency, et al., Defendants,* 8.

5. Ibid., 24.

6. *Texas American Bancshares, Inc., et al., Plaintiffs-Appellees v. Robert Logan Clarke, Comptroller of the Currency, et al., Defendants,* Federal Deposit Insurance Corporation, Defendant-Appellant, No. 90-1674, United States Court of Appeals, Fifth Circuit, February 27, 1992. Personal files of author.

7. Interview with Peter B. Bartholow, chief executive officer of MCorp during its bankruptcy, October 30, 1995.

8. "FDIC Barred from Seizing Affiliate of Failed Bank," *American Banker,* July 29, 1994.

9. Ibid.

Chapter 18

1. "Bank Stats: Industry Quarterly," George M. Salem, CFA, in *Research,* Prudential Securities, August 12, 1992, p. 26.

2. "Inaction on MCorp Costly, Report Says," *Fort Worth Star-Telegram,* March 17, 1992.

3. "Banc One in Texas Deal Valued at $782 Million," *American Banker*, March 24, 1992.

4. "Feds Get Friendly with Banks," *Dallas Morning News*, April 5, 1992.

5. "Tough Guys: 'Regulators from Hell' Frighten Some Banks But Also Win Praise," *Wall Street Journal*, April 27, 1993.

6. "Bank Blight Descends on East Coast," *Fort Worth Star-Telegram*, February 11, 1990.

7. Ibid.

8. "Financial Casualty: U.S. Recession Claims Bank of New England as First Victim," *Wall Street Journal*, January 7, 1991.

9. "Leeway Sought for Banks: New England Uses Its Political Clout," *Dallas Morning News*, March 17, 1991.

10. Ibid.

11. Ibid.

12. "Comptroller's Office Abandons 'Black Box' Loan Exams," *American Banker*, April 9, 1991.

13. "Banks Given Green Light to Roll Over Realty Loans," *American Banker*, June 21, 1991.

14. "Bank Regulators Are Set to Announce Changes to Ease Credit Pinch," *Wall Street Journal*, March 1, 1991.

15. "Leeway Sought for Banks: New England Uses Its Political Clout."

16. Ibid.

17. "Bias Against Texas Hurts Banks, MCorp Chief Says," *Fort Worth Star-Telegram*, October 13, 1988.

18. "In California, 'Unrelieved Despair,'" *American Banker*, October 6, 1992.

Chapter 19

1. *Federal Deposit Insurance Corporation 1992 Annual Report*, Washington D.C., 2, 4.

2. "Bancshares Plan to Recapitalize Falls Through," *Fort Worth Star-Telegram*, April 28, 1990.

3. "FDIC Utilizes New Measure to Scrap Bailout," *Wall Street Journal*, April 30, 1990.

4. "Judith Fellheimer Quits Equimark Post, In Surprise End to Husband-Wife Team," *Wall Street Journal*, May 30, 1990.

5. "Fellheimer's Fall: Attacked for Nepotism and Slumping Results, Equimark Chief Quits," *Wall Street Journal*, September 7, 1990.

6. "Equimark, FDIC Settle Management Fee Dispute," *American Banker*, February 3, 1992.

7. Ibid.

8. "Equimark Corp.," *Wall Street Journal*, November 16, 1990.

9. "Regulators Sell 9 NBC Subsidiaries to NCNB," *Fort Worth Star-Telegram*, June 2, 1990.

10. "Case Studies: How Not to Rescue a Bank," *American Banker*, February 2, 1989.

11. "BancTexas Seeking Injunction Against Federal Reserve Order," *Wall Street Journal*, February 5, 1990.

12. "Case Studies: How Not to Rescue a Bank."

13. Ibid.

14. "Hibernia Says Loan Quality Is in a 'Continuous Decline,'" *American Banker*, May 2, 1991; "Hibernia Seeks Acquirer, Plans to Sell Some Businesses: Top Management Quits," *Wall Street Journal*, July 31, 1991.

15. "Hibernia May Have to Sell Its Jewels," *American Banker*, May 9, 1991.

16. "Hibernia Running Out of Time to Heal Itself," *American Banker*, August 23, 1991.

17. "Creditors Agree to Take Stake in Hibernia," *Dallas Morning News*, December 20, 1991.

18. John W. Milligan, "Who Shot First City," *Institutional Investor* (March 1992), 38.

19. Ibid., 38.

20. Ronald R. Glanz and John C. Hockenbury, "FDIC Open Bank Transactions," *Financial Services Regulation*, vol. 4, no. 5, March 9, 1988 (New York: Standard & Poor's Corporation).

21. "Abboud Ousted from Top Posts at First City," *Wall Street Journal*, March 28, 1991.

22. Milligan, "Who Shot First City," 38.

23. "First City's Abboud Gets His First Taste of the Familiar Woes of Texas Banking," *Wall Street Journal*, July 2, 1990; "Abboud's Ouster Ends Three Stormy Years for First City," *Houston Business Journal*, April 1, 1991.

24. "Abboud Ousted from Top Posts at First City."

25. Milligan, "Who Shot First City," 35.

26. Ibid.

27. "FDIC Sells First City Banks for More Than Expected," *Dallas Morning News*, January 28, 1993.

28. "First City Takes Broad Aim at FDIC with $3 Billion Lawsuit over Seizure," *American Banker*, September 28, 1993.

29. "First City Suspends Litigation, Pursues Settlement Talks with FDIC," *Dallas Morning News*, October 9, 1993.

30. "First City Bancorp., FDIC Reach Accord Over Seizure of Banks," *Wall Street Journal*, June 24, 1994.

31. "First City Plans Merger with J-Hawk of Texas," *American Banker*, December 4, 1994.

32. "First City Cleared for Merger with J-Hawk in Last Chapter of Long Bankruptcy Saga," *American Banker*, May 17, 1995; Interview with Steven Goodwin, of Carrington, Coleman, Sloman & Blumenthal, June 15, 1995.

Chapter 20

1. "Blunt Regulator Thrives in the Banking Crisis," *New York Times,* December 22, 1990.

2. "Outside Control: Many Texas Banks Aren't Run from Texas. Is That Bad?" *Fort Worth Star-Telegram,* August 6, 1988.

3. The following information on NCNB Texas is from "NCNB Name Still Bruised After Leap into Texas Market," *Dallas Morning News,* October 13, 1991.

4. Ibid.

5. "Governor's Signature Makes Texas First State to Opt Out of Branching," *American Banker,* May 12, 1995.

6. "Branch Study: Conclusion Firm, Data Confusing," *American Banker,* March 19, 1992.

7. "FDIC Plans to Appeal Judgement Stemming from Bailout of Bank," *American Banker,* May 20, 1994.

8. Ibid.

9. "FDIC, Bank to Pay for Breaking Office Lease," *Dallas Morning News,* May 14, 1994.

10. "USB News: Washington," *USBanker* (August 1994), 12.

11. Deposition of Albert V. Casey, *Federal Deposit Insurance Corporation, Plaintiff v. H. R. Bright et al., Defendants,* United States Court for the Northern District of Texas, Dallas Division, Civil Action No. 3-91-1490-H, Washington, D.C., May 18–19, 1992, p. 311.

12. Ibid., 103.

13. *Federal Deposit Insurance Corporation 1992 Annual Report,* Washington, D.C., 3.

14. *Federal Deposit Insurance Corporation 1989 Annual Report,* Washington, D.C., 91; *Federal Deposit Insurance Corporation 1991 Annual Report,* Washington, D.C., 56.

15. Sandra L. Planisek, "History of Reconstruction Finance Corp. Holds Lessons for RTC," *American Banker,* November 1, 1989.

16. Ibid.

17. "Continental Bank Celebrates Return to Public Ownership," *Dallas Morning News,* June 16, 1991.

18. Ronald R. Glanz and John C. Hockenbury, "FDIC Open Bank Assistance Transactions," *Financial Services Regulation,* vol. 4, no. 5, March 9, 1988 (New York: Standard & Poor's Corporation), 41.

19. "Feds Get Friendly with Banks," *Dallas Morning News,* April 5, 1992.

20. "Seidman, Trump Urge Tax Breaks For Realty," *American Banker,* November 22, 1991.

21. "FDIC Plans to Guarantee New Loans in Northeast," *American Banker,* February 6, 1992.

22. "Crossland Sets Tone for Future FDIC Takeovers," *American Banker,* January 29, 1992.

23. Ibid.

24. "New Plans For S&Ls and Banks," *New York Times*, February 18, 1992.

25. "Feds Get Friendly with Banks."

26. Ibid.

27. "William Taylor of F.D.I.C. Dead at 53," *New York Times*, August 21, 1992.

28. "FDIC Closes Two Banks with Formula That Reduces the Expenses for Agency," *Wall Street Journal*, October 5, 1992.

29. "FDIC Statement of Policy and Criteria on Assistance to Operating Insured Banks," *Federal Register*, vol. 51, 44122 (Washington, D.C.: U.S. Government Printing Office, December 8, 1986); "FDIC Policy on Assistance to Operating Insured Banks and Savings Associations," *Federal Register*, vol. 55, 12559 (Washington, D.C.: U.S. Government Printing Office, April 4, 1990); "FDIC Statement of Policy on Assistance to Operating Insured Depository Institutions," *Federal Register*, vol. 57, 60203 (Washington, D.C.: U.S. Government Printing Office, December 18, 1992).

30. "FDIC Issues Policy That May Encourage Banks, Thrifts to Seek Aid to Bar Failure," *Wall Street Journal*, December 9, 1992.

31. "Crossland Bank Is Sold to Investors For $332 Million," *Wall Street Journal*, August 13, 1993.

Epilogue

1. The dialogue from the hearing has been reconstructed from the author's recollections and notes.

2. John L. Douglas, "Comment: Directors Shouldn't be Scapegoats," *American Banker*, June 30, 1992.

3. "Judge Rejects Most Negligence Charges Against Former Aides of a Failed Bank," *Wall Street Journal*, February 19, 1993.

INDEX